S

THE SINGER AND THE VOICE

The Singer and the Voice

VOCAL PHYSIOLOGY AND TECHNIQUE FOR SINGERS

ARNOLD ROSE

Foreword by Harold Rosenthal,
Editor of *Opera*

FABER AND FABER LIMITED

3 Queen Square

London

First published in 1962
by Faber and Faber Limited
Second edition 1971
Printed in Great Britain by
Western Printing Services Limited, Bristol
All rights reserved

ISBN   0 571 04725 4

Acknowledgments

It is a pleasure to express my gratitude to those who have helped in the preparation of this book. The specialized assistance and encouragement of Dr. J. Hasted of the Department of Physics, University College, London, has been invaluable. I am particularly indebted also to Professor D. Whitteridge of Edinburgh University for the laboratory and equipment he so generously made available for experimental purposes; to Dr. M. H. Draper who conducted the experiments described in Appendix II; and to the other members of the University staff who gave so willingly of their time and skill.

I acknowledge with special gratitude the co-operation of Dr. E. J. Moran Campbell of London whose insistence on a rigorous scientific methodology has been a constant inspiration and stimulus. In a field so uncharted and where the empirical approach is so much more tempting, this discipline was of the greatest value. I hope I have not fallen too short of the high standard he set.

I record also the skilled assistance of Mr. W. V. Rowe and Mr. C. de la Nougerede who were responsible for the execution of the technical drawings, and the expert help of Mr. C. R. Howe in revising the manuscript to ensure clarity of presentation.

Acknowledgment to those who have allowed the use of copyright material is made on the page on which it appears, and I would like to express my thanks to the publishers and authors who have kindly permitted this use of their work.

Contents

FOREWORD 11

PREFACE TO THE SECOND EDITION 15

Section One
THE TEACHING OF SINGING

I. TEACHERS AND TEACHING 19
II. THE LOST TRADITION 30

Section Two
PRINCIPLES OF SOUND

III. THE VIBRATOR 43
IV. RESONANCE 52

Section Three
DESCRIPTION OF THE VOCAL MECHANISM

V. THE BREATHING MECHANISM 69
VI. CONTROL OF THE BREATHING MECHANISM 94
VII. THE LARYNGEAL MECHANISM 104
VIII. THE RESONATORS 114

Section Four
CONTROL OF THE VOCAL MECHANISM

IX. PRINCIPLES OF BREATH CONTROL IN SINGING 135
X. CONTROL OF THE LARYNGEAL MECHANISM 145
Pitch, Intensity, Dynamics, Colour

7

CONTENTS

XI. THE VOCAL RESONANCE SYSTEM   168

XII. CONTROL OF THE RESONATORS   178
    Open Throat, Head Tone

XIII. ARTICULATION   193

XIV. INTENSITY, DYNAMICS AND COLOUR IN THE
    ART OF SINGING   201

XV. REGISTERS   206

Section Five

DEVELOPMENT OF THE VOCAL MECHANISM

XVI. DIALECTICS OF TENSION AND RELAXATION   223

XVII. DEVELOPMENT OF BREATH CONTROL   228

XVIII. PRACTICE   250

APPENDIX I   255

APPENDIX II   259

BIBLIOGRAPHY   262

INDEX   265

Diagrams

1. Sound waves *page* 44
2. Forms of vibration of a string 46
3. Fundamental and harmonics (unresonated) 60
4. Resonance curves (single resonator) 60
5. Sound spectrum (single resonator) 60
6. Resonance curve (double resonator) 61
7. Sound spectrum (double resonator) 61
8. Thorax 70
9. Enlargement of chest from back to front 71
10. Enlargement of chest from side to side 71
11. Lungs 72
12. Elongation of bronchi and divisions during inspiration 73
13. Diaphragm 75
14. Chest and diaphragm 76
15. Abdominal muscles 78
16. Latissimus dorsi 80
17. Breath volumes 81
18. Ventilation 83
19. Springs—resting, compressed and stretched 89
20. Springs—stretched by weights 89
21. Alveolar pressure due to elastic recoil 92
22. Diagrammatic representation of chest expansion 98
23. Diagrammatic view of the cartilages and muscles of the larynx 104
24. Cartilages of the larynx from the front 105
25. Cartilages of the larynx from behind 105
26. Cavity of the larynx in a frontal section 106
27. Elongation of vocal cords due to tilting of thyroid cartilage on the cricoid cartilage 106

9

DIAGRAMS

28. Action of the posterior crico-arytenoid muscles in rotating the arytenoid cartilages to open the glottis   107
29. Action of the lateral crico-arytenoid muscles in rotating the arytenoid cartilages to close the glottis   107
30. Form of vibration of vocal cords—posterior section adducted   108
31. Forms of vibration of vocal cords   110
32. Thin vocal cord—high note   112
33. Thick vocal cord—low note   112
34. Action of breath on vocal cords   112
35. Diagrammatic representation of vocal cords on low and high notes   113
36. Resonators   115
37. The mouth   116
38. Muscles of the neck—supra-hyoid   118
39. Muscles of the neck—infra-hyoid   119
40. Tongue in relaxed position   126
41. Open throat   126
42. Closed throat I   126
43. Closed throat II   126
44. Movements of thyro-arytenoid fold in a cat   135
45. Horizontal movement of vocal cords   137
46. Vertical movement of vocal cords   137
47. Vibration of vocal cords—less breath   138
48. Vibration of vocal cords—more breath   138
49. Tension concepts relating to pitch   148
50. 'Breath-intensity' curves of a well-produced voice   158
51. Lip position   184
52. Pitch quality zones   251
53. Chart showing partials of vocal notes in relation to vowel formants   252–3
54. Air pressure gauge   256
55. Manometer   257

Foreword

'Good taste is fast disappearing, the profession is suffering from a precipitous decline.' These words were not written in the 1960's or even in the 1860's, but in 1723 by Pier Francesco Tosi, the most famous of singing teachers in the so-called period of *Bel Canto*. When then was the 'Golden Age of Singing'? It has variously been suggested that it was always the era before the present; that it only existed in the minds of the critics and the singing teachers; and that it did once exist, but that it began to decline as soon as operatic art began to develop.

If we take the trouble to read musical criticism from the days of Tosi onwards, we find the same theme recurring again and again. Callas and Di Stefano are compared unfavourably with Ponselle and Gigli; Ponselle and Gigli cannot bear comparison with Destinn and Caruso; nor they with Patti and the De Reszkes, who of course were good, but not nearly as good as Grisi and Mario. And so it goes on, and so it will always go on.

We find critics at all times disagreeing among themselves; we certainly cannot trust our own personal memories, for the further away we get from an event, the rosier it seems in retrospect. And are we to trust the gramophone record? In its early days correct pitch was not always adhered to, and many great singers of the last century were past their prime when they made their first recordings. And today modern techniques magnify voices out of all proportion, and singers can remake those sections of a recording in which they ran into a bad patch.

Today the emphasis in opera has changed. Our Victorian grandparents enjoyed opera performances in which little or no thought was paid to acting or production. Styles and tastes have changed, the emphasis has shifted from merely singing the notes to singing with great dramatic intensity and meaning. Mere exhibitionism has given

11

way to singing with greater intelligence; and opera is not now treated as a vehicle for vocal display, but as a composite whole in which voice, orchestra, conductor and producer all assume equal part.

What are the attributes of a great singer? The voice teachers of the eighteenth century demanded four things of their pupils: beauty of tone, agility, true musicianship and the study of the text, in that order. Today more than ever, when opera singers must be able to do more than just stand on the stage and sing the notes, a firm vocal training is necessary.

I am not one of those people who believe that the good old days were the best in opera or in anything else, so I welcome a book which emphasizes the fact that the standard of singing today rests heavily upon the standard of teaching, that the problems of singing must be examined afresh and that the teachings of the past should not be simply taken for granted without very critical examination. I have heard too many promising young voices ruined because they have been misused by their owners, misused by operatic managements, and also unfortunately misused in the first place by the teachers in whose hands the owners of the voices placed themselves, due in great part to the fact that, as Mr. Rose points out, too few people both in and out of the profession realize the difference between the Teacher of Singing, i.e. the Teacher of Voice Production, and the Teacher of Music, the Vocal Coach, the Repetiteur.

The scientific and anatomical knowledge required by the Teacher of Voice Production may seem at first sight out of all proportion. But the Teacher of Voice Production no less than a skilled surgeon is a specialist in his profession, and one would not entrust oneself to an unskilled or untrained surgeon for a delicate operation. The human voice is a delicate instrument, and it deserves skilled and careful treatment. Unfortunately one cannot prosecute those so-called teachers who ruin voices; but the more the potential singer, the critic and even members of the public are conscious of what is required by the Teacher of Voice Production, the more hope there is that the standard of teaching and therefore of singing in this country, no less than anywhere else, will improve.

There is a pressing need for an authoritative standard textbook which can be universally accepted as a basis for training a voice, a need which has never been greater than it is today. In Mr. Rose's book new light has been thrown on the problems I have posed above and, with the help of the most up-to-date scientific advances, techniques of training have been carefully studied with great insight, and presented in such a way as to fill admirably the need for such a text-book. For this reason in particular, amongst others of equal merit, I welcome this book.

HAROLD ROSENTHAL
Editor *Opera*

Preface to the Second

In this second edition several important revis
have been incorporated. Of greatest importance
made since this book was first published in the u
colour and its control. Many singers today ca
vocal line but the number who can give intere
performances without destroying the line are
same time, much greater interpretative dema
upon the singer, in which control of colour pl
part. Greater understanding of the problem
therefore more urgently needed now than eve

Whereas colour control has traditionally be
tion of the resonators, deeper understanding
cords and resonators in voice production has
of emphasis. It is now evident that it is the la
not the resonators which plays the fundam
colour. This new approach gives the singer
positive command over this and other aspec

In addition to this fundamental change, n
rewriting of the relevant chapters, the ord
altered. Those chapters dealing with the the
production are now grouped together in
various facets of vocal technique can be mo
physiological and acoustic foundations of
and referred to in separate sections. The
taken to rewrite several other passages so
will be as easy for the beginner to un
advanced student.

London, 1971

15

SECTION ONE

The Teaching of Singing

I

Teachers and Teaching

Too many voices today are working at far below their maximum efficiency, both in tone and control. Furthermore, the interpretative powers of most singers are far from being fully realized and numbers of students beginning with fine natural voices, find themselves, after years of study, no nearer their goal than at the start. Some, in truth, are even farther away.

Why is progress in the teaching of singing virtually at a standstill when so much new scientific knowledge is available? One of the main reasons lies in the way in which singing is being taught. As will be shown, this is far from being conducive to the advancement of knowledge.

How is singing taught today? To answer this question, we must be very clear as to what is, and what should be meant by the title, Teacher of Singing. The teaching of singing involves two main aspects —first, *the teaching of voice production*, whereby the pupil learns to develop and control his voice so as to sing with the greatest possible beauty of tone and to express his feeling clearly without in any way destroying the purity of the vocal line; and second, *the teaching of musicianship*, which implies knowledge of musical theory, sight reading, languages, memorizing roles and songs and, finally, a deep understanding of what is sung in order to express the inherent message of the music in the most beautiful and powerful manner.

A Teacher of Singing, therefore, should be a person who teaches all these things to his pupils. A teacher who is mainly concerned with the first aspect should properly be called a Teacher of Voice Production, whilst a teacher who specializes in the second aspect is really a Teacher of Music, a Vocal Coach or a Repetiteur. Unfortunately, these terms are fast losing their real meaning and it is most important, in the interests of singing, that this should not happen.

Originally the term Teacher of Singing implied first and foremost, a teacher of voice production who usually, though not necessarily, also coached his pupils musically. The term Singing Coach was used to describe a teacher who tutored his pupils solely in musicianship, or musicianship and interpretation. Today, however, we have 'Teachers of Singing' who, in actual fact, only possess the qualifications of a singing coach. The general public often has very little understanding of the difference between a Teacher of Singing and a Singing Coach and the term Singing Coach is increasingly used to include all that was originally meant by Teacher of Singing. This is only one aspect of the confusion surrounding the teaching of singing today. To understand the serious implications of this confusion and to discover how it may be remedied, one must appreciate how the state of affairs arose.

There was a time when a teacher could, if he wished, be all things to all singers because the range of his knowledge did not need to extend beyond music of a certain type. It is true that great skill was needed in the execution of this music, but the field was limited, and both teachers and singers could devote their efforts exclusively to achieving perfection in this one style of singing.

In the last hundred years or so, however, singing has developed into many different and varied fields of expression. There are various types of opera—e.g. Mozartian, Italian and Wagnerian. There is oratorio and the concert field in general, including lieder, modern songs and many special branches in all languages, e.g. madrigals, French songs and early Italian songs—to mention only a few forms of Western classical music. These different fields of expression each require a different musical approach, and involve differences in the handling of the voice, all of which must be thoroughly understood by the teacher.

The effect of this greater complexity of music has resulted in conditions which call for a wider range of technical achievement by the singer today than his counterpart of more than a century ago. And further, while musical demands are much more varied, demands on volume and staying power are also much greater. A singer must concern himself with quantity as well as quality, especially in opera. Operas like those of Wagner and Strauss, for example, call for a very large orchestra above which the singer must be heard.

Thus, the knowledge and skill required by the teacher today is much more than was necessary in earlier days. There is urgent need for some teachers to specialize in the various branches of music and for others to specialize in voice production.

Yet, while the need for greater specialization among teachers has arisen, we find that the tendency has been in the opposite direction. Most teachers like to feel, even more so today, that they can still be all things to their pupils. They are so jealous of their prerogative that they would not dream of admitting their inadequacy in any field but claim mastery in every branch of the art. This is virtually impossible today.

Moreover, while singing has become ever more complex, and the demands on the singer increasingly greater, teachers have remained content with methods of teaching which, as I will show, have serious limitations, as they had even in the greatest days of singing when the demands made were of a more specialized nature.

A good coach today must have a very advanced musical education and a detailed knowledge of the operas and music he coaches. He may specialize in certain branches of music only, and in certain languages. He does not need specific knowledge of the production of the voice, but should have a deep understanding of music in its artistic and spiritual aspects. He should be able to convey to the student the type of tone necessary to express any part of the song, e.g. soft, loud, warm, bright, dark. If the pupil has been taught to have full control over his voice, he will be able to produce at will any type of tone, within his scope, that the coach requires.

On the other hand, a teacher of voice production today must know what psychological and physiological processes are needed by the singer to produce different tones, and must be able to diagnose the cause of bad tone. He must be able to assess the branch or branches of singing for which the pupil is most suited. He is primarily concerned with the production and development of the voice and development of the pupil's powers of expression. He must be able to give the pupil sufficient control over his voice so that, as I have said above, he is able to produce any type or colour of tone at will. This is most essential today as the ability to colour is more necessary than ever before. In order to be able to do this, he must have a deep artistic understanding of music. He must appreciate all the fine nuances and shadings and the range of dynamics needed in the voice to express any emotion and he must have the widest possible understanding of the mechanics of the voice. His knowledge of music must be adequate but not necessarily so detailed as that of the coach or repetiteur.

Adequate facilities for the training of a coach are available today, and his diploma or degree, in conjunction with his experience, will give a fairly accurate picture of his capabilities. Unfortunately, the

21

same cannot be said of the teacher of voice production. The diplomas given to teachers of singing today, and which are recognized as qualifications, do not satisfactorily equip their holders for their work. I shall give reasons for this, but first let me define the basic training requirements of a teacher of voice production and show to what extent they are met by present-day training courses.

Lamperti, one of the greatest teachers of yesteryear, said that the general requirements of a teacher are experience, sensitivity of ear, gift of intuition and individuality of approach. These hold good today, but to them must be added a high degree of scientific knowledge and the ability to apply it. Lamperti was a great man with great intuitive understanding, and that he took advantage of the scientific knowledge of his day can be seen from his diagrams on vocal anatomy. Teachers coming after him, with lesser intuitive gifts, have tried to apply his methods, but they have failed because they could not appreciate the true nature of his understanding and their own limitations. Lamperti's pupils must also have had a more intuitive approach than is likely to be found in this material age. But even Lamperti would have been able to achieve speedier and more far-reaching results if he could have benefited from the greater scientific knowledge available today.

For these reasons, and many others which will be found in later chapters, it will be appreciated that a teacher of voice production must have a much higher scientific training than was necessary of old. As well as the musical and artistic side, his training should include the necessary parts of physiology, psychology, physics and phonetics; and, above all, it should give him a constructive, scientific approach to his teaching and the individual problems of his students. Knowledge alone is not enough. He must have the ability to observe, analyse, and reject that which does not produce results. He must be able to test and apply new methods and have that spirit of enterprise and the desire to make researches into the developments arising from the work of other teachers or scientists.

It is also important that a teacher of voice production should himself sing. It is not necessary that he should have the backing of a singing career or a voice of world calibre, but he must be a singer with complete control over his voice and be able to demonstrate when necessary, to illustrate a particular problem. He should be able to demonstrate good and bad tone and command a wide range of colours. No teacher can hope to teach his pupils well who has no more than a theoretical knowledge of the problems involved. It is by overcoming his own problems of voice production that he will gain an understanding which no book or course can ever give him. A teacher of singing who is not a singer himself can never have the sympathy and intuitive understanding which is so necessary to his work. There will always be a lack of affinity between teacher and pupil which will not be conducive to the progress of the student. Only when a teacher has this understanding as well as a scientific approach together with the necessary knowledge can he be considered well equipped.

Let us now examine the present-day training of a teacher of voice production.

A glance at the syllabus of a well-known and representative musical institution will show that, in the training of a singing teacher, the musical side is heavily emphasized, but very little prominence is given to the technical problems of voice production. The final examination consists of oral and written work for which there are just over two hundred marks awarded. Of these marks, approximately fifty are awarded for answers on voice production. There is, in addition, a special written examination devoted entirely to musicianship. It is easy to see from this how heavily the balance is weighted. Then again, that training which is given is based essentially on orthodox, empirical methods with no adequate consideration given to the study of more recent researches. There are no opportunities for the student teacher to watch highly skilled teachers in the course of giving instruction to student singers having a variety of problems and at progressive stages of their training; and no opportunities for a student teacher to give instruction himself under the expert guidance of such master teachers. Yet the student teacher of singing needs such practical tuition and experience no less than does the student doctor.

The diploma for a singer-performer omits even this amount of technical emphasis. In the case of this diploma, emphasis is purely on music. If, in later years, the holder of such a diploma decides to teach, he will not even have the benefit of the limited understanding of technical problems which training for a teaching diploma would give him.

If one is interested in teaching and has gained such a teacher's diploma, there is no further course open as a teacher of voice production. There is a B.Mus. degree, but this is again purely musical. A science degree would be a useful asset for a teacher of voice production but is rarely taken for this purpose.

Small wonder then that a prospective singer has limited faith in a teacher with such qualifications. But where else can he turn?

One can study under a well-known singer, but this course is also fraught with extreme uncertainty. In the past more harm than good has been done to pupils studying under singers who have no qualifications other than the experience of their own voices and knowledge of their own sensations. Their experience has not been such as will give them any adequate understanding of the innumerable problems that can hamper the progress of different students. They can only base their training on their own individual experience. Indeed, they can have but little realization of the real nature of the many problems that exist, and must simply repeat the same formulas that they were given by their teachers. *If a pupil fails to respond after many years, it is assumed that he has no talent.*

A teacher must have much more extensive knowledge than he needs to pass on to any one pupil and his background needs to be entirely different from that usual for a singer.

A singer who is also a fine musician usually has all the qualifications required for a first-class singing coach, but he may have none of the qualifications required for even a low degree of efficiency in voice production. This has been proved over and over again by results. If a singer has had a good scientific background, his singing experience can prove invaluable as far as teaching voice production is concerned. Without it, however, his singing experience might well be of little value in its application to teaching.

Of course, a singer who decides to teach may undertake a serious study of the voice. Unfortunately, most singers do not do so nor do they think it necessary. The public cannot tell if the singer-teacher has made this study and seldom thinks to inquire. It is simply assumed that a singer should be able to teach. *The public are quite unaware of the fact that this pernicious system has ruined far more voices than it has created.*

The state of affairs I have just described would be sufficiently serious if those singers who do take up teaching had themselves achieved perfect production. In the vast majority of cases, however, they achieved their singing reputations without ever having had perfect production while others have lost the ability to produce their voices correctly by the time they start teaching. It is possible to sing for many years with a production which, while being acceptable to the general public, will eventually result in deterioration of the voice. The rapidity of the deterioration will depend on the extent and type of the singing. Whether, therefore, a singer of this type takes up teaching before or after he has actually lost his own voice, he will pass on a method which must eventually ruin the voices of his students at a comparatively early age. These students, as they in turn become teachers, will pass on the very methods by which their own voices have been ruined. What 'knowledge' is this to hand on?

As there are no satisfactory standard qualifications, it is natural for a student to turn to a teacher who has had a number of successes. But here again, history has shown that teachers having several successful pupils over a number of years, and even one or two brilliant successes, have yet failed to realize the potentialities of most of their pupils. Such teachers have even ruined numerous fine voices.

Results of Unscientific Training

It will be readily appreciated that few of the teachers described above, because of their lack of training, will have any real understanding of scientific methods. Unless they have undertaken such study on their own initiative, they will be in no way equipped to derive benefit from the constructive work of scientists and other teachers.

Many teachers boast that they have never read a book on singing. Clearly, such teachers must be quite satisfied with the limited methods at their command which on past records, cannot be reasonably expected to achieve a high standard of success except with one or two extremely gifted pupils—and even then, over a greatly protracted period. These teachers react to new knowledge like those who rejected Galileo's demonstration that the sun does not move round the earth. There is still a great deal not known about the voice, but those things which have been indisputably proved are rejected over and over again in favour of prejudices which can neither be proved nor produce results.

For the progress of science, many theories must be abandoned as they are shown to be incorrect. In singing, there is great unwillingness to discard anything. Indeed much effort is made by some to try to show that proven misconceptions are still valid. This attitude does not make for progress.

Incomplete knowledge may achieve satisfactory results in certain circumstances, but it will not do so in all cases and cannot be built into a sound system. Many well-known 'systems' of teaching have been built upon the success of a particular pupil with a particular clear-cut problem. The same problem does not necessarily apply to other pupils and, unfairly, their failure to respond is again assessed as lack of talent.

Now let us take the case of a teacher who is interested in learning more about his profession. Under the present system, his scientific background is likely to be so limited as to make it difficult, if not impossible, for him to gain any real benefit from his studies. Such teachers all too easily misinterpret the scientist or fail to discover the practical application of his findings. In fact, the language of the scientist may well be beyond their comprehension. It is essential that a teacher should have a good scientific background in order first that he may understand the work of the scientist, and further, he must be capable of passing on the results of his researches to his pupils in an understandable form.

This aspect of teaching is too often forgotten as most books intended for students clearly show. Terms and expressions are used which are not always clearly defined and the reader is often puzzled by a mass of words on various aspects which could be explained in a much clearer manner. Also, there are many valuable scientific works on the vocal mechanism available, but the average student is incapable of understanding their application to singing. It is a task for the teacher of voice production to interpret these to his pupils in such a way that they can understand and benefit from them. Instead, the contributions of the scientist, if not completely ignored or misinterpreted by the teacher, are passed on to the pupils in such a manner that they either misunderstand or do not understand at all.

Thus, while the teaching of singing is in the hands of such teachers, any contribution of value made by the serious teacher or scientist will fall on barren ground.

Progress in singing is also greatly hindered by the contention that the old teachers held knowledge which, if it could be rediscovered, would enable us to create once again the voices of the golden age. The futility of this hope will be demonstrated in the next chapter, but it can be said now that too much time is wasted in searching the sayings and records of the old masters for lost knowledge. At the same time, desperate attempts are made to demonstrate the truth of each and every statement made by them in the light of more recent discoveries.

Many of the sayings of the old masters are correct when considered in the light of present knowledge, but in their original context they are comparatively valueless as they are either too vaguely and ambiguously expressed and open to misinterpretation, or bound up with other conceptions of the voice which have since been proved groundless or incomplete and which therefore invalidate them.

It is an unscientific approach on the part of a teacher that leads to this uncritical attitude towards the old teaching traditions, and too great a tendency to accept them as the be-all and end-all of the teaching of singing. An open-minded investigator must try to understand the achievements of the past, but must see them in their proper perspective. The achievements and contributions of the old teachers have been given a prominence out of all proportion to reality.

Only by examining them critically is it possible to find anything of value, and only when we can see them in their correct perspective will we understand how little they can help us today and why we must proceed along new avenues of exploration.

The Contributions and Limitations of the Scientist and the Work of the Teacher-scientist

Much valuable work is being done by scientists which could be of help to the teacher of voice production. Unfortunately, as I have already stated, much of the new knowledge is not related to the problems of voice production. Neither is it presented in such a way that the average singing teacher can put it into practice with his students; whilst the possibility of the student's understanding the principles is often quite out of the question. Yet it is essential that these principles should be available in a readily understandable form for all teachers and students. The difficulty lies in the fact that the scientist seldom teaches singing and therefore has little or no appreciation of the problems that face a singing teacher who must put his knowledge into practice with *untrained and inexperienced singers*.

A scientist who has not had a wide teaching experience can be limited in many ways. It is even possible for him to cause considerable confusion. For instance, there are some scientists who have done much good work on one aspect of the voice, but who know little of its other aspects. Instead of simply presenting the facts on which they are an authority, however, many attempt without foundation to build up a complete system of voice training which only adds to the general chaos, and is one further reason why the work of the scientist has not had the impact which it deserves.

An example more to be followed is that of Dr. Oscar Russell. In addition to his own original contributions mainly in the field of resonance, he also attempted to give an all-round picture of the vocal mechanism as then understood. He presented the facts known to him clearly and concisely and did not make a single statement that was not based on scientific methods. He preferred to admit his ignorance of certain matters rather than fill in the gaps with empirical knowledge. If he brought forward a theory, he presented it as such. He did not claim it as a fact. His book[1] stands as an object lesson, and is at variance with most literature on singing in which theories are presented as facts and facts developed into impossible theories.

However, the scientific method does not end with the laboratory and the X-ray photograph. Scientific progress is not solely a matter of tabulating and describing what exists. It necessitates experimenting with various combinations in an endeavour to discover ever improved methods of procedure. The scientific method can and must be carried into the studio. Knowledge of the physiology of the voice is essential to the teacher and a very useful guide to the student. Nevertheless, it can only outline the broad principles. There is much that the physiologist and phonetician cannot tell us at the moment of the physical manifestations of the voice and there are many aspects of singing that may elude such analysis and require a somewhat different approach. For instance, the phonetician can explain what happens in the resonators of the voice but, so far, has not been able to tell us how to control them to make subtle differences to the tone. A singer needs strong and supple muscles, but he must also have the correct mental concepts for each and every tone he wishes to make. As a singer thinks, so does he sing. It is the work of the teacher to try to discover what mental concepts produce the best results.

It is not sufficiently recognized that the early attempts by famous singers to teach by trying to convey their sensations to their students were serious attempts within the scope of the scientific method, and they did produce certain limited results. Unfortunately, there it stopped. Scientific method implies that if an experiment fails, or produces only limited results, further experiments must be made in an attempt to improve upon it. However, little attempt has been made in singing to improve upon those early experiments, or explore the field further. Most teachers have contented themselves with the methods and results of the first experiments. Those who have been dissatisfied with the results have, in the main, turned their thoughts in a completely different direction—that of scientific observation and analysis from an external viewpoint rather than inward analysis of a

[1] *Speech and Voice* (Macmillan, New York 1931).

singer's needs. But as will be seen, both are necessary. Progress can only be made when these two avenues are each fully explored.

The questions that should have been asked are on the following lines:

1. Were the sensations of the singer correctly analysed and correctly conveyed?

2. Were they made by the singer under ideal conditions, i.e. when he was at the height of his fame and singing at his best, or were they made when his powers were leaving him?

3. Is it possible to describe and convey such sensations satisfactorily?

4. If those sensations described by the singer do not produce satisfactory results, are there any other sensations or concepts that will give better?

5. Are teachers overlooking anything which could be of greater importance to the student?

The first three questions are being asked today and some attempt has been made to answer them. However, the last two and most constructive questions are rarely asked and never sufficiently explored. Yet they hold out tremendous possibilities as will be seen.

It is in this field that the work of the pure scientist ends and the teacher-scientist must take over. The subtleties of these sensations are outside the scope of the pure scientist. They demand the knowledge and understanding of the experienced teacher with a scientific outlook, a teacher who must also be a singer because his work calls for extreme sensitivity of ear, intuitive understanding and great insight into the problems of his students.

But unless better facilities are provided for the training of singing teachers we cannot expect the standard of teaching to improve.

II

The Lost Tradition

From the lips of almost everyone interested in singing, we hear over and over again: 'Where are the days of the golden age of singing, the days that ended with Tetrazzini, Caruso, Melba, De Reszke and many others?' 'Why do we not hear voices like these today?' 'Something has gone. What is it?'

These questions are asked so often that one wonders if such voices do not exist today, or whether the old singing masters had secrets that have since been lost. The possession of an inherently great voice is not enough. It must be produced correctly before its greatness can be generally appreciated. Only when we have the combination of inherently great voices with correct production will we have singers comparable to the great of the golden age—singers who, besides producing tones of full, rich quality (not necessarily big, but with great carrying power), were able at will to swell them skilfully into a powerful fortissimo or caress them into the most delicate pianissimo on every note of their range, and maintain a flowing legato line.

First let me say that great voices still exist. There are today many potential Carusos and Melbas, but their voices are held back by incorrect production and their potentialities never fully realized. One of the most famous operatic tenors of today has a voice of Caruso-like proportions, but his voice is so throaty and rigid that this fact would never be guessed by the average untrained listener who can only accept a voice as he hears it and cannot differentiate between an inferior voice and one whose power and quality are reduced by incorrect production. Yet the voice of this tenor is so inherently great that, even with faulty production, he occupies a high place in opera today. One can well imagine its magnificent possibilities if produced correctly.

A perfectly produced voice is seldom heard today even on a smaller scale but, for reasons that I will give later, contemporary teaching is far more likely to produce accurate results with a small voice than with a big one. In fact, the chances of a big voice being allowed to develop fully are very remote, unless some fundamental misconceptions are removed.

Is there a secret that can make the possessors of voices such as the one I have described into singers as great as those of old? Again we ask, did the teachers of old have knowledge which we lack? Until this question has been satisfactorily answered, little progress will be made in the understanding of the voice because, while people believe that the answer to the problem lies in the past, they will direct all their inquiries into the sayings of the teachers of those days instead of into an attempt to formulate their own methods and to base them on a thorough investigation of the structure and nature of the voice. Furthermore, in these circumstances, any new knowledge is accepted and will continue to be accepted, only when it seems to agree with a teacher's interpretation of the sayings of the teachers of old, whether or not it can be proved that their success was actually due, in any shape or form, to many of the things they may have professed. This book will demonstrate the futility of these researches into the past and will show that only when our investigations are placed on a truly scientific basis can we come to a real understanding of the 'secrets' of this bygone age.

Before trying to answer our question, let us be quite clear as to the achievements of the golden age of singing. We have very little record of the actual knowledge of the great teachers of the golden age. We have a few books and some maxims, but these are of little assistance as, collected together, they would form a very incomplete teaching method, even though much of what was said might be quite correct. As far as results are concerned, we know only of a comparatively small number of singers who became great after studying with these teachers. We have no evidence of the numbers of failures they may have had. From the time of Caruso onwards, we do have records of the position, and we know that very few pupils of the teachers of this period survived. Many of these teachers may have been great singers, but as teachers (with the exception of Lamperti and Garcia) their record is that of failure after failure with many fine voices ruined for every one which was enabled to reach the heights. It is quite reasonable, therefore, to assume that the earlier teachers may have had a similar low proportion of successes. This would seem to imply rather fortuitous methods in which successes were due to many other factors and not to a real and complete understanding of the voice, nor an ability to correct badly produced voices and develop the immature.

We know, too, that many of the greatest singers possessed correctly produced voices, or alternatively developed them, without studying under a teacher. Adelina Patti, for example, had a perfectly produced voice from early childhood. We have records that she was singing and giving concerts at the age of nine, after which she went from strength to strength. Tetrazzini was self-taught and refused the services of a teacher. Gallicurci also rejected singing teachers entirely. Even today, a singer of the calibre of Mario del Monaco chose to train his own voice because he had no confidence in the methods of contemporary teachers. This shows that it was quite possible for a talented and intelligent singer to develop to the highest standard without tuition, although it is very likely that there was someone on whom they could rely to advise them whether they were producing good or bad tone. It is very difficult, in these circumstances, to assess accurately to what extent was the success of singers who did study under teachers due to their own inherent greatness, and to what extent was it a result of their tuition.

Let us now return to the original question—what has been lost? It is usually assumed that what has been lost is a method of teaching, a way of conveying to the pupil what is required and showing him clearly how to achieve it. But from the evidence I have given, it would appear that the real secret lies much deeper. Let us rather, therefore, ask the two following questions. *How was it possible for the golden age singers to sing so well in spite of having very limited technical knowledge?—and why has it not proved possible in more recent years?*

One explanation of the first question, based on a considerable amount of evidence, is that a teacher of those days was more able to recognize a correctly produced natural voice and was wise enough not to interfere with it. He would have given exercises and scales for flexibility and would have concentrated on the development of the pupil's artistry. His knowledge of how to produce a voice was extremely limited, but he did recognize the need for scales and exercises. He was humble when a great voice was brought to him, and guided it in the correct channels rather than produced it. He had intuitive knowledge and understanding of the psychological needs of the student.

Most voices have to be 'produced' as few are faultless. There have, however, been great natural voices that needed to be guided rather than produced. Many students come to teachers today with equally fine natural voices but, for reasons which will soon become obvious, the teachers cannot recognize their greatness. They try to impose their pet theories and in the process they mangle, mutilate and mistreat these voices until they are distorted and destroyed out of all recognition.

In the very early days, it is probable that teachers did not really worry, in the sense we do today, about producing a voice. They may scarcely have realized that it was possible to do so. Instead, they accepted the voice as it was and proceeded to give the student all the other things required by a singer, such as flexibility, artistry and musicianship. Years of scales and exercises must improve the voice and the skill of any singer to some extent, but they alone are unlikely to improve greatly a badly-produced voice. The important thing in the case of these teachers, however, was that they did not ruin or in any way interfere with a fine natural voice. They allowed it to develop naturally, if slowly. The practice of scales and exercises over a sufficiently long period of time makes the muscles so flexible that the ability of the pupil to adjust his resonators unconsciously is greatly increased; this enables him to approximate to a more perfect production and achieve great improvement in tone without any specific instruction.

Before the second question I have posed above can be answered, it should be appreciated that a teacher's knowledge must be twofold. He must have, first and foremost, a clear and accurate knowledge of the correct tones essential in a singing voice, and, secondly, he must be master of the technique by which the pupil can be shown clearly how to make these tones. The first aspect is rarely, if ever, discussed but, if the teacher has an incorrect conception of the tones to be acquired, no amount of technical knowledge will enable him to obtain the correct tones from his pupil. If a teacher has the correct concepts of tone, the possibility of his obtaining the desired results is greater (even if he knows practically nothing about the physiological structure of the voice) as he will encourage the pupil when he makes the right tones and discourage all others. It is my contention that the old masters knew very little about the physical nature of the voice but they did know very clearly what were the right tones. It is this conception of tone which is in danger of being lost, perhaps more so now than at any other time.

To understand why this is so, it is necessary to know something of the physical nature of sound and singing tone and something of the musical traditions of the golden age as compared with those of the present day.

A singing tone, described in scientific terms, is composed of air

33

vibrations at the frequency of the fundamental pitch, and upper partials of tone or harmonics which are multiples of the frequency of the fundamental. The quality of the tone we hear is determined by the distribution of energy among these harmonics when amplified by the resonators. The lower harmonics give roundness and robustness. They form a hard, steely core and give the tone a rich, sonorous quality. The higher harmonics give ring and carrying power, and a velvety sheen to the tone.

The quality of a singing tone is also affected by the acoustics and area of the studio or hall. In a large hall, the higher harmonics of tone die away very rapidly as they have little energy content, and the lower harmonics are damped and mellowed by the resonance of the hall. In a small studio, the voice sounds more pleasing with much less energy in both the higher and lower harmonics than is needed in a concert hall. A true operatic voice heard in a small studio sounds hard because of the full impact of the lower harmonics and rather overpowering because of the higher harmonics. The closer one is to the singer the greater the impact, particularly of the lower harmonics, and the harder the sound becomes. This is very important—a well-produced operatic voice in a small studio does not simply sound too loud for the size of the room: *it takes on a different quality.*

On the other hand, the difference between a throaty voice singing in a studio and the same throaty voice singing in a hall is mainly in a loss of power, and thereby a lessening of effectiveness; there is not the same great difference in quality as the tone is already damped in the resonators. If there was always a distinct quality change no matter what the production, these facts would have been more obvious and the present state of affairs might never have arisen.

So unless the singing teacher fully understands these facts, he concentrates on trying to give a voice the same quality in the studio as he wants it to have on the stage, i.e. after it has been mellowed by the conditions of the hall.

In these circumstances, a teacher usually does one of two things. He can make the singer produce his voice with a balanced harmonic relationship, but on such a small scale that the strength of the different harmonic components are insufficient to produce, even in a small studio, the hard sound he rejects. In other words, the singer will be using his voice correctly in relation to the room in which he is singing.

If, on the other hand, the teacher tries to build up the power of the voice for opera without emphasizing the various harmonics in the correct proportions, he can do so only by placing unnatural restraints upon the voice and ultimately producing a constricted tone. The tragedy is that the bigger the voice, the harder it must necessarily sound in a small studio and the more harm it will suffer from such restrictions.

A teacher must therefore be able to relate the tones made in the studio to the sound of the same tones if heard in a concert hall, in a large opera house, or in whatever circumstances the singer will be heard publicly. He should be able to teach his students to produce the voice so that, no matter where they sing—small hall, large hall, opera house, they can adjust the tone accordingly. It is not important how the voice sounds in the studio. What is important is how it will sound from the stage, and this is one thing the old masters fully realized. They knew that a voice is like a rapier, the steel of which must be hardened to a very high degree before it can be tempered to produce steel of high quality, with suppleness as well as strength. They knew that, if the tone of the singer was forged to the right degree of hardness in the studio, it would be tempered and mellowed by the acoustics of the opera house, but that if the degree of hardness in the studio was too low, the voice would lack ring and power on the stage, making it ineffective and unexciting.

The effect of this fundamental error has been that present-day teachers completely lose sight of the characteristics of tone they should be trying to attain in the studio. It is this lack of knowledge that constitutes one important reason for the deterioration of singing standards.

Another reason for this loss of correct conceptions is inherent in their very nature. These conceptions form a tradition that cannot be written in a book or recorded on disc or tape because the harmonics of tone are affected to a lesser or greater extent when they are mechanically recorded, depending on the fidelity of the recording and reproducing equipment. It is a tradition that must be handed down by memory alone from generation to generation and carried in the minds of the teachers.

How faithful are the minds and ears of the listener, and can they be relied upon to record faithfully the right singing tones?

Helmholtz[1] noted that a musically trained ear will not necessarily be able to hear upper partial tones with greater ease and certainty

[1] *On the Sensations of Tone*, p. 49 (translated by A. J. Ellis, Dover Publications, Inc., New York, 1954).

than an untrained ear. Similarly, a musician will not necessarily be able to analyse the harmonic components of individual notes without specific training and experience in such analysis. However, a musician is, by his training, more easily able to perceive the type of sounds with which he is in constant touch. He is able to analyse musical tone more sensitively just as the engineer is able to analyse the sound of an engine accurately and to hear sounds the average layman will fail to hear until they are pointed out to him. The more intimate one is with any particular type of sound, the more accurate will one be in recognizing and memorizing it.

In the golden age of singing, a singing teacher was most vitally concerned with the vocal tones needed for the operatic stage of his day. There were other forms of singing and music but these were of secondary importance to him. He lived in an atmosphere permeated by the noble tones of the great singers. The faculties responsible for registering and remembering these sensations of tone were, therefore, very highly developed and his ability to perceive these sounds was very acute. Thus, he did not need to be conversant with acoustics or the nature of sound.

Today, a teacher very rarely hears anything comparable to the tones of the golden age—the few recordings made then have less fidelity than those of today. Furthermore, he is surrounded by many other types of sound. Concert singing and oratorio both call for different types of tone as they are sung under different circumstances from opera. In grand opera, as well as beauty and clarity of tone, the main vocal objective of a singer is carrying power and a high intensity. There is a certain quality of tone necessary to an opera singer, a steely vibrancy, that is not required to quite the same degree in concert singing.

In this profusion of different tones, the faculties concerned with analysing any one tone in particular do not receive the same intense memory stimulation. It is readily understandable, therefore, why so many aspiring operatic singers use a tone which, though it might be more correct for the concert hall, is inadequate for the operatic stage. In most cases, they will have been taught by teachers who have grown unaccustomed to true operatic tone through schooling in an oratorio or concert tradition.

Even more important, however, is the fact that so much of the singing surrounding teachers today is bad singing. This unhappy state of affairs works its insidious influence to such an extent that the conceptions of good singing tone are gradually watered down and bad, not good, singing becomes the criterion. This applies to a great extent in England but it is also true on the Continent. If bad singing is heard frequently enough it is soon accepted as being correct, just as an oft-repeated lie is frequently accepted as the truth, except by those who are sufficiently aware of the danger. In this confusion it is no mystery that correct tones are forgotten and teachers prefer a throaty production to fine, free ringing tones. Did not academicians, familiar with grime-covered old masters and their muted shades, frown heavily upon those who sought to bring back vitality and freshness into their palette!

What is the solution? First, there must be more consciousness of the problem, a thorough realization of what has happened and why. Then the nature and physical composition of vocal tone must be studied and time spent in conscious analysis of the tones of different singers under differing circumstances, and the differences between concert tone, studio tone and operatic tone.

In the heyday of singing, it was not necessary for a teacher to analyse tone scientifically or consciously. He was in close touch with the right tones for the type of singing with which he was concerned and was able to conceive and recognize them accurately without any difficulty. Today, especially in countries where the great operatic tradition is more remote, it is essential that a teacher studies the matter conscientiously. Without knowledge of the composition of a tone, he will be less able to recognize and analyse the fundamental characteristics of good tone even when he hears it. An average listener to Gigli, for example, would have described his voice as soft and mellow. This it was on the surface, but someone who understands the nature of sound and who knows for what to listen, would have heard also the innate hard core of the tone. This ability to hear correctly gives a teacher a clearer picture of what he must demand of his students.

A teacher who does not understand these things and who is accustomed to more muted tones is not only unable to produce the right tones from his students but is also unable to recognize tones of true greatness when he hears them. *If a singer of old on the grand scale were to come to the studio of the average singing teacher today, he would almost certainly be taught to modify the very qualities that made for greatness in the golden age.*

It is extremely significant that the old masters used to refer continually to the steel, ring, brilliance and mellowness of the voice whereas contemporary teachers speak almost exclusively of mellowness and roundness. One can see at once how the emphasis has shifted.

The foregoing are only some of the reasons for the decline in singing. There are many sociological factors which must also be taken into account before the problem can be fully understood. The student of today is a product of a different age and has different problems to overcome; for instance, he is, in this more material technological age, the less able to use his intuitive faculties. In former days, much knowledge and understanding could be acquired intuitively, whereas today the student must be approached rather differently. He must be given a clear and logical understanding before he is able to act, and teaching which has no logical foundation is unlikely to succeed. That is why it is important that a student has a basic understanding of the working of his voice. Teachers who do not admit this necessity are harking back to a period which cannot be recaptured. If we, of the twentieth century, wish to equal and surpass the achievements of our predecessors, we can no longer rely on intuition. We must have sound knowledge as well.

In earlier times, a singer was able to devote more time to study. Many of the singers came from the aristocracy and wealthy classes and had the background, leisure and money to work for many years. Others were helped by wealthy patrons who enabled them to study under advantageous conditions. Today, undoubtedly, there are many more people able to study singing, but few have the means to spend a lengthy time in study. There is only a very remote chance of aid from a patron, and scholarships cannot give the same opportunities for concentrated and prolonged study.[1] The primary consideration of most people, even if they possess very fine voices and great natural talent, is to earn a living, and singing can only be undertaken in such time as is left. Many of those who can afford to study singing seriously are not prepared to devote to it their full energies because of the uncertainty of success. This is particularly so under present methods of training by which, even after many long years of arduous work, it is quite usual for a singer still to have insufficient control over his voice for a successful career, even though his voice may have great potential merit. Therefore, one finds that most people who would wish to be singers must devote their energies first and foremost to the acquisition of a skill, or the study of a profession in which there is more certainty of reaching an adequate standard at the end

[1] There are some full-time scholarships which make provision for only one one-hour lesson per week for voice production, the remainder of the time being devoted exclusively to musical and dramatic studies.

of a specific period of training, and in which a subsequent career is more assured.

In former days it was usual for pupils to receive lessons every day and some pupils lived with their master so that they could be under their constant surveillance. Today, because of the financial and other difficulties discussed, lessons are, in the majority of cases, taken no more than once a week. It follows that the student must undertake the main part of his practice without supervision. In these circumstances, true conceptions of tone easily fade from memory with the consequence that the progress of a student taking lessons at such prolonged intervals is much more difficult, particularly until a certain amount of control has been gained and proper conceptions have been firmly established. It is not surprising, therefore, that even the most enthusiastic student is often daunted and needs extreme faith, courage and perseverance to continue.

We are today faced with the fact that much less time can be spent in study by the average student, and methods that may have succeeded over a long period in earlier times can no longer be successful, since most singers are unable or unwilling to spend the time required by earlier methods. Every effort must therefore be made to evolve methods by which correct conceptions of tone can be instilled quickly, surely and accurately, and scales and exercises used to full advantage in order that voices can be trained with more certainty of success and in the shortest possible time.

There are no short cuts in the training of a singer in musicianship and artistry, but much time is wasted by inefficient methods of voice production in the establishment of a singer's basic technique. One well-known singing teacher tells his pupils that learning to sing is very like progress along a dark tunnel. 'One must press on and on with faith until suddenly one beholds the light!' What nonsense is this to tell a student! This ruinous waste of time travelling through dark ignorance must be brought to an end if we are to make progress. The light of knowledge must be shed upon the whole journey so that instead of stumbling steps in the dark, firm steady strides can be taken towards the goal.

Those people who were privileged to hear the great singers of days gone by speak nostalgically not only of their vocal prowess but also of a certain spiritual quality which was so characteristic of these singers—a stately, regal bearing very rarely found today.

Here we can gain further insight into the successes of the past, because this inspiring quality born of service to the ideal of beauty, by a subtle alchemy of spirit, helped the singer to achieve the correct production essential to beauty of tone.

In the golden age of singing, the singer lived in a world rejoicing in the creation and appreciation of beauty. Life was more leisurely, less artificial, and pursuit of the beautiful had real significance. It was an exuberant age in which the influence of the Renaissance was felt in all branches of art. It was an age which produced great painters, sculptors, architects, musicians as well as great singers.

A singer gave himself to his art in a spirit of dedication and all his efforts were concentrated on the mastery of the fundamentals and intricacies of his means of expression. Such intensity of feeling not only enhanced the nobility of his interpretation but also gave him powers of concentration and other qualities essential for perfect control in the production of the voice. People of such stature could survive even the most protracted training under a teacher of limited technical knowledge.

What do we find today? The answer is that appreciation of the beautiful and the desire to create beauty, innate in humanity, is often today too deeply buried in the subconscious. The student lives in a world of technology where the artist is tolerated but admired rather for his fees than his art, except by the perceptive few. Many look upon preoccupation with beauty as negative or effeminate. Most people never think seriously about the question at all, and the attitude of the public and the atmosphere of the age certainly do not encourage them to do so. Yet it can be one of the most positive forces in the whole of the singer's training as the mental attitude of a singer is closely bound up with his physical responses.

In these circumstances, the teacher today has an added responsibility to his student. He must try to develop his spiritual awareness as well as his technique. It is the teacher's duty to awaken in his student first and foremost, an appreciation of beauty. The student must be encouraged to acquire understanding of philosophy and of other forms of art, to broaden his outlook, widen his interpretative powers and stamp his rendition of a song with that indefinable quality that only comes from mature understanding. It will also give his production a surety born of inner confidence and purpose.

SECTION TWO
The Principles of Sound

III

The Vibrator

Physically, the phenomenon of musical sound is a series of regular vibrations or pressure pulsations in the air. These pulsations are formed by alternate condensation and rarefaction of the air. Sound may be caused by any means capable of setting up these vibrations. For instance, a vibrating string will alternately compress the air when swinging in one direction and rarefy it when swinging back in the opposite direction. Vocal sound originates from the vibrations of the vocal cords which displace the air in such a way as to alternately condense and rarefy it, thus producing sound waves. In normal circumstances, these sound waves travel outwards at a speed of between 1,100 and 1,200 feet per second.

It must be understood, however, that the air itself does not travel with the sound. It is sound energy which is transmitted, not air motion. To make this quite clear, let us imagine a stone dropped into a pond. The stone hits the surface of the water, the water on each side is pushed aside and forced upwards, and the force of this displaced water in turn presses against the surrounding water. As the water is alternately pushed out and up and then allowed to return, waves are formed which radiate in all directions. The up and down wave motion gives the onlooker the illusion of the water moving outwards but, in fact, the water does not travel. After the waves have passed, each particle of water will be in the same place as before, providing that no other factor is involved. We may also compare the transmission of sound to a bump given to the first carriage in a long line of coupled cars. The shock will be transmitted to each car in turn, although the train as a whole remains in the same position. Sound vibrations are transmitted in a similar manner except that they do not simply move in one direction or radiate on a flat surface. They are transmitted outwards in all directions so that if a series of sound waves could be made visible, they would appear as a series of progressively larger

43

balls, one outside the other, and would be made up of alternate layers of condensed and rarefied air (Fig. 1).

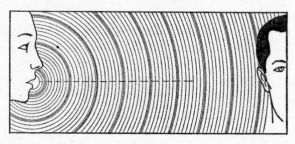

FIG. 1

As stated above, the vibrations travel outward at a uniform rate of approximately 1,100 feet per second. This is the same no matter how big the sound wave so that a soft note is heard as quickly as a loud note. It means that if there was only one vibration per second, each vibration would have travelled 1,100 feet before another vibration commenced or, in other words, it would have a wavelength of 1,100 feet. If the air is vibrated a hundred times per second, the sound waves would be following each other at a distance of 11 feet and we would say that the sound had a wave length of 11 feet. A sound with a repeated vibration or frequency of 1,000 vibrations per second is approximately C^3—two octaves above middle C on the piano. The higher the frequency (i.e. the greater the number of vibrations per second), the shorter the wavelength or distance between sound waves.

At each vibration of the vocal cords during phonation a tiny puff of air escapes between them. Although the pressure of the breath behind the vocal cords has been instrumental in determining the nature of the sound waves, once this has been accomplished, the escaping air no longer serves any useful purpose. The stone once it has created the waves, sinks and is lost but the waves go on. The sound waves produced at the vocal cords travel outwards at a speed of about 1,100 feet per second, but the escaping air leaves the mouth at a speed of a few inches per second and is soon dispersed. If the puff of air leaving the vocal cords could in some way be conveyed or diverted to a closed container, there would be no appreciable differ- ence to the sound. Unfortunately, while the stone thrown into a pond sinks in an entirely different direction from the course of the waves, the air leaving the vocal cords must take its course out of the mouth before it can disperse. This has led to the theory that the voice is physically carried on the breath and many unfortunate attempts to direct the breath in various ways in an endeavour to control the tone. As we can see, any system of directing the flow of breath is not needed even if it were possible. *In fact, any theories of the voice being carried physically on the breath are absurd because if this were so, the sound could not be heard more than a few feet from the singer.* The old saying that 'the voice floats on the breath' probably applied to a singer's attitude of mind, i.e. the conception that the sound, once it has been produced at the vocal cords, floats out by itself without being pushed or directed in any way by the singer. Any striving to achieve correct production by a student who believes that the sound is carried out on an air-stream whose direction he can control usually leads to very bad straining. Here is an example of the way in which the sayings of the old masters can be misinterpreted to produce most harmful results.

When considered from a musical point of view, sound has three main attributes: pitch, quality or timbre, and intensity.

PITCH

In a stringed instrument, the pitch of the tone is dependent on the rate of the vibration of the string, e.g. 264 vibrations or cycles per second will be heard as middle C. If the frequency of any pitch is doubled, the resulting note will be an octave higher and if the frequency is halved, the resulting note will be an octave lower. The greater the number of vibrations per second, the higher the pitch. The smaller the number of vibrations per second, the lower the pitch. The ear normally hears only frequencies of between 20 and 15,000 vibrations per second.

Now, let us say that we had three tuning-forks, one with a frequency of 264 c.p.s.,[1] the second vibrating at twice this rate or 528 c.p.s., and a third vibrating at half this rate or 128 c.p.s. per second. If we sounded all three tuning-forks simultaneously, the ear would hear the tone as one octave below middle C (132 c.p.s.), i.e. the tone corresponding to the tuning-fork having the lowest number of vibrations per second. This lowest frequency is the fundamental of the tone. The sound from the other two tuning-forks is heard as harmonics giving a change of quality to the note. However, whilst

[1] C.P.S. = cycles (or complete vibrations) per second.

THE VIBRATOR

a tuning-fork emits almost a pure tone, i.e. the tone having only the frequency or pitch for which it is designed, this is not true of the tone produced by vibration of the vocal cords nor of the vibrations from any stringed instrument. This is because when a string vibrates, it does so not only at its full length to produce the fundamental but also segments into halves to produce the first harmonic which has twice the frequency of the fundamental; into thirds producing the second harmonic which has a frequency of three times the fundamental and into fourths, fifths, sixths, sevenths, eighths, etc., to produce series of higher harmonics. Other forms of vibrating material such as membranes and air cavities also segment to produce harmonics.

Another name for these harmonics is overtones or partials. When this term is used, it must be remembered that the fundamental is the first partial and the first harmonic is the second partial. All partials from the second onwards are also known as upper partials as their frequency is higher than that of the fundamental.

Fig. 2 will help in understanding the forms assumed by a vibrating string. The dotted lines show the position of the string at the end of half of a complete cycle. In all the cases illustrated the strings are vibrated in a special way so that they do not segment but perform

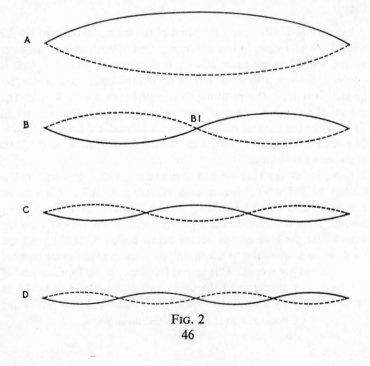

FIG. 2

simple pendular oscillations. In (*a*) we see the form of vibration if the whole of the string vibrates and does not segment, in which case we would hear a single simple tone with no harmonics. In (*b*) the string has been touched at b¹ and each half of the string is set in vibration separately. Each half of the string would therefore vibrate simultaneously at twice the frequency of the whole string and would be heard as a simple tone one octave above the note of (*a*). In (*c*) the string has been touched at two points so that it is divided into three equal parts, each simultaneously producing the twelfth above form (*a*). In (*d*) the string is divided into four equal parts, each producing a note two octaves above note (*a*). A string may be subdivided in this way until the sections are too short and stiff to be capable of vibration. Very fine strings are therefore capable of division into a greater number of vibrating sections than thicker ones.

Normally, however, a vibrating string does not merely perform simple pendular oscillations as above, but assumes a form which may be regarded as a compound of the above simple vibrations and many more. As a result of these complex forms of vibration, a great number of harmonic upper partials are heard at the same time as the fundamental or prime tone represented by form (*a*) above. The thinner the string, the greater the number of these higher tones will be produced.

QUALITY OF TONE

The quality of a tone is dependent on three factors, the pitch of the note, the energy distribution of the fundamental and upper partials produced by the vibrator, and the way in which these vibrations are affected by resonance.

Quality: Pitch

If we look at the following table, we can see that the pattern of the sound waves is different for each note of the scale.

Pitch	Frequency of Fundamental or 1st Partial	Frequency of Upper Partials			
		2nd P.	3rd P.	4th P.	5th P. etc.
c¹	264	528	792	1056	1320 etc.
b¹	495	990	1485	1980	2475 etc.
c²	528	1056	1584	2112	2640 etc.
f²	704	1408	2112	2816	3520 etc.

Furthermore, as the thickness of the string alters with the pitch, the total number of upper partials produced will vary as well as their frequency. This will also affect the pitch character of each note as far as quality is concerned.

The difference in pitch quality characteristics resulting from these variations can be observed in a piano where we find a gradual change in quality as we go from the lowest to the highest note. The ear, however, is somewhat limited in its ability to analyse the harmonics of tone and it hears these changes mainly as a proportion of the predominant character of the lower notes and that of the higher notes, the predominant character of the lower notes being dark and mellow while that of the higher notes is brilliant and silvery. Now, although these changes in pitch quality attributes are even and gradual, they are usually divided in the mind of the average listener into two groups, i.e. those notes where the dark, mellow character is dominant and those notes where the bright character of the higher frequencies is greatest. To make this quite clear, let us compare the musical scale with a colour chart gradually shaded from yellow to green in which each colour in the scale has a little more green and a little less yellow. The shades having a higher proportion of green will usually be described as green and vice versa, even though they all have a certain proportion of the other colour.

The understanding of these pitch quality attributes is of paramount importance to the singer. The point at which there is an equal balance between these two quality characteristics is also most important as we shall see later. In the following pages, the notes below this point of equal balance will be called the *lower pitch quality zone* while those notes which lie above this point will be grouped under the term *upper pitch quality zone*. The point at which one zone merges into the other is approximately C264.

Quality: Energy Distribution of Fundamental and Upper Partials

The quality of the tone is dependent, in the second place, on the energy distribution of the fundamental and various partials produced when the vocal cords vibrate. A thicker string produces a stronger fundamental and stronger lower harmonics, with less higher harmonics. A thinner string produces a weaker fundamental and weaker lower harmonics, but a greater number of higher harmonics and these have relatively greater strength than those produced from a thicker string. As the richer quality lies in the lower harmonics, we may say

48

that the thicker the string, the richer the musical quality. However, although the lower harmonics are most necessary for rich quality, a certain proportion of higher harmonics are essential to add brilliance to the tone. For this reason, it is important that the thickness of the string on any given pitch be such as to produce the best proportion of higher and lower harmonics.

It is found that the most satisfying tone is derived from a string which also has the right amount of elasticity. In this case, a greater thickness of string can be employed with much less reduction of higher partial quality as a supple string produces more and stronger higher harmonics than one of less flexible material. If there is too great a proportion of higher harmonics, as with a very fine string, the tone suffers. This is overcome, by the use of a thicker string with the necessary elasticity so that there is a combination of the most desirable attributes of the thicker and the thinner string. The importance of elasticity is recognized, as we all know, in the choice of the most suitable material for the strings of a violin. If the string is too thin the tone will be thin and not sufficiently mellow. If it is too thick or not sufficiently supple, the tone will be dull.

The more supple the vocal cords, the greater will be the mass vibrated with less volume of breath and with less tension of the cords. The necessary flexibility must be obtained by suitable exercises.

If the voice is used correctly, the energy content of the upper partials will be perfectly balanced but if the breath is used incorrectly so that the vocal cords vibrate at an unsuitable thickness, this will not be so.

Quality, as affected by Resonance

Thirdly, the quality of the tone is dependent on the manner in which the vibrations from the vocal cords (fundamental and upper partials) are modified by the resonators. As we shall see, the shape of the resonators can be altered so as to intensify certain partials and dampen others in varying degrees. In a well-produced voice, the resonators are shaped so as to amplify those partials which give best quality to the voice but—and this is most important—the pattern of pitch quality change must not be interfered with. Certain variations are permissible to give variety and colour to the tone but any attempt to invest a note with the pitch quality attribute of a note at the other end of the scale is to force the voice into unnatural channels not in accord with the nature of the instrument. If a teacher has no understanding of pitch quality attributes, he can very easily acquire an incorrect conception of the best quality for any note.

INTENSITY

The third attribute of sound is intensity. This depends on the amplitude of the vibrations and thus, the degree to which the air particles are rarefied and compressed. The greater the swing of the vibrator, the greater the amplitude of the vibrations and the greater the intensity of the note. The loudness of the sound we hear depends on its intensity but the two terms must not be confused. Intensity refers to the actual measurable rate of the energy flow while loudness is a subjective, psycho-physiological response to sound intensity and depends on several things such as ear sensitivity and pitch.

The intensity of the sound as heard, as well as its quality, is also dependent on the resonators and, of course, the acoustics of the room or hall.

VIBRATION OF STRINGS IN RELATION TO PITCH

It is necessary to explain the manner in which a vibrating string or membrane alters according to pitch. When a string vibrates, it generates a pitch which is determined by its length and tension. The greater the tension, the higher the pitch of the note produced when the string is vibrated. The pitch of the note in a singing voice can therefore be raised in the larynx if the tension on the vocal cords is increased, just as the pitch of a violin string is elevated by tightening the string when it is tuned. Because of the limits of elasticity inherent in any vibrating string, elevation in pitch can be carried only so far by this act of increasing the tension. When this limit has been reached, further elevation in pitch can be accomplished as a result of a phenomenon similar to fingering a violin string on the finger-board and thus shortening the length of the string which is free to vibrate. The pitch rises an octave if the length is halved or if the tension is doubled.

Another factor which affects the pitch of a vibrating string is its thickness or mass. If the mass is decreased the pitch rises and if the mass is increased the pitch will be lowered because of the greater inertia induced by the greater mass. If the pitch is to be held constant while the mass is increased it will therefore be necessary, either to shorten the string or increase its tension proportionately. *If the adjustment is made by increasing the tension, it is obvious that the maximum thickness of the string will depend on the tension it is capable of sustaining.* The possible thickness of the string will also depend on its elasticity. As a flexible material produces less inertia, a greater mass can be employed before the limit of its tension is reached.

From the foregoing we can also see that a note of the same pitch can be produced from strings of varying lengths and of differing tension and mass—providing that the ratio between these three elements is correct for the pitch concerned. The tone quality in each case, however, will be somewhat different and this accounts in part for the difference in tone quality between various instruments, even of the same type, for instance, between different makes of pianos.

DEFINITION OF AN EVENLY-RISING SCALE

A normal scale may be defined as one in which the intensity rises in direct proportion to the rise in pitch. If the intensity of each note in such a scale were recorded, the pitch intensity curve of the scale should rise smoothly and evenly. In other words, as the pitch ascends, so does the degree of loudness. However, because the ear expects this rise of intensity with the rise in pitch, a scale sung in this way would be heard as a smooth, unbroken musical line. It is important, however, that the rise in intensity should not only be smooth, but in a definite ratio to the rise in pitch. If the intensity rises too slowly in relation to the rise in pitch, no matter how smooth it is, the scale will appear to the listener to get softer. If the intensity rises smoothly but too steeply, the scale will appear to grow louder. Of course, if the intensity increases unevenly in a series of jerks, the result is an uneven scale. *The ability to sing an evenly-rising scale is the foundation of a singer's technique.* Until he can achieve this, he cannot be said to have any adequate degree of control over his voice.

IV

Resonance

All musical sound, as we saw in Chapter III, originates from some mechanism which causes a series of regular vibrations or pressure pulsations in the air. However, these pulsations, whether they be caused by a vibrating string, a reed or a tuning-fork, are too slight to affect the ear of the listener to any great extent. In order to affect the ear of the listener with such strength as to give him the sensation of hearing a louder sound, these pulsations must be made more powerful. This is achieved by placing the vibrator or initiator of sound in relation to a resonator whose function is not only to increase the strength of the vibrations but also to affect the quality of the tone.

As sound waves are initiated by vibrating an elastic material, resonation is a phenomenon also made possible by the elasticity of air[1] and other materials. A resonator may consist of the same type of elastic material as an initiator of sound, e.g. one piano string may resonate sound waves from another; an air column may be vibrated to produce its own note or it may be used to resonate a note produced by, say, a tuning-fork. In the case of an initiator of sound, the elastic material is vibrated mechanically by a bow, a hammer, air pressure, etc.; in the case of a resonator, the elastic material is caused to vibrate by the energy of sound waves which have already been set up by another vibrating material. On the one hand, we have what is known as 'free vibration' and on the other, 'forced vibration'.

Free Vibration

If a weight suspended from a spring is raised from its position of rest and then allowed to fall, it will start to return to its original position. By the time the weight reaches this position, it is travelling

---

[1] Elastic in the sense that it can be compressed and will recover from the compression.

so rapidly that it overshoots and stretches the spring until the tension of the spring gradually brings it to a momentary stop and then starts lifting it again. By the time the weight returns to its normal resting position, it is going so fast that it once more overshoots, this time in the opposite direction. This process would be repeated indefinitely were it not for the fact that the motion of the spring is gradually stopped by the friction of the air and the friction of the spring itself. The frequency, i.e. the number of complete up-and-down movements or vibrations per second, is called the natural frequency of the system. This natural frequency depends on the mass of the weight and the stiffness of the spring.

As we saw in the last chapter, a taut string possesses this quality and when vibrated by a bow, a hammer or by any other such means, will oscillate at a frequency which depends on the length, thickness and tension of the string. It is in this way that a string can be made to modulate the air to initiate sound waves, the amplitude of which will depend on the force with which it is made to vibrate by the hammer or bow.

A column of air in a tube also has this springy quality and, when agitated by blowing across an opening or tapping the container, is thrown into what is called stationary vibration, i.e. the air surges backwards and forwards from one end of the tube to the other at a rate or frequency which depends on the length of the tube and the number of openings. It will produce a sound corresponding to the frequency of these surgings which is the resonant pitch of the tube. This can be easily observed by blowing across bottles whose air spaces have been varied by filling them with different amounts of liquid. If the length is halved, the vibrations are enabled to travel twice as many times per second and produce a note of twice the frequency.

The formation of upper partials has already been described in the vibrations of a string. Upper partials are also formed when a column of air vibrates and may be visualized as subdivisions of the column of air vibrating in the tube. Each subdivision consists of sound waves surging to and fro in the same way as the sound waves of the prime which occupy the whole length of the tube. Thus, if the partials prominent in a note include the second, third, fourth and fifth, we may visualize the column of vibrating air in the tube as divided simultaneously into halves, thirds, fourths, fifths of its total length, each division producing sound waves which occupy its own length. Differences in the number and relative strength of the partials produced, and thus the quality of the tone, depend on the size, shape and material of the tube.

FORCED VIBRATION (RESONANCE)

As stated above, forced vibration occurs when a freely vibrating force is applied to a vibratory system, i.e. to a material or body capable of being vibrated by such free vibration. We shall differentiate between two kinds of forced vibration (a) when the frequency of the vibrating force corresponds to the frequency of the system, and (b) when the frequency of the vibrating force differs from that of the system.

If we take a weighted spring as described on page 89 and apply to it a very small pulsating force whose frequency is the same as that of the spring, we shall find that its movement will gradually build up until it oscillates through a considerable distance or amplitude. If, on the other hand, a pulsating force of the same strength or magnitude but of a frequency either much higher or much lower be applied to the weight, very little movement will result.

If this principle is translated into the realm of sound and a pulsating force be applied to a suitable elastic system (one capable of producing sound waves) we find that if the period of the pulsating force corresponds to the natural frequency of the system, there is an enormous amplification of the original sound. Fill a bottle with water until the pitch of the note elicited by blowing across the mouth is g. Then take a series of tuning-forks from c to c^1, strike each one in turn, and hold it over the mouth of the bottle. The response will be small for c and c^1 but greater for notes nearer to g, and greatest of all for g itself. If all the forks are made to vibrate simultaneously at the same amplitude, the g will be picked out, and heard above all the other forks. The air in the bottle is said to respond by resonance.

Strictly speaking, the term resonance applies only to (a) above and is the particular case of forced vibration when the force and the system are in unison; when the natural frequency of the vibrator and that of the system correspond. The term is, however, more generally used to describe both types of forced vibration.

FORCED VIBRATION (vibrator and resonator having different natural frequencies)

If the frequencies of the vibrator and that of the resonance system do not correspond, then one of two things may happen, depending on the manner in which the two are coupled, their relative size and the materials used, as follows:

(a) *The vibrating force may be pulled out of its natural frequency so that it vibrates more or less in the period of the system.* Most wind instruments fall into this group, the pitch of the note depending not on the natural frequency of the reed or other vibrator, but on the natural frequency of the air column to which it is coupled. In these circumstances, the function of the vibrator is simply to agitate the body of air in the resonating tube more or less powerfully, after which the resonator alone determines the pitch of the note. This means that the natural frequency of the resonating tube must be different for every note. In the organ, there is a pipe of different dimensions for each note played by the instrument; in most other wind instruments, there is only one pipe or tube, the dimensions of which can be altered by covering finger-holes or manipulating other devices for altering the natural frequency of the tube.

(b) *The vibrating force may compel the system to vibrate at a frequency related to its own, no matter what the natural resonant pitch of the system may be.* If a sounding tuning-fork is held over the mouth of a bottle of different resonant pitch, we shall hear a sound from the air in the bottle, and the sound will have the pitch of the fork. The air in the bottle will not vibrate freely at its own resonant pitch but, instead, its vibrations will be forced and the sound waves from the tuning-fork will determine the pitch of the note. Examples of this type of vibration are to be found in many musical instruments, e.g. bowed string instruments and the piano. When a violin is played, the sound comes mainly from the body of the instrument and partly from the contained air. These vibrating systems give the pitch of the note of the string. They are in forced vibration. The body of the violin and the contained air both have a tone of their own but their vibrations are not free; they are controlled by the vibrating string. In a piano, the vibrating string imposes its frequency on the sounding board.

The resonance of the human voice is of this type; the pitch of the note is determined by the frequency of the vocal cord vibrations and the resonators are in forced vibration.

DAMPING

When an elastic material is struck, a certain amount of energy is communicated to it and this energy appears in the vibrations. The energy is dissipated in two ways. A certain amount is used up in overcoming the resistance of the air to the vibrating material, and some of it is communicated to the air as sound waves and conveyed through the air away from the vibrator. As the energy is thus lost, the vibrations die away and the note ceases to be heard. The rate at which the vibrations die away varies considerably and these differences are due to what is known as damping. In the case of a tuning-fork, which is lightly damped, they last for a long time; with piano strings rather less; while those of an air cavity, which is more heavily damped, die away more rapidly.

If either of the above sources of energy-loss is increased we say that the rate of damping has been increased. For instance, if a large tuning-fork be struck and held in the air, its rate of damping is very slow. If it be given a blow of the same strength and then placed with its shaft on a table or in a resonance box, the rate of damping is increased; the sound produced is much louder, sound waves are carrying energy more rapidly away from the fork, so that the vibrations decay more rapidly and the duration of the sound is appreciably shortened.

Thus, a lightly damped resonator will give greater amplification of the original free vibrations, and reduced duration; a heavily damped resonator will give less amplification of the free vibrations and increased duration.

Damping is increased by a soft surface, and higher frequencies in particular are weakened in these circumstances, the reason being that a soft surface when compressed takes longer to recover its original state. This slowness of movement makes it impossible for a soft surface to vibrate strongly, if at all, to the very rapid frequencies of the higher harmonics, and we say that they are absorbed by soft surfaces, or that soft surfaces do not respond to these frequencies.

The amount of damping, as far as the voice is concerned, is also affected by the amount of breath passing through the cavity. The higher the ratio of breath to cavity size, the greater will be the damping.

In the voice, the question of damping is also closely related to the size of the cavity because as the throat cavity is enlarged the soft surfaces become more taut and the damping decreases.

SELECTIVITY OF RESONANCE

As explained above, if the tuning of the vibrator and the resonating system is accurate, i.e. if the pitch of the vibrator and that of the system correspond, we get a very marked amplification of the original vibrations. If the tuning is not accurate, i.e. if the frequency of the two systems do not correspond, the response is less marked. If, however, the above experiment is tried with different materials, one important fact emerges.

In some cases (e.g. in that of the tuning-fork and the bottles) we find that although the response is more marked at correct tuning, it is also quite appreciable when the vibrator is a semitone, a tone or even a third or fourth from the pitch of the resonating system.

In other cases (e.g. when one tuning-fork is used to resonate another) we find a very marked response at correct tuning and almost no response when the tuning is even slightly inaccurate.

In the first case, the resonance is said to be general—the response does not vary greatly with the correctness of tuning and is still notice-able when the mistuning is considerable; there is a good response over a wide range of pitch without very marked response at correct tuning. In the second case, the resonance is said to be highly selective.

The above differences in selectivity are, of course, due to differences in the degree of damping of the resonator. A lightly damped resonator is very selective and, as the damping increases, the selectivity de-creases. Thus, a very lightly damped resonator responds strongly to the frequencies to which it is tuned and gives little response to neigh-bouring frequencies. A heavily damped resonator responds over a large range of wavelengths without marked response at any. Too selective a response will give a thin tone lacking in richness of partials; too highly damped a resonator will give a muffled, dull quality. The damping of the resonator must therefore be somewhere between these two extremes to provide the most pleasing tone.

In a musical instrument, it is essential that all notes are resonated satisfactorily and a resonating system which transmitted one note at strong intensity and others feebly would be quite useless. Even an air column does not have a sufficiently general response.

Except on an organ, it is not generally practicable to have a sepa-rate vibrator and individual resonator for each note to be played by a musical instrument. Nor would this necessarily be desirable. In wind instruments, as indicated above, this problem is overcome by being able to alter the frequency of a single resonating tube to cor-respond to each pitch required on the instrument and, as we know, the vibrator is forced into the frequency of the resonator.

In instruments where the pitch of the note is the function of the vibrator, there are two ways in which a more general response can be obtained. Firstly, by ensuring that the natural frequency of the resonating system is outside the range over which a general response is required, i.e. of greater (higher) frequency. Secondly, as with the sounding board of a piano or the box of a violin, and also in the case of the voice, by having a responding system with a series of overlapping regions of pitch so that the resonance is distributed. Here the degree of damping is an important factor.

RESONANCE OF UPPER PARTIALS

In our account of resonance so far, we have considered only the fundamental pitch of the note. However, as we know, the vibrator of a musical instrument vibrates not only at its full length to produce sound waves having the frequency of the fundamental, but also segments into halves, thirds, fourths, fifths, sixths, etc., thus producing sound waves having 2, 3, 4, 5 and 6 times, etc., the frequency of the fundamental. How are these upper partials affected by resonance?

An elastic material will vibrate sympathetically to a note having a corresponding natural frequency, but it will also vibrate sympathetically to a note, one of whose partial tones corresponds to its own natural frequency. Suppose that one goes to the piano and holds down the key for the tone middle C (264 cycles) without sounding it. This will raise the damper from the strings of middle C, enabling them to vibrate freely. If the C an octave below (132 cycles) is struck and then damped out by letting the key come up immediately, middle C (264 cycles) will be heard to ring out. The string can only have been brought into vibration in sympathy with a sound source which produced its own natural frequency, in this case, the first upper partial of the note which was struck. A similar phenomenon occurs when the G key, a fifth above middle C is held down. In this case it will respond to the second upper partial of the low C string.

Basically, upper partials respond to the same laws of resonance as the fundamental of the tone. The previous paragraph gives us the key to the understanding of general resonance. If the frequency of the resonator corresponds to the frequency of the note, then the note will be reinforced mainly on the fundamental. If the frequency of the resonator corresponds to one of the upper partials of the tone, then this partial will carry the greater part of the sound energy of the note. If the frequency of the resonator does not correspond exactly to the frequency of any partial of the tone, it will be forced into the frequency of the partial with which it most nearly coincides. Thus, just

RESONANCE

as a resonator may give a more selective response to notes of a closely related frequency, so are certain partials of a note more favoured than others by different systems according to their tuning and selectivity. By altering the tuning of the resonator, it is possible to shift the emphasis on to different partials of the note.

Distribution of Sound Energy

By far the greater part of the energy or intensity of a musical tone may be contained in one or more of its upper partials reinforced by resonation and only a small part be contained by the fundamental.[1] It is a peculiarity of the human ear that whatever may be the pitch and relative proportions of the partials contained in a note, we normally perceive the pitch of the fundamental or prime only.

This is because no matter which partials of the note carry the greater proportion of sound energy, all partials can be mathematically related to one, and only one, fundamental frequency. This is so even in notes which are an octave of each other. Compare, for example, C 264 and C 528.

Partial	Frequency	
1 (fundamental)	264	528
2	528	1056
3	792	1584
4	1056	2112
5	1320	2640
6	1584	3168
etc.	etc.	etc.

(Note. All partials of both notes are divisible by 264 but not all partials of the lower note are divisible by 528.)

It is this harmonic relationship which establishes in our mind the sensation of hearing the fundamental frequency and not the frequency of the partial tone which happens to be strongest.

Let us take, for example, a note having a fundamental frequency of 66 c.p.s. The original unresonated sound may be illustrated as follows, the thickness of the lines giving an idea of the possible

[1] A striking example is C. Seashore's analysis showing the distribution of energy among the partials of the note when played on the open string of a violin. It was found that the fundamental contained only *one-tenth of one per cent* of the energy of the tone, the first and second partials containing twenty-six per cent and forty-five per cent respectively. (*Psychology of Music*, McGraw Hill 1938.)

difference in amplitude between the various partials of the tone, the spacing between the lines representing pitch.

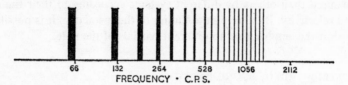

FIG. 3. *Fundamental and Harmonics (unresonated)*

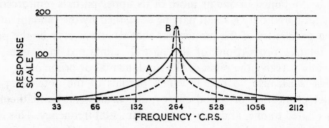

FIG. 4. *Resonance Curves (single resonator)*

Let us now imagine this to have passed through a resonant cavity tuned to 264 c.p.s. (Fig. 4—higher curve), or another of the same frequency but of greater damping (lower curve). In each case, the selectivity is such that the response in the case of the higher curve is negligible except for frequencies very close to 264 c.p.s. In the case of the lower curve which is more highly damped, the selectivity is not so great. Fig. 5 gives an idea of the proportionate increase of sound energy due to resonance on the fundamental and upper partials in the case of the lower curve.

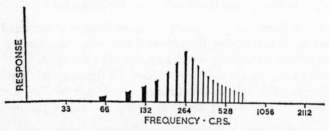

FIG. 5. *Sound Spectrum (single resonator)*

If the original sound is passed through a series of coupled resonators, it is possible to get an increased output of sound over a rather wide frequency band, or multiple resonant effects where there may be several regions of pitch in which the partials are strengthened. Thus, if we have a pair of resonators as shown in Fig. 6 the sound illustrated in Fig. 3 would emerge with the characteristics illustrated in Fig. 7.

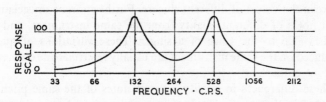

FIG. 6. *Resonance Curve (double resonator)*

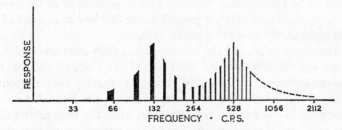

FIG. 7. *Sound Spectrum (double resonator)*

In both cases, the fundamental pitch of the note is 66 c.p.s. and it is this note that we consciously hear, although in Fig. 5 the seventh partial (264 c.p.s.) and adjacent partials receive most of the emphasis, and in Fig. 7 the third and fifteenth partials (132 and 528 c.p.s.) and adjacent partials are reinforced more strongly.

If one or more resonators in a series is capable of being separately tuned to different frequencies, an enormous variation in the distribution of sound energy is possible.

PARTIAL TONES AND MUSICAL QUALITY

'If a note of given pitch is played successively on two different musical instruments, and played with exactly the same loudness, we can distinguish between the two sounds and refer each to its appropriate instrument. The basis of this judgement is the "quality" of the sound. The piano, the violin, the voice, the flute, etc. each has its own characteristic "quality". The German word for it is "klangfarbe", the French word (frequently borrowed in English) is "timbre".[1]

In addition to these differences between different kinds of musical instruments, we can also distinguish differences of 'quality' or 'timbre' between different instruments of the same kind—between two different pianos, between a Stradivarius and a modern violin, between the voices of different singers. Furthermore, a musician can elicit notes of different quality from the same instrument, and this applies also to the voice of a singer. These variations of quality produced on the same instrument are usually referred to as differences in 'tone colour'.

These differences in quality between notes of the same pitch are reflected in the energy distribution on the various harmonics of the tone. It is generally agreed by the more recent investigators that, in order to be effective and pleasing, a large percentage of the energy of the musical tone must, in general, be carried by one or more of its first eight partials, omitting the seventh.

According to Jeans,[2] the second partial adds clearness and brilliance but nothing else; the third partial again adds brilliance, but also contributes a certain hollow, throaty, or nasal quality; the fourth adds yet more brilliance, and even shrillness; the fifth adds a rich, somewhat horn-like quality to the tone, while the sixth adds a delicate shrillness of nasal quality. The first six partials are all part of the common chord of the fundamental, but this is not so of the seventh, ninth, eleventh and higher odd-numbered partials. The higher harmonics also add qualities which contribute to the beauty and brilliance of the tone, unless the emphasis is on the odd-numbered partials which add dissonance and a certain harshness.

The distribution of energy is determined by the nature of the vibrations which initiate the tone and then by such factors as size, shape, tuning, damping and selectivity of the resonators.

If there is too much emphasis on the higher harmonics, the tone is inclined to be 'plummy'; if too much emphasis on the lower harmonics, the tone has a hard, open quality. In a correctly produced voice where the emphasis is correctly apportioned, the tone has a mellow, open quality—the lower harmonics giving body and strength, the higher harmonics clothing the tone with a brilliant sheen.

[1] Alexander Wood, op. cit., p. 61.
[2] Jeans, *Science and Music*, p. 86 (C.U.P. 1937).

RESONANCE

AMPLITUDE—VIBRATOR *v.* RESONATOR

Before going any further, the reader must be quite clear as to the respective parts played by the vibrator and the resonator in the loudness of the tone we hear, and we shall use a violin as an example to illustrate this point. If we detach a violin string from the body of the instrument and stretch it between two points in mid-air to the same tension as when it is on the violin, and then draw the bow across it, there would be very little audible difference between the sound produced by this isolated string when bowed as for a pianissimo note or a fortissimo note. In both cases, we should hear a very feeble sound that would not carry far.

If the string is returned to its position on the box of the violin and bowed in exactly the same manner as before, we find that there is an enormous amplification of both notes but that there is an appreciable difference in loudness between the pianissimo note and the fortissimo note, although this difference was barely perceptible when the notes were played on the isolated string.

Thus, differences in dynamics are essentially a function of the vibrator. The resonator acts as an enlarger or amplifier of the dynamics inherent in the embryo note produced by the vibrator.

Some resonance systems are, of course, more efficient than others in the amplification of sound, depending on such factors as size, degree of damping and accuracy of tuning. It is possible to reduce or increase the power of the sound by altering the above resonatory factors. It must be remembered, however, that such changes also affect the distribution of sound energy among the various partials and thus affect the quality of the tone (Figs. 3–7).

In most cases, slight changes in these resonatory factors will make very little difference to the amplification of the tone but may cause a considerable change in quality. Because of these inherent quality changes, the scope of a resonator in varying the amplitude of the tone by the above means is negligible.

Once the size, damping and tuning of the resonator has been established according to the type of tone desired, increases of power, often quite considerable, can be accomplished only by increasing the amplitude of the original tiny vibrations.

SIZE OF RESONATOR

The size of the resonator or resonators must, of course, be correctly related to the amplitude of the original vibrations. A reed organ pipe which effectively resonates the vibrations of its own reed would be much too large to be affected by the vibrations of a clarinet reed—to give an extreme example. On the other hand, the effect of a resonator too small in relation to the original sound can be likened in some ways to the distortion produced were we to hear a large organ in a room much smaller than that for which it was intended. The tone would sound muffled.

In musical instruments, the relationship between resonator and vibrator makes allowance for a certain range of dynamics, e.g. the sounding board of a piano will effectively resonate the vibrations of the strings whether they be struck lightly or with greater force. When we come to examine the resonating system of the human voice, we shall have to consider *whether one setting of the resonators is capable of effectively resonating the whole range of dynamics in the original tone from the vocal cords or whether the setting must be altered as the amplitude of the vocal cord vibrations increases.*[1]

Vowel Quality

The human voice alone among musical instruments is capable of colouring the tone in such a way as to produce qualities which we recognize as vowel sounds. As with differences in musical quality, the differences between vowel sounds are a result of variations in the relative strength of the partials of which the tone is composed. However, the pattern of emphasis resulting in vowel formation possesses certain characteristics which differ from those patterns that affect the musical quality of the tone. Different vowels may be sung to the same note and, in all cases, except for the differences in vowel quality, the general character of the notes may remain the same. On the other hand, we may vary the quality of the tone while singing the same vowel. *We shall therefore distinguish between 'vowel quality' and 'instrumental quality' and our study of resonation of the human voice is largely concerned with this distinction.*

The instrumental quality of a tone as defined above, depends on the order of the partial strengthened and this, of course, varies on every pitch. In the case of middle C (c^1, 264 c.p.s.), the second partial adding clarity and brilliance will be c^2 (528 c.p.s.); in the case of d^1 (330 c.p.s.), the second partial adding the same qualities will be d^2 (660 c.p.s.).

On the other hand, each vowel sound is associated with an empha-

[1] See pages 172 and 175.

sis on partials in the same pitch regions, no matter what the frequency of the note being produced. A region of pitch in which all partials are strengthened is called a formant, and for every vowel there are two formants of fixed pitch.

The frequencies of these vowel formants have been studied by many investigators using various methods. The results vary somewhat, but not significantly. The results for a number of observers have been summarized in the following table by H. Fletcher.[1]

Characteristic Frequencies of the Vowel-sounds

Speech Sound	Low Frequency	High Frequency
u (pool)	400	800
u (put)	475	1,000
* o (tone)	500	850
a (talk)	600	950
o (ton)	700	1,150
a (father)	825	1,200
a (tap)	750	1,800
e (ten)	550	1,900
er (pert)	500	1,500
a (tape)	550	2,100
i (tip)	450	2,200
e (team)	375	2,400

* In these vowels the higher formant is much weaker and, for this reason, the earlier experimenters did not detect them.

It must be remembered that the frequency given is, in every case, the centre of a range of pitch within which all partial tones are strengthened, and this range is sometimes considerable.

These differences in harmonic structure give to each vowel not only its distinguishing sound but also a distinctive quality or tone colour, in the same way as differences in harmonic structure are responsible for differences in the pitch quality characteristics of various notes.

[1] *Speech and Hearing* (Macmillan).

Description of the Vocal Mechanism

V

The Breathing Mechanism

Voice is primarily a result of the vibrations of the vocal cords, the nature of the vibrations being dependent to a great extent on the flow of breath and the action of the respiratory muscles.

Although the larynx is described in detail in a later chapter, it must be understood that, strictly speaking, it forms part of the respiratory mechanism as it provides a variable resistance to the air flow and therefore plays a part in the mechanics of breathing. It cannot be wholly divorced from discussion on breathing and a certain minimum will come into this chapter.

DESCRIPTION OF RESPIRATORY MECHANISM

When we breathe, the air is alternately taken into and expelled from the lungs. The lungs are suspended within the thorax (chest cavity) to which they are held by the pleural tissues. The thorax, lungs and the muscles which affect their shape and movement will be described below.

THORAX

Although the lungs take up most of the volume within the thorax, the thorax also houses the heart and other structures. It is barrel-shaped, but narrower above than below. It is longer behind than in front, and wider from side to side than from front to back. The top and sides are formed by the first ten pairs of ribs (costae) which are attached to the thoracic vertebrae of the spinal column at the back, and directly or indirectly to the sternum (breast bone) at the front. The base of the thorax is formed by the diaphragm—a dome-shaped muscular and membraneous sheet forming a partition between the thorax and abdomen.

69

THE BREATHING MECHANISM

The ribs are all firmly connected to the spinal vertebrae at the back by extremely strong ligaments which enable them to operate at that point as if they were on hinges, that is, allowing each rib to move freely as the front end or middle of the rib is raised or lowered.

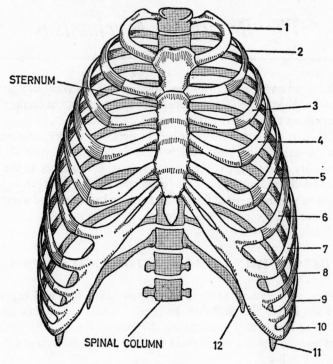

FIG. 8. *Thorax*

The ribs are not horizontal. They curve first in a wide sweep outwards at the back, then forward and slope steeply downwards towards the front. Because of this slope, any raising of the front ends of the ribs results in an increase in the front-to-back (antero-posterior) diameter of the thorax (Fig. 9). As each rib has a larger circumference than the one above, raising of the middle of the rib towards the position of the smaller rib above results in an increase in the side-to-side (transverse) diameter of the thorax (Fig. 10).

The ribs may be sub-divided into three groups according to the manner of their front (anterior) attachment, their shape and direction, all of which slightly modifies the above movements.

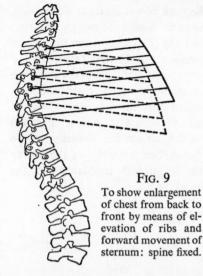

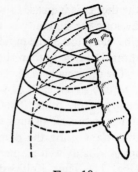

FIG. 9

To show enlargement of chest from back to front by means of elevation of ribs and forward movement of sternum: spine fixed.

FIG. 10

To show enlargement of chest from side to side by raising of the middle of the rib.

1. First pair of ribs. These form the inlet of the thorax and are attached by their cartilages to the manubrium sterni (upper section of the sternum). Up and down movement of the front ends of the ribs causes a raising and lowering of the sternum and a slight change in the antero-posterior diameter of the thoracic inlet. No movement occurs during quiet breathing.

2. The upper (vertebro-sternal) ribs. These comprise the second to sixth ribs which are all connected directly to the sternum by their cartilages. These ribs move about both axes described above. Raising of these ribs is associated with a forward movement of the sternum and an increase in the measurement of the thorax both from side to side and from back to front.

3. The lower ribs (seventh to tenth). With the exception of the seventh ribs, none of the ribs in this group is connected directly to the sternum. The eighth, ninth and tenth are all joined together in front, and attach to the seventh by their upward-curving cartilages. The seventh is at one point fastened to the sixth by a small cartilage. These ribs rotate essentially on the same axes as those of the vertebro-sternal ribs, but differences in shape and direction result in slight differences in their movement. Raising the anterior end of these ribs is associated with a backward movement of the sternum and thus a slight decrease in the antero-posterior diameter of the thorax. Rotation on the second axis causes the middle of the rib to move backwards as well as upwards and outwards so that the measurement of

the thorax is increased towards the back as well as from side to side. Because the obliquity of the downward slope increases in the lower ribs, elevation of the middle of these ribs results in greater increase of thoracic capacity than similar movements in the upper ribs.

The differences in the anterior attachments of the ribs divides them into two units, each of which can move to a great extent independently of the other. This independent movement is affected by the different muscle groups that attach to each unit, one of the most important being the diaphragm which affects the elevation of the lower ribs as well as increasing the vertical diameter of the thorax (Fig. 11). Thus Keith[1] divides the inspiratory mechanism of the thorax into two main parts as follows:

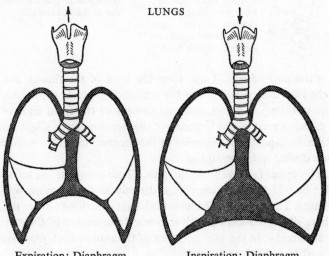

LUNGS

Expiration: Diaphragm
high, chest narrow.

Inspiration: Diaphragm
descended, chest wider.

FIG. 11. *Increase of thoracic capacity resulting from elevation of the ribs and descent of the diaphragm*

(*a*) an upper mechanism connected with the expansion of the upper lobes of the lungs, and consisting of the second, third, fourth and fifth ribs and their attached muscles;

(*b*) a lower mechanism designed for expansion of the lower lobes, and consisting of the sixth, seventh, eighth, ninth and tenth ribs and their attached muscles, including the diaphragm.

[1] Arthur Keith, 'Mechanism of Respiration in Man', article in *Further Advances in Physiology* (Leonard Hill, London 1909).

The first ribs are part of another mechanism which plays little part in normal respiration. The eleventh and twelfth ribs are functionally part of the abdominal wall.

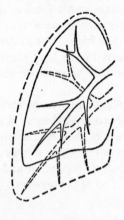

FIG. 12

Diagrammatic representation of the elongation of two main bronchi and divisions during inspiration. Note also the slight movement of the lung root.

The costo-sternal and diaphragmatic walls of the thorax move most freely and it is here, i.e. at the front, sides and base, that greatest expansion is possible. The regions bounded above by the cupola and behind by the bodies of the vertebrae and the vertebral ends of the ribs (especially the upper ribs) can expand very little.

LUNGS

The lungs—one on the right and one on the left—are suspended in the thorax within closely fitting elastic tissue called the pleura. The thorax walls are also lined with pleural tissue. The shape of the lungs follows the shape of the thorax walls to which they are held by their pleural surfaces so that enlargement of the thorax is accompanied by corresponding increase in the area of the lungs.

The lungs are packed with minute air cells (alveoli). Air enters the trachea (windpipe) through the glottal opening of the larynx, thence into the main bronchial tubes. After the bronchial tubes enter the lungs, they divide and subdivide into a branching tree of tubes. The main tube and first few branches are termed bronchi, while the succeeding and smaller branches are termed bronchioles. It is through the bronchioles that the air reaches the air cells where oxygen is exchanged for carbon dioxide from the blood.

The lungs also contain blood vessels which bring the blood into the network of capillaries which surround the air cells, and conduct it out of the lungs after the above gas exchange has taken place.

The greater the expansion of the lungs, the more air is enabled to enter and take part in gas exchange. The upper regions of the thorax can expand very little and expansion of the upper lobes of the lungs is made possible by a downwards and forwards movement of the root of the lung during inspiration, rather than by increase in the volume of the thorax in those areas. The parts of the lung most free to expand as a result of increase in thoracic volume are the costo-sternal and diaphragmatic.

The trachea and bronchi are made of extremely tough cartilages in small rings. They cannot be voluntarily controlled so as in any way to vary their characteristics but, because of their ring arrangement, are capable of bending in any direction as the body assumes different positions. They dilate and elongate during inspiration and narrow during expiration as a result of contraction of the bronchial muscles.

RESPIRATORY MUSCLES

The respiratory muscles may be divided into two groups, those whose action results in increase of the thoracic capacity and thus assist inspiration, and those whose action causes reduction of thoracic capacity thus helping in expiration. It must not be assumed, however, that respiration is simply a matter of alternating tension and relaxation of these muscles as inspiration follows expiration. The inspiratory muscles are active not only during inspiration and the expiratory muscles are not necessarily always active during expiration.

The Diaphragm is a dome-shaped muscular and membraneous partition that separates the cavities of the thorax and abdomen. Its lower edges are attached by means of muscular fibres around the full circumference of the chest. These muscular fibres arch upwards and inwards to end in tendinous fibres which interlace and form the central tendon of the diaphragm. They are divided into three parts: (1) *the vertebral*, which arise from the lumbar vertebrae of the spinal column; (2) *the costal*, which arise from the costal margin; and (3) the *sternal*, which arise from the tip of the sternum.

Contraction of all parts of the diaphragm results in descent of the central tendon and enlargement of the chest cavity in a vertical direction. The descending diaphragm presses downwards and forwards on the upper abdomen.

74

Contraction of the costal fibres of the diaphragm, i.e. the fibres inserted into the ribs or rib cartilages, causes an upward and outward movement of the lower ribs. Conversely, any movement of the lower ribs, due to action of other muscles, will affect the circumference of the diaphragm accordingly. If the ribs are held fixed in any way, then contraction or relaxation of the diaphragm will result only in upward or downward movement of the dome.

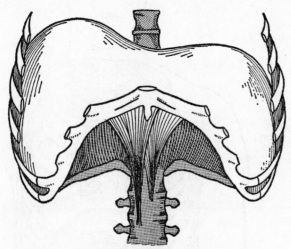

FIG. 13. *Diaphragm*

While contraction of the musculature of the diaphragm causes it to descend, it possesses no muscles capable of raising it. Ascent of the diaphragm is due to relaxation and other forces acting on the diaphragm, i.e. abdominal compression whereby the contraction of the abdominal muscles presses on the abdominal contents and raises intra-abdominal pressure which forces the diaphragm up from below.

The diaphragm is probably the principle muscle of inspiration and, during quiet breathing, may be the only respiratory muscle in action.[1] However, it is not the only one as inspiration can still be produced if the diaphragm is paralysed. The muscles which contribute most towards increase of thoracic capacity, after the diaphragm, are considered by most authorities to be the intercostal muscles.

The Intercostal Muscles. The space between each rib is filled with two layers of muscles.

[1] E. J. M. Campbell, *The Respiratory Muscles and the Mechanics of Breathing*, p. 12 (Lloyd-Luke, London 1958).

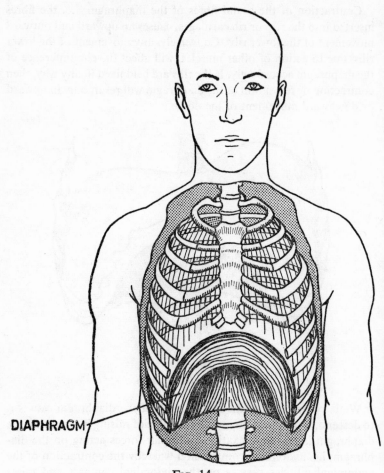

DIAPHRAGM

FIG. 14

The outermost, the *external intercostal muscles*, slope obliquely downwards and forwards from the upper rib to the one below.

The innermost, the *internal intercostal muscles*, slant in the opposite direction, namely downwards and backwards. The internal intercostals can be subdivided into (*a*) a *posterior* or interosseous portion, where the bony part of the ribs slope downwards and forwards, and (*b*) an *anterior* or intercartilaginous portion, where the costal cartilages slope upwards and forwards.

The exact role of the individual intercostal muscles has not been definitely established. One of the most widely accepted theories is that

76

the external intercostals and the anterior or intercartilaginous internal intercostals raise the ribs, and the posterior or interosseous internal intercostals depress the ribs.

There is activity in the external intercostals and probably the intercartilaginous internal intercostals during inspiration and there is reasonable evidence that this activity contributes significantly towards the upward and outward movement of the ribs (Campbell). The activity of the intercostal muscles increases progressively during graded voluntary inspiratory efforts. They are powerful and probably second in importance only to the diaphragm as inspiratory muscles.

Their activity during expiration is more complex. Green and Howell[1] have shown that contraction of the intercostal muscles persists into expiration during quiet breathing and dies away as the rate of air flow rises to a maximum. However, Campbell shows that *this activity is not expiratory in function but is a continuation of inspiratory activity which opposes expiratory forces and results in a lower rate of airflow than would be the case if these muscles ceased to contract at the end of inspiration.*

In addition to the above activity at the beginning of expiration, their action during expiration is as follows. The intercostal muscles are inactive throughout expiration in quiet breathing and when the depth of respiration is considerably increased, i.e. up to ventilation rates of 40 L./min.

The intercostal muscles of the lower spaces contract towards the end of expiration when the depth of respiration is increased beyond this. They also contract during voluntary maximum expiration and, probably, during graded voluntary expiratory efforts. It is not clear whether the above activity of the intercostal muscles during the latter part of expiration aids or opposes the expiratory forces. *It should be noted, however, that activity of the intercostal muscles during expiration occurs in more or less the same circumstances as increase of activity of the abdominal muscles and roughly in the same proportion.*

Abdominal muscles. The abdominal wall is composed of muscular sheets, one above the other, the fibres of each layer being differently directed. They consist of the transversus abdominis, the internal oblique, rectus abdominis and external oblique. Together, these muscles form a wall which protects the abdomen and supports its various organs in position. All are attached to ribs or rib cartilages above and end in ligaments in the pelvic region below.

[1] Campbell, op. cit., pp. 66–67.

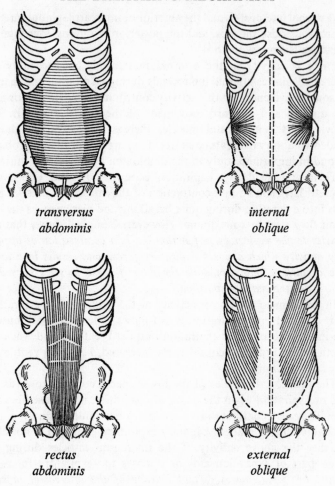

transversus
abdominis

internal
oblique

rectus
abdominis

external
oblique

FIG. 15. *Abdominal Muscles*

The innermost of these muscles is the *transversus abdominis*, a broad muscular sheet of mainly horizontal fibres encircling the upper and lower abdomen. It has attachments to the spinal column at the back and its upper border is attached to the cartilages of the six lower ribs.

The fibres of the *internal oblique* radiate from the hips. Their ascending fibres are attached to the cartilages of the seventh, eighth and ninth ribs.

The *rectus abdominis* is a double muscle sheet running vertically upwards from the crest and symphysis of the pubis to be inserted into the anterior surfaces of the tip of the sternum and the cartilages of the fifth, sixth and seventh ribs.

The *external oblique* is the outermost of the abdominal wall. It originates from the eight lower ribs by slips which interdigitate with the serratus anterior and latissimus dorsi muscles and descends some-what obliquely on either side of the rectus. These muscles have the following actions:

(*a*) *Compression of abdominal contents.* When the abdominal con-tents are compressed, intra-abdominal pressure is increased and up-ward pressure is brought to bear on the diaphragm. If the diaphragm is relaxed, this pressure will cause it to ascend and reduce thoracic capacity. If, however, the fibres of the diaphragm are contracted, the diaphragm will press down and help further increase intra-abdominal pressure from above. In this way, the diaphragm and abdominal muscles are antagonistic to each other. The degree of intra-abdominal pressure and the amount of movement of the diaphragm and ab-dominal walls will depend mainly on the relative amount of activity in each of these two groups of antagonistic muscles although other muscles may also be involved.

(*b*) *Depression of the ribs.* Contraction of the abdominal muscles draws downward the lower ribs to which they are attached, thus assisting in expiration. If, however, the ribs are held fixed, the action of the abdominal muscles in compressing the abdominal contents will be facilitated.

(*c*) *Flexion of the trunk*

The actions of the abdominal muscles in depressing the ribs and increasing intra-abdominal pressure against the diaphragm results in reduction of thoracic capacity and constitutes their expiratory ac-tivity. They are in fact the most important and the only indisputable muscles of expiration.[1]

The abdominal muscles have various separate functions in con-nexion with movements of the trunk but, in expiration, the degree of contraction of the various muscles depends on the strength of the expiratory force desired. The greater the expiratory force, the greater the extent and degree of the contraction.

There is a certain amount of postural activity in the abdominal muscles during inspiration but no significant respiratory activity. The circumstances of their contraction during expiration is as follows. During quiet breathing, expiration is produced by elastic recoil of the

[1] Campbell, op. cit., p. 40.

lungs and there is not usually any expiratory activity in the abdominal muscles. *When the depth of respiration is increased considerably, the abdominal muscles contract only towards the end of expiration when the force of elastic recoil is at a minimum.* As the ventilation is further increased, the intensity of contraction increases and begins earlier in expiration. Vigorous contraction occurs in all voluntary expiratory manœuvres such as the expulsion of reserve air, maximum voluntary ventilation, and in such activities as coughing, straining and vomiting. Contraction of a slight to moderate intensity has been noted during ordinary speech by Campbell, although quite a loud sound can be produced without the use of the abdominal muscles if a maximum inspiration is used to obtain maximum elastic recoil.

Contraction of the abdominal muscles is necessary to develop any significantly raised intra-thoracic (intrapleural) pressure because, if the intra-abdominal pressure were not raised in conjunction with reduction in the volume of the bony skeleton of the thorax, a rise in intra-thoracic pressure would be dissipated by depression of the diaphragm.

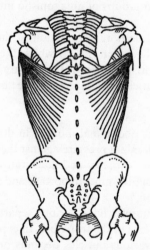

FIG. 16. *Latissimus dorsi*

Accessory Muscles of Respiration

There are a number of accessory muscles which may take part but which do not, in normal circumstances, play a significant role in inspiration. The most important of these are the *scaleni* and the *sternomastoid* muscles. These, and other muscles which normally only contract at the end of a maximum inspiration, connect the upper ribs and sternum to the collar-bone and neck. Contraction of these muscles helps to raise the upper ribs and thus increase the capacity of the upper chest to a certain extent. In addition to actual respiratory efforts, any action which raises the shoulders and tenses or bends the neck brings these muscles into tension.

Another muscle of respiration over which the singer has voluntary control is the *latissimus dorsi*. This muscle contains fibres which arise from the lower three or four ribs and which might be able to elevate the ribs, thus facilitating inspiration. Contraction of the muscle as a whole, however, compresses the lower thorax and can therefore assist expiration. The main mass of the muscle can be felt to contract quite vigorously during coughing, but it is not normally active in respiration except during deep inspiration. When voluntarily tensed, this muscle can be felt by placing the hands in the small of the back. This muscle is brought into play more strongly whenever a high support is necessary (see page 103).

PHYSIOLOGY OF RESPIRATION

In order that the normal functions of the body may be carried out, it is necessary that all the tissues are continuously supplied with sufficient amounts of oxygen. At the same time, the carbon dioxide produced in the tissues must be removed. Oxygen is obtained from the air taken into the lungs during inspiration and exchanged for carbon dioxide which is removed at the succeeding expiration. In

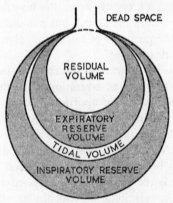

FIG. 17. *Breath Volumes*

order that bodily needs may be met, it is necessary that sufficient air is taken into the lungs.

The amount of air inspired during each respiration is called *Tidal Volume*. In a resting adult this is approximately 500 c.c. (1 pint). After a normal inspiration, the maximal amount of air that can be inspired by voluntary effort is called *Inspiratory Reserve Volume* and is roughly 1,600 c.c. (3 pints). A similar amount of air can be expelled from the lungs at the end of a normal expiration and this volume is termed *Expiratory Reserve Volume*. At the end of a maximal expiration, there remains a substantial amount of air in the lungs (around 1,000 c.c.) which is known as *Residual Volume*.

VENTILATION

The process whereby, as inspiration alternates with expiration, fresh air enters the respiratory tract and an equal amount of pulmonary gas is exhaled is known as ventilation. The respiratory tract is composed of the conducting airway (nose, mouth, pharynx, larynx, trachea, bronchi and brochioli) and the alveoli. Rapid gas exchange of oxygen (O_2) and carbon dioxide (CO_2) occurs only in the alveoli— not in the conducting airway. It is the amount of inspired air that enters the alveoli each minute (alveolar ventilation) which is of greatest importance.

Alveolar ventilation depends not only on the total amount of air inspired but also upon the frequency of respiration. The same total amount of air may be inspired, for example, in 32 shallow breaths or 16 deeper breaths and, in each case, there will be a considerable difference in the amount of alveolar ventilation.

This is because at each breath, no matter how deep, about 150 c.c. of fresh air never reaches the alveoli but remains in the conducting airway which, for the purposes of calculating alveolar ventilation, is termed respiratory dead space.

During the following expiration, this fresh air in the dead space is exhaled first, to be replaced as expiration proceeds, by gas from the lungs—air containing a high proportion of carbon dioxide. At the beginning of the next inspiration, this alveolar gas from the dead space is drawn back into the lungs before the incoming fresh air.

Exactly the same quantity of dead space air is thus 'lost' in a shallow breath as in a breath of greater depth, and the shallower the breath, the greater is the proportion of inspired air which does not take part in alveolar ventilation. Also, the greater the number of breaths per minute, the greater the amount of dead space loss.

In the following examples (Fig. 18) we have three different types of breathing: (A) rapid and shallow, (B) normal, and (C) slow and deep. In each case, the minute volume (total amount of inspired air per minute) is 8,000 c.c. However, in A, where this volume has been produced by 32 shallow breaths, the difference between alveolar ventilation and total inspiration is 32 times the dead space volume of 150 c.c.—a total of 4,800 c.c. In B, where the 8,000 c.c./min. has been obtained in only 16 breaths, the difference is only 16 times 150 c.c. or 2,400 c.c. while in C, the loss is only 1,200 c.c.

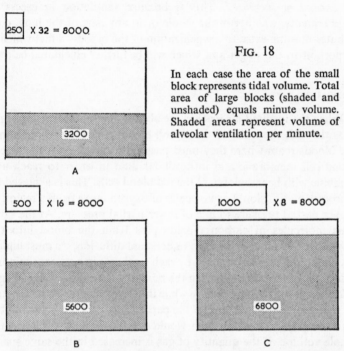

250 X 32 = 8000

3200

A

500 X 16 = 8000

5600

B

1000 X 8 = 8000

6800

C

FIG. 18

In each case the area of the small block represents tidal volume. Total area of large blocks (shaded and unshaded) equals minute volume. Shaded areas represent volume of alveolar ventilation per minute.

These figures show that if the normal frequency is halved, the depth of respiration need only be increased by approximately 70 per cent (not doubled) in order to obtain the same degree of alveolar ventilation. *This fact is of importance in singing where the frequency of respiration is decreased.*

DISTRIBUTION

Another factor in ventilation—one, however, over which the individual has no control—is the distribution of air in the lungs.

It is important not only for sufficient air to reach the alveoli, but this air must also be evenly distributed. The form of the human lung is very complex, the airways being divided and subdivided a great number of times. In such a lung, even though it is healthy, alveolar ventilation is not absolutely uniform. In various disorders, alveolar ventilation may be decidedly uneven. Thus, in the same individual, poorly ventilated areas may exist side by side with areas in which the ventilation is excessive. *In such a case, bodily requirements may not be met even though the minute volume and total alveolar ventilation be normal or increased.* This is because ventilation in excess of requirements, whether in the whole or in any part of the lung, contributes nothing extra to oxygenization of the blood—a fact which is important to the singer and which will be further elucidated below.[1]

DIFFUSION

When the inspired air reaches the alveoli, the molecules of oxygen pass through the walls of the alveoli and capillary membranes into the bloodstream where they must pass through the plasma, the red blood cell membrane and intracellular fluid in order to reach and combine with haemoglobin in the red blood cells. This is achieved by a process of diffusion, i.e. molecules of oxygen move from a region of higher partial pressure to one of lower partial pressure. At the same time molecules of carbon dioxide pass from the blood into the alveoli by the same process. To understand diffusion, we must understand that the pressure exerted by each single gas in a gaseous mixture is independent of other gases in the mixture. The pressure of each gas is known as the partial pressure while the total pressure of the mixture of gases is equal to the sum of the partial pressures, i.e. a sum of the separate pressures which each would exert if it alone occupied the whole volume. If the quantity of gas is increased in the same space, the pressure rises proportionately. The symbol P will be used below to denote the partial pressure of the gas.[2]

The following examples will serve to describe the above process. Let us say that a certain volume of alveolar gas with high PO_2 (high oxygen pressure) comes in contact with a certain volume of venous blood with low PO_2. Molecules of oxygen will pass from the alveoli into the blood until the pressures are equalized. If the PO_2 of the same quantity of blood was lower before diffusion, the alveolar PO_2 and blood PO_2 would also be lower after diffusion had taken place

[1] See pages 86–87.   [2] See Appendix I.

84

because a greater quantity of oxygen would have to be transferred to this same quantity of blood before the pressures would be equalized. If, on the other hand, the PO_2 of the blood remained the same but the total quantity of blood coming into contact with the alveoli is increased, a similar result would be obtained, i.e. lower PO_2 in both blood and alveoli after gas exchange had taken place. In this case, the quantity of inspired air (i.e. ventilation) or the alveolar PO_2 would have to be increased in order to oxygenate the blood to the same degree. Diffusion of carbon dioxide occurs in a similar manner except that the molecules of carbon dioxide pass from the blood into the alveoli.

BLOOD CIRCULATION

Venous blood flows from the tissues to the lungs in order that there it may give off carbon dioxide and receive oxygen from the alveolar air. It is important that the flow of venous blood passing through the pulmonary capillaries be equally distributed through the lungs so that all the blood comes in contact with the alveolar air. If this were not the case, some of the blood would pass through the lungs and be pumped back to the tissues with little or no change in gas composition.

Assuming that the pulmonary capillary flow is evenly distributed it is also necessary that the amount of blood passing through the lungs per minute is in such relationship to the amount of fresh air reaching the alveoli each minute that adequate gas exchange takes place. If the amount of blood passing through the lungs is correctly balanced with alveolar ventilation, the blood leaving the lungs will carry the correct amount of oxygen and carbon dioxide. If the blood flow and alveolar ventilation increases proportionately, the same will apply. If, however, increased or normal blood flow is in excess of ventilation, the amount of oxygen in the blood and alveoli will decrease, and the amount of carbon dioxide will rise above normal levels.

The amount of blood passing through the lungs depends on the requirements of the tissues. During activity of any kind, the tissues produce proportionately more carbon dioxide and need greater amounts of oxygen. In these circumstances, the heart beats faster and the blood circulates more quickly so that a greater volume passes through the lungs each minute. When this occurs, the alveolar ventilation must be increased in order to oxygenate the increased volume of blood.

THE BREATHING MECHANISM

BLOOD GASES

When the oxygen from the air enters the blood, it no longer retains the same form. It combines with the blood in two ways: (1) it is dissolved in the watery parts of the blood, and (2) it combines chemically with haemoglobin in the red cells of the blood.

A liquid is capable of dissolving only a certain amount of gas. A simple example is in a bottle of aerated water where gas has been compressed into the bottle. As soon as the bottle is opened, the gas in excess of the amount which can be dissolved leaves the surface of the water. The amount of oxygen which can be dissolved in the watery parts of the blood is in direct proportion to the PO_2 to which it is exposed (i.e. alveolar PO_2) but, no matter how high this rises, breathing ordinary room air, the amount is insignificant in relation to the oxygen requirements of the body.

Fortunately, the haemoglobin in the red blood cells is capable of combining chemically with much greater quantities of oxygen than could be dissolved in the same amount of liquid. One gram of haemoglobin can combine chemically with 1·34 c.c. of oxygen. The actual amount of oxygen combined with the haemoglobin depends on the partial pressure of oxygen in the blood. The amount of oxygen taken up by the haemoglobin, however, does not rise in direct proportion to a rise in partial pressure but rises quite steeply until the haemoglobin is almost completely saturated, the last part rising somewhat less steeply than at the beginning. If the subject is inactive, this point is reached during quiet breathing of room air. From then on, the partial pressure may rise considerably if ventilation is increased but there will be very little addition of oxygen to the red blood cells because an increase in ventilation after the saturation point is neared will not result in a corresponding rise in oxygen content of the red blood cells.

The manner in which oxygen combines with haemoglobin means that the ventilation may fall somewhat below normal without causing a significant reduction in the oxygen content of the blood.

The carbon dioxide content of the blood, on the other hand, rises and falls in direct proportion to alterations in alveolar PCO_2. This means that a change in alveolar ventilation will be more directly apparent in the measurement of carbon dioxide than in oxygen content, whether this be a rise or fall.

To summarize, *ventilation in excess of requirements* will cause the

86

carbon dioxide content to fall below the normal level[1] and will not enable the singer to create an oxygen reserve because, once saturated, the oxygen content of the blood cannot be increased significantly. *Inadequate ventilation* results in reduction of oxygen content and increase of carbon dioxide in the blood, the latter reaching significant proportions before the former.

CHEMICAL AND VOLUNTARY REGULATION OF VENTILATION

It is important that the gas content of the blood be kept at the correct levels. In the resting state, the amount of air taken into the alveoli is sufficient to supply the oxygen needs of the body and to remove the carbon dioxide which must be given off in a similar quantity. If blood flow increases and alveolar ventilation is inadequate the body has mechanisms which sense this. These are chemically controlled centres in the brain that are sensitive to the gas content of the blood which reaches them. If, through inadequate ventilation, the oxygen content of the blood falls and the carbon dioxide content rises, these chemo-receptors will stimulate activity in the respiratory system so that there is an increase in ventilation through increased tidal volume and perhaps also an increase in the rate of breathing. If inadequate ventilation is due to voluntary decrease in the rate of breathing (as in speech) then the increased ventilation resulting from stimulus from the cerebral centres will be achieved by an increase in the depth of respiration only. These chemo-receptors, while not quite so sensitive to oxygen lack, are extremely sensitive to a rise in carbon dioxide which, as stated above, is more closely indicative of a variation in ventilation.

In certain types of activity, even though the ventilation is increased considerably, it may still be insufficient to meet the bodily needs. In this case, certain physiological processes are set in motion which allow bodily processes to continue, but an oxygen debt is created which must be repaid by a continuation of increased breathing after the activity has stopped. After a certain point, the existence of an oxygen debt causes a decrease in the efficiency of muscular contraction. In some cases, the type of activity may make it impossible for ventilation to be increased greatly even though the need for increased ventilation may be considerable, e.g. in running, a sprinter runs 100 yards without taking a breath, but performance in all races over 400

[1] Overbreathing, by washing out the carbon dioxide from the blood, may make people dizzy and faint.

yards (or one minute) is limited by the capacity of the lungs and heart to transport oxygen and carbon dioxide.

The normal ventilation of severe muscular exercise, although very high, does not reach the level of ventilation which is possible when a person voluntarily uses all his breathing reserves. Thus, while it is not possible for the reasons just given to create an oxygen reserve, in some cases it may be possible and desirable consciously to increase ventilation during activity over and above the increase which would result reflexly from the activity. In fact, training in many sports includes the acquiring of certain breathing habits which delay, as far as possible, the building up of a high oxygen debt without hindering the carrying out of the activity.

MECHANICS OF BREATHING

The factors governing mechanical movement of the thoracic cage are not only muscular. During inspiration, muscular effort enlarges the thorax, causes expansion of the alveolar gas and reduction in pressure so that air at atmospheric pressure flows in. However, this muscular action is opposed by certain forces which may be divided into three components as follows:

(a) *Force to overcome elastic resistance.* Elasticity is a property inherent in certain matter that causes it to return to its resting shape after external pressure, tension or distortion. If we take a spring as in Fig. 20 we find that the degree to which it can be stretched varies proportionately to the amount of force used until the elastic limit is reached or exceeded. At the same time, force is needed to compress a spring if the resting position allows of this (Fig. 19).

Some tissues of the lungs and thorax also possess the property of elasticity. Like the springs, these tissues must be stretched during inspiration by an external force (muscular effort) and when this muscular force ceases, these tissues recoil to their resting position. The greater the muscular force, the more the tissues are stretched and the greater the volume increase on inspiration. The relation between muscular force and amount of stretch depends only upon change in distance or volume and is not affected by the speed at which the stretching action is carried out.

Fig. 20 shows single elastic systems since in each case there is only one spring or one set of springs. However, the lungs and thorax each possess a different set of springs with the resting levels at different

points. As the lungs and thorax are held together by the pleural surfaces, the combined resting level is at a point where the lung springs
are somewhat stretched and the thoracic springs are somewhat compressed. In singing, however, we are only concerned with the combined resting level of the lungs and thorax which is at the end of a
normal quiet expiration. This balanced or neutral position is called
the *resting expiratory level,* and the volume of air contained in the
lungs at this level is the *functional residual capacity.* Muscular effort is
required to stretch the springs towards inspiration or compress them
towards further expiration.

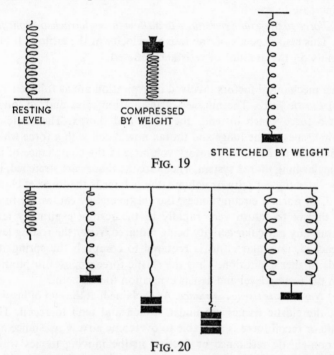

RESTING LEVEL

COMPRESSED BY WEIGHT

STRETCHED BY WEIGHT

FIG. 19

FIG. 20

(b) *Force to move non-elastic tissue.* Muscular force is also required
to overcome inertia within the tissues that move during inspiration,
such as the rib cage, diaphragm, abdominal contents. Unlike the
force required to overcome elastic resistance, it is dependent on
velocity of motion and therefore on the rapidity or quickness of
breathing, i.e. the greater the speed of the respiratory movement the
greater the muscular force. At the beginning of a normal inspiration,
when air flow is just beginning, it is at a minimum. It is greatest at the

time of greatest airflow (even though maximum inspiratory volume has not yet been reached). It is zero at the end of inspiration when flow and movement stop, although it is at this point that the muscular force needed to overcome elastic resistance must be the greatest because maximal volume has been reached. End inspiration is, therefore, a result of reduction in muscular effort sufficient to cause no further inspiratory movement, but not so great a reduction as will allow the elastic forces to cause the elastic tissues to recoil towards the resting position. If it is desired to increase the speed of the inspiratory movement, the muscular effort must be increased proportionately to the increase in speed.

(*c*) *Force to overcome resistance to airflow through tracheo-bronchial tree.* This also depends on the rate or velocity of the airflow. It also depends on the amount of resistance offered.

The mechanical factors involved in expiration are as follows:

(*a*) *Elastic force.* The muscles of inspiration relax and no longer exert a force which distends the lungs and thorax. The stretched elastic tissues of the lungs and thorax now recoil with a force which depends on their end-inspiratory volume and the compliance of the particular lung thorax system. The more the tissues are stretched, i.e. the greater the capacity or volume, the greater is the force of elastic recoil. In normal circumstances, the elastic energy causes the lungs and thorax to return very rapidly to the resting expiratory level without any muscular activity being required. After the resting level is reached, muscular effort is required to compress the springs towards further expiration. Thus the elastic force opposes inspiration from the resting level and assists expiration to this point.

(*b*) *Non-elastic tissue resistance.* As explained, at the end of inspiration, the elastic tissues are under stretch and tend to recoil. This elastic or recoil force is available to overcome airway resistance and the non-elastic resistance or friction in the moving tissues which exists during expiration as well as during inspiration and which, again, is greatest at the moment of maximum airflow. If, during expiration, there is any continuation of tension in the inspiratory muscles, this also opposes the expiratory elastic forces.

(*c*) *Resistance to airflow through tracheo-bronchial tree.* As in inspiration, this depends on the resistance offered as well as the rate or velocity of flow. In phonation, resistance is also offered by the coming together of the vocal cords, a factor which will be discussed in detail below.

THE BREATHING MECHANISM

INTERACTION OF ELASTIC PROPERTIES AND RESPIRATORY MUSCLES

The forces moving the lungs and chest wall during breathing may come, then, from three sources: muscles of inspiration, muscles of expiration, or passive elastic forces. The direction, speed and magnitude of the respiratory movements are a result of the action of all these forces, and the activity of the respiratory muscles can only be really understood when studied in relation to these elastic forces. Certain patterns can be observed during quiet and increased breathing which can be summarized as follows: Inspiration is produced by contraction of the muscles of inspiration opposed by the elastic recoil of the lungs and thorax, the speed and magnitude of the inspiratory movement depending on the extent of the muscular force. In quiet breathing and considerably increased pulmonary ventilation, expiration is produced solely by the elastic recoil of the lungs with no need for activity of the expiratory muscles. When activity does occur, it is late in expiration when the force of elastic recoil is at a minimum. More vigorous contraction of the expiratory muscles occurs in those circumstances where elastic recoil is insufficient to produce the desired expiratory force, i.e. in maximum voluntary expiration and when it is desired to increase the speed of expiration, also in such activities as coughing, straining where the abdominal muscles act in conjunction with contraction of the diaphragm to raise intra-abdominal pressure.

ALVEOLAR PRESSURE DURING ORDINARY BREATHING (UNPHONATED)[1]

Ignoring for the moment the effects of resistance to airflow, the pressure of air in the lungs during ordinary breathing (unphonated) depends on the extent of the elastic forces (which, in turn, depends on the volume of air in the lungs) and also on the degree of participation of the respiratory muscles. These factors are summarized in the pressure-volume diagram (Fig. 21) after Campbell.

If all muscles are relaxed at the end of a maximum inspiration, so that expiration is produced by elastic forces, the pressure in the alveoli at any lung volume during expiration is as shown by the dotted line. Early in expiration when the volume is 1,200 c.c. above the resting or relaxation volume (F.R.C.) the pressure is approxi-

[1] See Appendix I.

mately 1 cm. mercury above atmospheric. When the volume drops to 600 c.c. above the functional residual capacity, the pressure is only ·5 cm. mercury above atmospheric. At the resting level (i.e. when the muscles of breathing are inactive)[1] the pressure in the alveoli is atmospheric. Beyond this point, the pressure drops below atmospheric. Thus, the greater the volume, the higher will be the pressure of air in the alveoli as a result of elastic recoil. (This is obviously brought about because at the beginning of expiration, air pressure is increased by the force of elastic recoil faster than it is decreased as a result of air escape through the open glottis. As expiration proceeds the ratio between these two factors decreases.) If, however, the activity of the expiratory muscles is consciously intensified at any point, the pressure at any volume will be correspondingly higher.

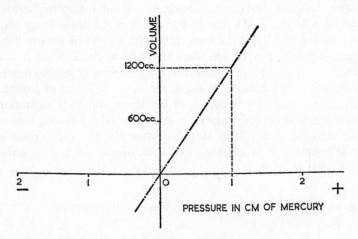

FIG. 21. *Alveolar Pressure due to Elastic Recoil*

When reading the above diagram, it should be noted that the pressure figures are given in relation to 0 which here stands for atmospheric pressure (76 cm.). Lung volumes are also given in relation to 0 which, on the vertical scale, stands for the functional residual capacity (approx. 2600 cc.)—see page 29 for definition of F.R.C. To ascertain the pressure at any volume a horizontal and vertical line should be taken from a point on the diagonal dotted line. In this example when the volume is 1200 c.c. greater than the F.R.C. the pressure will be approx. 1 cm. mercury greater than atmospheric, i.e. 77 cm.

---

[1] Quiet breathing is a reflex activity. Therefore, the fact that the muscles are not consciously brought into tension does not necessarily indicate that they are inactive.

THE BREATHING MECHANISM

Expiratory pressures and airflow as well as the action of the respiratory muscles during speech have been the subject of recently published studies by Draper, Ladefoged and Whitteridge. These are summarized briefly in the following extract.

'During a steady level of loudness of speech, the mean tracheal pressure is kept remarkably steady. The pressures needed varies from 2 cm. of water for very quiet speech to 30 cm. for parade-ground shouting.

'To attain a steady level of 2 cm. of water throughout an expiration the inspiratory muscles—the external intercostals—at first oppose the relaxation pressure (there is usually a short period when all muscles are inactive and the relaxation pressure acts alone); then expiratory muscles, beginning with the internal intercostals and later involving other muscles, such as the rectus abdominis, reinforce the diminishing relaxation pressure.'[1]

[1] M. H. Draper, P. Ladefoged and D. Whitteridge, 'Expiratory Pressures and Air Flow during Speech', *British Medical Journal*, 18 June 1960, pp. 1837–43.

VI

Control of the Breathing Mechanism

The next step in gaining an understanding of the vocal mechanism is to know as clearly as possible the full extent of voluntary control that is possible over the movements of respiration.

Considerable voluntary control, of course, exists in that the rate and depth can be altered at will and breathing can be arrested for a limited time. At the same time the muscular forces affecting the movements of inspiration and expiration can be distributed in various ways to produce different patterns.

These variations have been observed by Duomarco, Rimini and Recarte, 1944, who interpreted intra-abdominal pressure in terms of three mechanisms (1) action of the diaphragm; (2) movement of the ribs, and (3) action of the abdominal muscles. Campbell[1] has reversed normal patterns of abdominal pressure by deliberate alteration of normal breathing patterns.

Different movements can also be observed in the external appearance of the thorax and abdomen during inspiration in different individuals who are breathing naturally and without any attempt at conscious control of their breathing pattern. *However, all these patterns of expansion can be produced at will when voluntary control is exercised.* In all cases, the exact muscular patterns underlying these differences of external movement of the thorax cannot, on present evidence, be absolutely defined. In describing these patterns, therefore, we can only do so in terms of the outward appearance and the mental concepts producing such patterns. For example a certain pattern may be obtained by the individual trying to direct tension to the diaphragm or other muscles which in fact may or may not be affected in the way he imagines. Also, when a singer takes in a breath in which protrusion of the abdominal wall is more evident, and then a breath showing greater expansion of the ribs, he may not necessarily

[1] op. cit., p. 36.

94

be selectively using the intercostal muscles in one case and the diaphragm in the other. *In fact, it is possible that the actual movement of the diaphragm be the same in both cases while the difference in movement may be brought about by other accessory muscles.*

However, each different pattern affects the singing tone similarly in different individuals and we give below a description of the basic patterns that can be obtained.

INSPIRATION

The pattern of inspiration is determined by the extent to which the individual consciously or unconsciously (*a*) expands the upper chest; (*b*) raises the lower ribs; (*c*) causes descent of the diaphragm, and (*d*) tenses the abdominal muscles.

Natural, uncontrolled breathing depends on the above factors but may vary with different individuals. When breathing is consciously produced, one or more of the above factors may be intensified in varying degrees. These factors will now be discussed separately in so far as their merits in singing are concerned.

(*a*) *Expansion of the upper chest.* In normal quiet breathing, there is very little movement of the upper chest, expansion taking place mainly in the lower chest; some individuals obtain this expansion more by descent of the diaphragm and others more by raising of the lower ribs. When the depth of breathing is voluntarily increased but without conscious thought as to the particular pattern of expansion, the inspiratory effort is usually concentrated on increasing the capacity of the upper chest, i.e. on raising the upper ribs. The total amount of air that can be inspired in this way is very limited, even though a great deal of muscular effort may be employed, as these ribs have a very small range of movement and affect only a small area of the lungs. Much of the apparent expansion is produced by extension of spine and shoulder. Furthermore, if attempts are made to exploit this area of expansion to the full the amount of air which can be inspired is reduced rather than increased as the muscles of the lower chest are inhibited and the efficiency of the lower unit of thoracic expansion is minimized.

For reasons which will be explained below, the singer needs to take in a great deal of breath and this cannot be provided by expansion of the upper chest alone.

An even more important reason against excessive raising of the upper ribs is that the muscles which achieve this object can also interfere with the working of the larynx and with the resonation of the tone.

One further objection to the sole use of upper chest breathing is that if this method of inspiration is adopted, there can be no effective control over the expiratory phase. In upper chest breathing, no antagonistic forces are present and descent of the upper rib cage is brought about fundamentally by relaxation of the muscles which raise it. In lower chest breathing, on the other hand, it is possible to set up a balanced set of antagonistic forces which provides a variable adjustment of expiration much more delicate than the simple relaxatory collapse of the thorax and there is much greater control over intra-thoracic pressures. These antagonistic forces also affect movements of the larynx which are essential to correct production. *Correct production, as we shall see, demands the existence of antagonism to the abdominal muscles*. Without such antagonism the laryngeal mechanism is operated in quite a different manner from that which produces best tone, while powerful tones, particularly, can only be produced by methods which are injurious to the larynx.

The remaining factors in inspiration—diaphragm, lower ribs and abdominal muscles—cannot be considered separately as they each affect the others. If, for instance, the lower ribs are raised by contraction of the intercostal muscles, the circumference of the diaphragm moves. Contraction of the muscular fibres of the diaphragm can affect the movement of the ribs, the nature of this movement depending on the degree of activity in the abdominal muscles as well as the degree of activity in the intercostal muscles.

The diaphragm and the muscles responsible for raising the lower ribs are antagonistic to the expiratory abdominal muscles. If activity of the abdominal muscles is greater than the inspiratory forces, then the movement will be one of expiration. If, however, the inspiratory forces predominate, then activity of the abdominal muscles during inspiration results in alteration of the pattern of expansion.

(b) *Raising of the lower ribs*. If inspiratory effort is concentrated on trying to raise the lower ribs, the lower chest expands to some extent and, of course, the circumference of the diaphragm follows the movement of the ribs. If, however, no attempt is made to tense the diaphragm, the movement of the ribs is rather limited.

(c) *Descent of the diaphragm*. If inspiratory effort is concentrated on trying to depress the diaphragm, there is marked protrusion of the abdominal wall and little raising of the lower ribs. Expansion of the lower chest takes place in a rather more vertical direction.

(d) *Abdominal muscles*. Voluntary control of the individual ab-

96

dominal muscles is not possible,[1] except perhaps indirectly, and the singer can only conceive of tensing the abdominal muscles as one co-ordinated group. When he does so, however, there may be variations in the individual muscle tensions due to conceptions which he is trying to put into effect concerning the other respiratory muscles, e.g. if the ribs are held extended, the tension among the various abdominal muscles may be distributed differently than if the ribs were allowed to descend. Thus there is a possibility that the transversus can maintain abdominal pressure and provide a check to the descent of the diaphragm without interfering too much with the ribs, because its lines of force are not directed downwards from the ribs. Further, when one tries to tense the abdominal muscles, one may be adding tension to other muscles besides.

If, during the inspiratory effort, the singer tries to increase tension on the abdominal muscles, the pattern of inspiration changes so that there is greater lateral expansion of the lower chest and less increase in a vertical direction. The movement of the diaphragm is felt much higher—between the tip of the breast bone and the navel. Maximum lateral expansion of the lower chest is, in fact, accompanied by recession of the abdominal wall.

In inspiration, the lower chest can be expanded to the full in so far as it does not in any way interfere with other parts of the vocal mechanism, as can excessive expansion of the upper chest.

The method of inspiration which provides adequate increase of thoracic capacity, without causing any interference with other aspects of voice production, is thus a combination of all four factors, namely expansion of the lower chest by simultaneous efforts to (*a*) raise the lower ribs, (*b*) depress the diaphragm, and (*c*) tense the abdominal muscles; and expansion of the upper chest by raising of the upper ribs naturally and without force (more as a result of good posture and less as a result of conscious muscular effort).

Exercise on these lines makes it possible to increase the flexibility of the lower rib cage so that the capacity of the lower chest can be further increased to a very considerable extent. Whereas, if inspiratory effort is concentrated on descent of the diaphragm, no great increase of capacity can be obtained by exercise attempting to increase the extent of this movement.

Once a full breath has been taken in, the upper chest should be

---

[1] Direct voluntary control of the individual abdominal muscles can be achieved by long and arduous training. However, this is well outside the scope of the singer's needs.

kept raised whilst singing except for a slight, scarcely noticeable rise and fall that occurs when the breath is expelled through ascent of the diaphragm and descent of the lower ribs. This enables a fresh breath to be taken in more or less unnoticeably and in the shortest possible time. If the upper chest is allowed to fall, the amount of extra breath available is very small and *cannot be effectively controlled*, while a distinct disadvantage is the resultant loss of time and useless expenditure of energy at the next inspiration.

The upper chest is elevated not so much for the air contained in it as for the fact that its elevation is necessary to enable the lower chest to expand to its maximum. This it cannot do if the upper chest is quite relaxed because of the way the two mechanisms are connected. The upper chest mechanism in a sense forms a pivot for the movement of the lower chest. If the upper chest is not raised, the pivot from which the lower ribs can expand is much lower. Thus, what seems to be a negligible reduction of upper chest movement may result in considerable restriction of lower chest expansion (Fig. 22). This also provides an important reason for increasing the size of the upper chest.

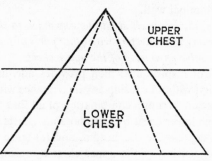

UPPER CHEST

LOWER CHEST

FIG. 22

Much is often made of the fact that well-known singers do not look as if they are taking in much breath, and pupils are often told that it is unnecessary and even harmful to take in deep breaths. This shows complete misunderstanding of the vocal mechanism. *Deep breaths are only harmful if they are obtained by excessive raising of the upper chest and if the singer is unable to control these deep breaths correctly.* If the upper chest is raised correctly as explained above and not allowed to fall, it is possible to take in very deep breaths by expansion of the lower chest without a great deal of noticeable movement taking place, as movement of the upper chest is always more obvious than that of the lower chest. As the measurements of the upper chest increases as a result of developing exercises, expansion of the lower chest becomes less and less obvious as it occurs 'under cover' of the increased framework of the upper chest. *So we find that the greater the physical stature of the singer and the more breath he is able to take in, the less noticeable his breathing becomes.*

Distribution of Muscular Tension on Completion of Inspiration

One further factor in inspiration remains to be discussed—the question of the distribution of muscular tension on completion of inspiration. This varies according to the method of inspiration employed. For example, if the upper chest only is used, there is scarcely any tension on the abdominal muscles or diaphragm at the end of inspiration. If the inspiratory effort is concentrated on the diaphragm, there will be little tension on the abdominal muscles and what there is will be rather differently distributed from that which occurs when inspiration is produced by greater activity of the abdominal muscles. If inspiration is produced by tension of the inspiratory muscles only, then expiration is mainly a result of relaxation of these muscles. If inspiration is produced, as recommended above, by the downward force of diaphragmic tension being opposed by an upward force resulting from contraction of the abdominal muscles, then at the end of inspiration, instead of there being one group of muscles tensed and the other relaxed, both groups will be under tension in balanced antagonism.[1] *In this case, it will be possible to increase tension on both sets of muscles with no actual movement taking place, just as when one holds the palms of one's hands together one may increase the muscular force directed at moving the hands towards each other, without any actual movement taking place.*

The above analogy is not absolutely accurate because the abdominal contents are situated between the diaphragm and the abdominal muscles, so it would seem that simultaneous increase of tension on the diaphragm and abdominal muscles would tend to increase intra-abdominal pressure unless other factors prevent this. Excessive pressures developed by straining can cause a fall of blood pressure and fainting and, if the subject has been overbreathing (see page 87), the effects combine. Duomarco and Rimini suggest that the upward and outward movement of the ribs during inspiration increases the volume

[1] The greater the depth of inspiration, the greater the tension on the muscles at completion of inspiration.

99

of the abdomen more than descent of the diaphragm reduces it.[1] My own experience has shown that it is possible, whilst singing, to make great efforts to increase tensions simultaneously on the abdominal muscles and the diaphragm without any untoward physical effects. This is probably because, unlike in straining, efforts are being made to keep the ribs raised which, according to Duomarco and Rimini, help to reduce abdominal pressure.

If inspiration is produced by a method in which the abdominal muscles are not consciously employed, attempts to tense them on completion of inspiration and during expiration are not as effective as if they had been tensed during inspiration.

Both method and extent of inspiration, therefore, are determined not only by breath volume requirements for the phrase but also by the distribution of muscular forces needed for correct vocal production during the expiratory phase. In fact, it is an even more important factor because it affects the tone continuously and not only at the end of phrases when the breath capacity is diminished.

EXPIRATION

The same muscular forces are present in expiration as in inspiration but the movement is in an opposite direction; whereas in inspiration the elastic forces oppose muscular effort, in expiration they are of assistance. There do not appear to have been any studies of attempts to voluntarily control the nature of expiration similar to those described during inspiration on page 94. However, there would appear to be no reason why the inspiratory muscles cannot be used to affect the pattern of expiration just as the abdominal muscles can affect the pattern of inspiration, and why the pattern of expiration cannot also be controlled by varying the tension ratio between the two major muscle groups of inspiration in relation to abdominal tension.

Variations in the ratio of activity in these muscle groups have been noted in ordinary speech by Draper, Ladefoged and Whitteridge and I have found that much better results are obtained in singing by a student who thinks of his respiratory mechanism (both inspiratory and expiratory) in terms of a ratio between these three major muscle groups than by a student who thinks in terms of only two, i.e. inspiratory and expiratory. *The former is in command of a greater number of tension relationships affecting pressure and volume.*

During inspiration, singers are only concerned with taking in cor-

[1] Campbell, op. cit., p. 36.

rectly the necessary amount of breath in the shortest possible time. Understanding of the expiratory phase, however, is much more complex as delicate control is required over breath volume and breath pressure for every note. It is therefore necessary to know how both breath volume and breath pressure are affected by these three tension concepts. In this section we shall deal only with the way in which the singer can control breath volume, i.e. the reduction of thoracic capacity.

As in inspiration, we must think of the abdominal muscles as being in antagonism to two separate forces (diaphragm and intercostal muscles) which may be used either separately or together. All movements can be conceived as being the result of a mental concept of a particular ratio of tension between these forces.

Normally, a greater flow of breath is obtained by relaxation of the inspiratory muscles, so that expiration is produced mainly by elastic recoil of the lungs and thorax, the flow being increased by any activity of the abdominal muscles. If such relaxation occurs during singing, however, it is impossible to produce powerful tones which, as we shall see, are produced only when the tension on the abdominal muscles is greatly increased.

The maximum degree of tension which may be placed on the abdominal muscles when the inspiratory muscles are relaxed is not very high. This is because the lower ribs form the upper attachments of the abdominal muscles. If the ribs are allowed to descend rapidly during expiration, the point of fixation of the abdominal muscles moves. As a result, the abdominal muscles are rapidly shortened, making it impossible to maintain a high degree of tension. If tension on the abdominal muscles is to be increased considerably, then the ribs must be held fixed against this abdominal pull. If effort is being made to hold the ribs extended, then any attempt to increase tension on the abdominal muscles is automatically accompanied by an increase of tension on the rib-holding muscles so that equilibrium is maintained, the downward pull of the abdominal muscles being countered by the upward pull of the ribs. In this case, increase of tension on the abdominal muscles does *not* increase breath flow. *Indeed thoracic movement may virtually stop although tension on the abdominal muscles continues to increase.*

If breath flow is to be increased without reducing the tension on the abdominal muscles, and without destroying the equilibrium between the abdominal muscles and the ribs, this can be achieved by relaxation of the diaphragm. As explained above (page 74) contraction of the diaphragm results in ascent of the ribs as well as descent of the central tendon. Thus, if the diaphragm is allowed to relax, the ribs must descend. However, if the ribs descend as a result of the inward pull of the diaphragm rather than as a result of relaxation of the intercostal muscles, then they remain more firmly held against the pull of the abdominal muscles.

In practice, if the singer thinks in terms of holding the lower ribs extended as he varies abdominal tension, they will hold against these tensions without any necessity for trying to control the ribs independently. This means that if the singer thinks in terms of keeping the lower ribs extended, he then only has two muscle groups to control consciously—abdominal muscles and diaphragm. *If he establishes this 'hold' on the lower ribs, he then has very delicate control over the diaphragm and abdominal muscles and can vary their respective tensions to a fine degree.* If, however, he tries directly to lessen the tension in the intercostal muscles or thinks in terms of regulating the speed of the descent of the ribs by gradual relaxation of the rib muscles, he tends to relax and lose control over the abdominal muscles and he is unable to maintain the same delicate control over breath volume as he can when the descent of the ribs is brought about more indirectly by concentrating on relaxation of the diaphragm.

It should be realized that if effort is made to hold the ribs extended and to tense the abdominal muscles, the natural tendency is to tense the diaphragm as well. In these circumstances, the greater the abdominal tension, the less breath is likely to be used. If an increase in breath volume is required at the same time as high abdominal tension is needed, then the singer must learn to control this natural tendency to increase tensions generally, and learn to increase or decrease tension on the diaphragm while he is maintaining the same tension on the intercostal muscles and abdominal muscles.

In fact, the acquiring of breath control in singing is no more or less than acquiring the ability to control these tensions independently instead of allowing the natural co-ordinations to take place. An unskilled singer tends to increase tension or decrease tension simultaneously on all muscles while a well-trained one has a much greater independent control. The greater the tensions used, the more difficult this independent control becomes; but it must be acquired if the singer is to be able to produce the required tones.

Briefly then, if the singer wishes to have fullest control over the tension of the abdominal muscles as well as fine control over breath volume, he must first 'set' the ribs and then think only of controlling the abdominal muscles and diaphragm. To use more breath while maintaining the same abdominal tension, he decreases tension on the diaphragm; to use less breath, he increases tension on the diaphragm. In some cases, the volume of breath passing through the vocal cords will be sufficient even when the singer is placing as much tension on the diaphragm as he is capable of. In other cases, he will have to use careful control in order to increase the breath flow at the same time as abdominal and inspiratory intercostal muscles remain tense. The greater the expansion of the thorax, the more easily breath tends to flow as the force of elastic recoil is greater. The greater the strength of the abdominal muscles and the greater the tension placed on them, the less easily the breath tends to flow as the tension on the antagonistic inspiratory muscles increases in proportion.

Latissimus Dorsi

When an additional expiratory force is required without relaxing those inspiratory muscles which are antagonistic to the abdominal muscles, the latissimus dorsi can be brought into tension (see page 81).

VII

The Laryngeal Mechanism

As can be seen from Fig. 23, the vocal cords are attached to the arytenoid cartilages at one end and the thyroid cartilage at the other. These cartilages are controlled by the arytenoid muscles and the

PCA—posterior crico-arytenoid
LCA—lateral crico-arytenoid
CT—crico-thyroid

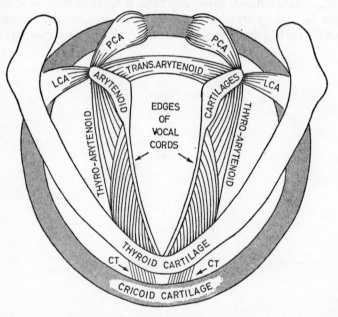

FIG. 23

Diagrammatic view of the cartilages and muscles of the larynx from above. The cricoid cartilage actually lies below the thyroid cartilage which would hide it from view at the sides and front when seen from this angle. In the diagram, it has been drawn outside in order to show the crico-thyroid muscles which link the two cartilages, so that the general working of the larynx can be seen at a glance.

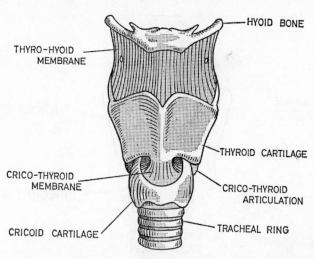

FIG. 24

Cartilages of the larynx from the front

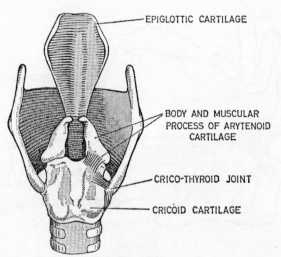

FIG. 25

Cartilages of the larynx from behind

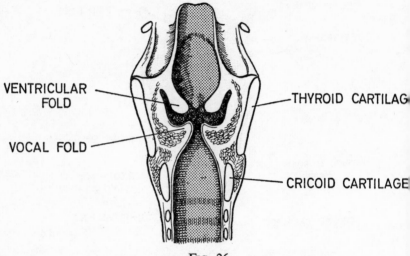

FIG. 26

Cavity of the larynx in a frontal section

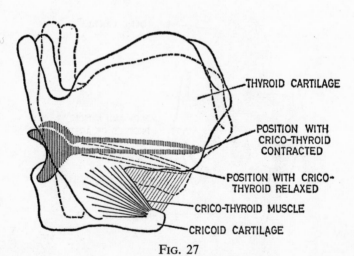

FIG. 27

Elongation of vocal cords due to tilting of thyroid cartilage on the cricoid cartilage

crico-thyroid muscles respectively. There are also muscles inside the vocal cords themselves called the thyro-arytenoid muscles. These three sets of muscles make up the *intrinsic muscles* of the larynx and are primarily responsible for the working of the vocal cords when production is correct.

Crico-thyroid Muscles

When the crico-thyroid muscles tense, they tilt the thyroid cartilage and the cricoid cartilage in such a way as to stretch and lengthen the vocal cords.

Arytenoid Muscles

The action of the *trans-arytenoid muscle*, when it tenses, is to draw the arytenoid cartilages together thus helping to close the posterior portion of the glottis.

When the *lateral crico-arytenoid muscles* tense, they draw the outer end of the arytenoid cartilage downwards and out in such a way as to also adduct the vocal cords (Fig. 29).

The *posterior crico-arytenoid muscles*, when they tense, draw the arytenoid cartilages backwards and inwards, thus abducting the vocal cords (Fig. 28). This muscle is the only abductor of the vocal cords as a whole.

The posterior crico-arytenoid muscles and the lateral crico-arytenoid muscles are antagonistic to each other but, working together, they draw the arytenoid cartilages towards the cricoid cartilage.

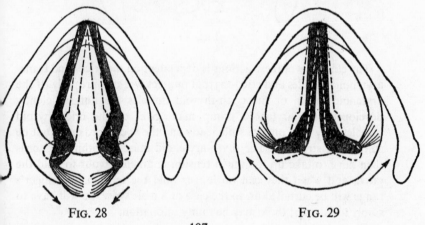

FIG. 28   FIG. 29

The arytenoid group as a whole act antagonistically to the crico-thyroid muscles and, when working properly, hold the arytenoid cartilages against the pull of the crico-thyroid muscles. If the arytenoid muscles were too weak they would not be able to hold, but when the crico-thyroid muscles tensed to stretch the vocal cords, they would 'give' thus reducing the efficiency of the stretching action of the crico-thyroid muscles.

Thyro-arytenoid Muscles

The thyro-arytenoid muscles lie within the vocal cords and are very complex. Acting as a whole, they would seem to draw forward the arytenoid cartilages, thus relaxing the vocal cords. However, they can also tense and adduct a posterior section of the vocal cords and leave only a relaxed, anterior portion free to vibrate. They can vary both the length and thickness of the vibrating segment (Fig. 30).

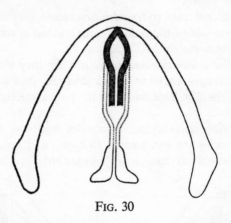

FIG. 30

The efficiency of these actions is dependent on the crico- and trans-arytenoid muscles and crico-thyroid muscles working properly. If the arytenoid group or the crico-thyroid muscles are not sufficiently developed, the arytenoid group may 'give' or the crico-thyroid muscles may not contract sufficiently and the vocal cords may not be sufficiently stretched. The thyro-arytenoid muscles within the cords then have to take up too much tension in an endeavour to hold the pitch, and when they can no longer hold the tension, the singer's range will be curtailed or, in the case of a male voice, he will have to resort to falsetto; there may be faulty intonation.

The correct action of these muscles in singing is also dependent on the correct working of the extrinsic muscles of the larynx. In fact what is usually ascribed to weakness of the larynx is more likely to be misuse of these extrinsic muscles which are attached to the larynx but which lie outside it. As these muscles also control the shape of the resonators they are described in the following chapter. Control of the extrinsic muscles has an important effect on the working of the intrinsic muscles of the larynx and much greater harm can come to the vocal cords as a result of misuse of these muscles than from incorrect breathing or any other factor in the production of the voice. It is misuse of these muscles which is responsible for the formation of nodules and eventual deterioration of the voice.

ACTION OF THE LARYNX IN RELATION TO PITCH

In other stringed instruments, the ratio between mass, length and tension for any pitch is pre-determined by the makers of the instrument; it is constant and cannot be altered. In the voice, however, this ratio can be altered at will by the use of the breath to produce a greater variety of tones. Herein lies the main difference between the voice and other stringed instruments. It is a most important difference, one which endows the vocal instrument with a greater potential of effectiveness but also one which, if not understood, is a source of danger to the singer. No matter how badly one plays a piano or a violin, little harm can come to the instrument because the ratio chosen by the makers is one which will withstand any strain to which it is likely to be subjected during use, and this ratio cannot be tampered with. If the laryngeal mechanism is not understood, however, a ratio can be chosen which will impose too great a strain on the muscles involved, resulting in limitation of the potential of the voice and its eventual deterioration. *In fact, we may say that knowledge of these ratios is one of the most important keys to voice production. It is a question which must be thoroughly understood by the teacher if the potential of the voice is to be fully developed and the health of the vocal mechanism preserved.*

Pressman has demonstrated the following changes that occur in the appearance of the vocal cords while singing up the scale but points out that these changes *are almost always gradual*—not sudden as many writers imply.

In the production of the lower notes, the glottis is open widest in its posterior part and the vocal cords are short and thick. All the laryngeal muscles are under the least tension on these notes. As the pitch rises, the crico-thyroid muscles tense so that the vocal cords gradually lengthen and grow thinner. At the same time, the trans-arytenoid muscle and crico-arytenoid muscles take up added tension in such a way as to gradually draw the vocal cords closer together so that the glottis gradually narrows until, in the middle notes, the opening is usually linear in shape. As this process continues, the tension on the vocal cords increases until a certain point when the tension becomes too great and further elevation in pitch is achieved in a manner similar to fingering a violin string on the finger-board, i.e.

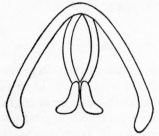

First Aspect (Low Notes)

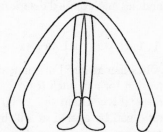

Second Aspect (Middle Notes)

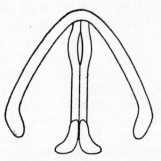

Third Aspect (High Notes)
FIG. 31

the posterior sections of the vocal cords are tightly adducted and the length of vocal cord left free to vibrate is shortened. This is achieved mainly by the action of the thyro-arytenoid muscles within the vocal cords themselves. At the commencement of the third aspect only the posterior tip of the cords is approximated, thus leaving relatively long vibrating segments anteriorly. As the higher tones are produced in a gradually ascending scale, the approximated posterior section becomes longer and longer and the vibrating portion correspondingly shorter.

The changes in tension of the vocal cords have not been clearly demonstrated although it is usually assumed that this increases as the pitch is raised as a result of the lengthening and consequent stretching of the vocal cords. The fact that shortening of the vocal cords takes place on the higher pitches tends to confirm this assumption as it is a phenomenon which only becomes necessary when tension becomes excessive.

Thus the general pattern of change as far as pitch is concerned conforms with the laws of vibrating strings except that the vocal cords grow longer from the lower to the middle tones instead of shorter. However, this is compensated for by the fact that they also become thinner which tends to raise pitch and one must assume that any further adjustment necessary is brought about by the increased tension which probably accompanies the lengthening of the vocal cords.

When considering the above, it must be remembered that the pitch at which one aspect of the vocal cords merges into another will depend on the intensity and nature of the sound produced (see page 109).

If, whilst singing, the mental concept of pitch is altered the vocal cords undergo changes in mass, length and tension as above, according to the breath pressure being employed at the time. Similarly, if the breathing ratio is altered while singing the same note, the vocal cords will undergo changes in mass, length and tension according to the rules in Chapter III.

That these complex changes occur is indicated by the observations of J. J. Pressman who has shown that the length of the vibrating section of the vocal cords can vary for a note of exactly the same pitch if the tension on the breathing muscles is altered. Pressman says:

'Extra pressure tends to elevate pitch. If the pitch is to be maintained constant in the face of added pressure, some compensatory change in the configuration of the vocal cords must take place to lower pitch in the same degree that increase in pressure tends to elevate it. Thus the cords would, for example, have to become less tense or something equivalent. Under these circumstances, if the pitch is to be maintained but volume increased by extra expiratory pressure, such increase in volume is accompanied not only by wider movement of the cords but also by changes to a pattern of vocal cord position characteristic of a relatively lower pitch.'

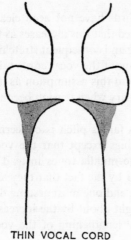

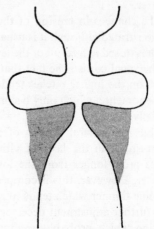

THIN VOCAL CORD
HIGH NOTE

Fig. 32

THICK VOCAL CORD
LOW NOTE

Fig. 33

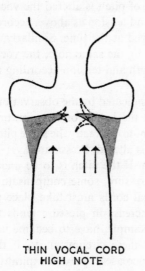

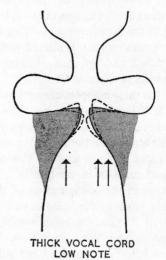

THIN VOCAL CORD
HIGH NOTE

THICK VOCAL CORD
LOW NOTE

Fig. 34

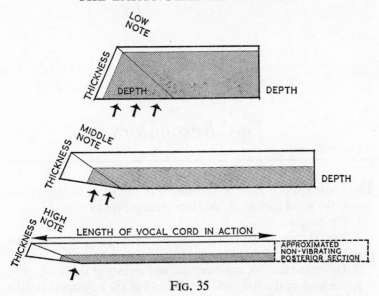

FIG. 35

These observations discount the theories of many writers who base their teaching on the assumption that certain changes always take place on the same notes of the scale. The experiments that would seem to prove this assumption, however, give no analysis of the tones produced and it is more than probable that in all cases, the breath pressures used were similar.

It should be noted that as the pitch rises, the glottis not only changes its shape but the opening becomes smaller and smaller.

113

VIII

The Resonators

The cavities which must be considered in our study of the resonation of the voice may be divided into three groups as follows:
1. The mouth.
2. The throat (comprising the laryngeal pharynx and oral pharynx).
3. The naso-pharynx, nasal cavities and sinuses of the head.

Alterations in the size and shape of any of the adjustable cavities may affect the size and shape of the adjacent cavities and their respective openings, e.g. alterations in the position of the base of the tongue affect the size and shape of both the throat and mouth cavities; movement of the jaw may affect the mouth cavity alone or it may affect both the mouth and throat cavities; raising or lowering of the soft palate involves changes in all cavities in these three groups. Furthermore, although the non-adjustable cavities cannot be altered in shape, differences in the shape of the adjustable cavities result in differences in the degree of stimulation received by the non-adjustable cavities.

Thus, in order to understand the actions of the vocal resonators, it is necessary to visualize the actions not of individual muscles or individual cavities, but to visualize the actions of several muscles acting simultaneously and making changes in two or maybe more cavities at the same time.

Before going further, a word about the above grouping. The laryngeal pharynx and oral pharynx have been grouped together because we cannot control either of these separately; anatomically they may be divided into two, but for purposes of control they can only be thought of as one. In the third group, only the entrance to the naso-pharynx is adjustable; the other cavities are connected to it and may be affected only indirectly by alterations in the entrance to the naso-pharynx.

114

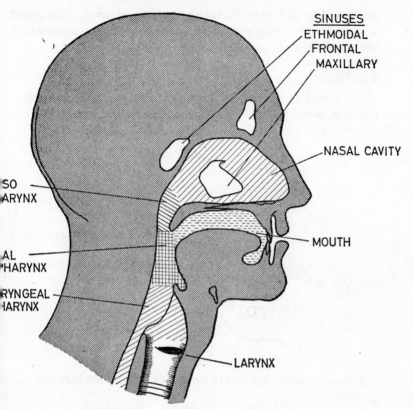

FIG. 36

THE SINUSES AND NASAL CAVITIES

The post-nasal cavities, the cavities behind the nose, open at the back through the post-nasal apertures into the naso-pharynx. They are long and high in shape but very narrow where they are most bony, and much of their internal space is taken up by the conchae, soft tissue which is not very resonant. They are connected by air channels with the sinuses or hollows in the frontal bones of the head.

The largest and most important of the sinuses are the maxillary sinuses situated on either side of the nose, below the sockets of the eyes and above the upper molar and wisdom teeth. They are separated from the mouth cavity by the hard palate which forms their floor, and are connected with the nasal cavities by air channels which run from their upper portions into the nose.

The other sinuses are the ethmoidal, sphenoidal and frontal. These

115

are also connected by air channels with the nasal cavities. The largest of them are the frontal sinuses, situated in the brow, on either side of the top of the nose.

THE MOUTH

The mouth is bounded externally by the lips and cheeks and is roofed in by the palate. Within it lie the teeth and the greater part of the tongue.

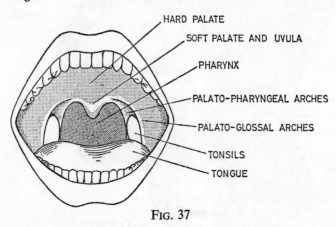

HARD PALATE

SOFT PALATE AND UVULA

PHARYNX

PALATO-PHARYNGEAL ARCHES

PALATO-GLOSSAL ARCHES

TONSILS

TONGUE

Fig. 37

The *palate* is divided into two portions, namely the hard and soft palates.

The *hard palate* has a bony foundation and represents the anterior two-thirds of the whole. It arches backwards from the upper teeth and forms a division between the mouth and nasal cavities.

The *soft palate* has a fibro-muscular basis and represents the posterior third. The superior surface of the soft palate continues the floor of the nasal cavities backwards and downwards and forms the floor of the naso-pharynx; the inferior surface continues the roof of the mouth.

The hinder part of the soft palate is freely mobile, moving like a door on its hinge near its junction with the hard palate. It forms an arch which is interrupted in the middle by a conical projection called the *uvula*. The soft palate extends backwards into the cavity of the pharynx, forming a partial division between the oral and nasal parts of the pharynx.

On each side, the soft palate is connected with two folds of mucuous membrane, extending downwards and forming a double arch, known as the *palatine arches*. They are separated on each side by a triangular interval occupied by the tonsil. The front folds—the *palato-glossal arches*—descend to the dorsum and sides of the tongue. The posterior folds—the *palato-pharyngeal arches*—descend from the posterior edges of the soft palate and are lost on the side walls of the pharynx.

The uvula and, if the tonsils have been removed, both palatine arches can be clearly observed through the open mouth.

The aperture through which the mouth communicates with the oral part of the pharynx is known as the *oro-pharyngeal isthmus*. It is bounded at the sides by the palato-glossal arches, above by the inferior surface of the soft palate, and below by the upper surface (dorsum) of the tongue.

Closure of the oro-pharyngeal isthmus is effected (*a*) by elevation of the posterior part of the dorsum of the tongue against the soft palate, (*b*) slight lowering of the soft palate and (*c*) by movement inwards of the palato-glossal folds. The muscles which bring about these various movements are the *palato-glossal muscles* lying within the palato-glossal arches, and the muscles concerned in elevation of the tongue. Wider opening of the oro-pharyngeal isthmus may be brought about (*a*) by depressing the base of the tongue and/or (*b*) by raising of the soft palate.

The size and shape of the front aperture of the mouth—the *oral fissure*—depends on the distance between the teeth and the shape of the lips. The shape of the mouth cavity also depends on the shape and position assumed by the front part of the tongue.

Thus, the factors affecting the shape and size of the mouth cavity are (*a*) the distance between the teeth, (*b*) the shape of the lips, (*c*) the size of the oro-pharyngeal isthmus and (*d*) the shape and position of the front part of the tongue.

PHARYNX

Structurally, the pharynx is a fibro-muscular bag lined with mucuous membrane and is of conical form—wide above and narrow below. It lies behind and communicates with the nasal cavities, the mouth and the larynx, and is continuous below with the oesophagus or gullet. The fibrous wall of the pharynx is firmly fixed above to the base of the cranium, but is not otherwise attached except to the hyoid bone and the skeleton of the larynx.

The muscular wall of the pharynx is composed of two strata. The external or circular layer consists of a series of three overlapping muscles—the *constrictor muscles* of the pharynx which, by their contractions in swallowing, force the food down into the oesophagus— their constriction at one level being accompanied by relaxation at the level immediately below. The internal or longitudinal layer consists of two accessory muscles which blend with the wall but are also attached to the larynx, namely the fibres of the *palato-pharyngeus* and *stylo-pharyngeus* muscles. The former arises in the soft palate and joins the pharyngeal wall through the palato-pharyngeal arch, after which it is joined by the salpingo-pharyngeus and descends downwards alongside the stylo-pharyngeus to the larynx. The latter runs from the styloid process (a projection on the skull close to the joint of the jaw bone) to the larynx, entering and blending with the wall of the pharynx in the interval between the superior and middle constrictor muscles.

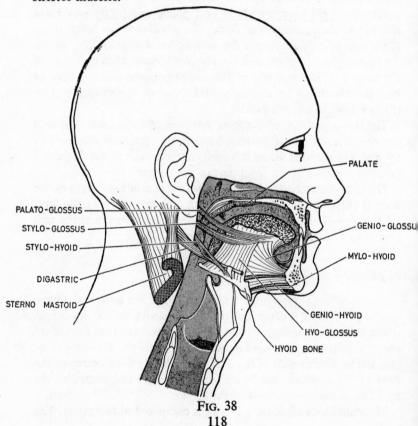

FIG. 38

THE RESONATORS

In the middle part of the pharynx, the pathway for respired air between the nose and the larynx crosses that of food and drink from the mouth to the oesophagus. The inferior portion below the opening of the larynx is exclusively a part of the alimentary tract, and the portion above the level of the soft palate (naso-pharynx) is used for respiration only.

In our study, we have divided the pharynx into two sections (*a*) the naso-pharynx, and (*b*) the throat—comprising both the laryngeal pharynx and the oral pharynx. The reason for this division into two sections is that we have separate voluntary control of the naso-pharynx and of the throat as a whole. We cannot voluntarily control the laryngeal pharynx independently of the oral pharynx.

The naso-pharynx is the highest part of the pharynx, situated behind the nasal cavities. It communicates with the nasal cavities through a pair of large fixed openings in its anterior wall. It differs from the rest of the pharynx in that its cavity is, under all conditions, an open chamber incapable of obliteration, since all its walls, with the single exception of the floor (soft palate) are immovable.

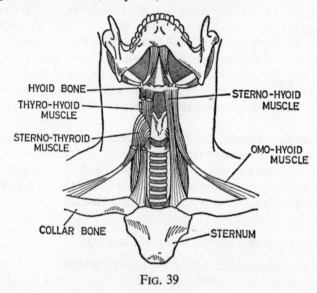

FIG. 39

The nasal pharynx communicates with the oral part of the pharynx through a passage bounded by the free, posterior margin of the soft palate and the back wall of the pharynx. This aperture is known as the *pharyngeal isthmus* and its closure is effected by raising the

119

posterior part of the soft palate so that it comes into contact with the posterior wall of the pharynx. The muscle responsible for raising of the soft palate and separation of the oral part from the nasal part is the *levator palati*, a muscle originating at the base of the cranium. The muscles which pull the palate away from the posterior wall of the pharynx are the *palato-pharyngeus* and the *palato-glossus* (both in the palatine arches), and the *tensor palati*[1] which is antagonistic to the levator palati.

Although it is a portion of the true pharynx, the naso-pharynx is functionally a part of the respiratory tract. Thus, the pharyngeal isthmus remains open during the act of breathing, and is closed during the act of swallowing in order to prevent the introduction of food and liquid into the nasal cavity.

During speech, the pharyngeal isthmus may be closed for all sounds except for the consonants m, n, and ng, which require nasal resonance for their correct pronunciation. Russell[2] shows in his X-ray experiments that in speech, the use of the nasal opening varies, some subjects opening the nasal passage for some vowels and not for others, while other subjects show either a closed passage or an open passage for all vowels. He states that the uvula may be raised or lowered by many individuals and that this seems to be especially true of professional singers who have trained themselves to pull it up out of the way, also of certain girls or even women, and of some Italians, Spaniards, and other Romance-language speaking peoples whose language requires the production of ringing or bright qualities in some vowels, etc.

Where the uvula and soft palate is raised, both they and the palatine arches become more tensed and present a taut, harder surface. When the uvula and soft palate hang down, their surfaces and those of the palatine arches become softer. The effect of these differences in surface quality on the tone will be discussed later.

THROAT (laryngeal pharynx and oral pharynx)

The oral pharynx lies behind the mouth, between the soft palate above, and the inlet of the larynx below. Its posterior boundary is

---

[1] In certain circumstances, the tensor palati assists the levator palati in raising the soft palate, e.g. in swallowing, when the palato-glossus and palato-pharyngeus are contracting to narrow the oro-pharyngeal isthmus. Contraction of these latter muscles normally result in lowering of the soft palate but, in this case, are prevented from so doing by the tensor palati which keep the soft palate tense.   [2] Russell, op. cit., p. 42.

the back wall of the pharynx, which has no distinguishing feature. It communicates above with the nasal pharynx through the pharyngeal isthmus. Anteriorly, it is bounded by the pharyngeal surface of the tongue, above which it communicates with the mouth through the oro-pharyngeal isthmus. Each side wall is a triangular area, bounded by the palatine arches, and named the tonsillar sinus as it is occupied by the tonsil.

The laryngeal pharynx is behind the larynx. It is wide above, but at the level of the cricoid cartilage it narrows rapidly as it passes down to the join the oesophagus. Its anterior wall is formed throughout by the larynx. Movements of the larynx as it rises for high notes and is pulled down for low notes, therefore, affects the shape of the throat cavity.

It is the movements of the tongue, however, which play the major part in altering the size and shape of the throat cavity. In its normal resting position the back part of the tongue lies quite close to the back wall of the pharynx and almost closes the oro-pharyngeal isthmus. The great enlargement of the throat cavity and the oro-pharyngeal isthmus when the base of the tongue is drawn forwards can be seen in Fig. 41.

In its normal resting position, the walls of the throat are relatively undamped. When the throat is opened, the palatine arches become more tense and the surface tension of the pharyngeal walls increases; the surfaces become harder and the degree of damping is reduced.[1]

If the throat is constricted, the palatine arches and the pharyngeal surfaces become bunched up, soft and flabby; the degree of damping is increased.

THE TONGUE

The tongue is a mass of interlacing bundles of muscle mingled with fat and entirely enclosed in mucuous membrane, except the posterior half of the lower part attached to the floor of the mouth, which is called the *root*, and through which the extrinsic muscles, the blood vessels and the nerves gain entrance to the tongue.

The *dorsum* or upper surface of the tongue can be divided into (1) a *palatine part* which looks upwards and is the surface seen in the open mouth, and (2) a *pharyngeal part* which looks backwards into the cavity of the pharynx and forms part of its anterior wall.

[1] See Resonance, page 56.

The intrinsic muscles within the tongue, details of which need not concern us here, alter the shape of the tongue.

The extrinsic muscles, arising outside the tongue (from the lower jaw bone, the hyoid bone and the styloid process) alter the shape and also produce changes in its position. They may be divided into two groups as follows:

(a) *Elevators of the tongue—stylo-glossus and palato-glossus.* Both these muscles arise from origins above the tongue. The *palato-glossus* descends from the soft palate, through the palato-glossal arches, to be inserted into the dorsum and sides of the tongue. The *stylo-glossus* descends from the styloid process (near the joint of the jaw bone), sweeps forwards on each side of the pharynx, and is inserted into the sides of the tongue, its fibres spreading out to mingle with those of the palato-glossus and hyo-glossus.

(b) *Depressors of the tongue—genio-glossus and hyo-glossus.* Both these muscles are attached to the hyoid bone at the base of the tongue. The *hyo-glossus* arises from the hyoid bone and is directed upwards and forwards to be inserted into the side of the tongue, its fibres interlacing with the fibres of the stylo-glossus and intrinsic muscles of the tongue. The *genio-glossus* arises from the inner tip of the lower jaw bone and radiates into the tongue, the posterior (lowest) fibres directed downwards and backwards to be inserted into the body of the hyoid bone, the anterior (intermediate and highest) fibres curving forwards to the tip of the tongue and radiating to the substance of the tongue in its whole length.

Actions. The posterior fibres of the genio-glossus draw the hyoid bone upwards and forwards towards the point of the chin and are active in protrusion of the tongue.

The tongue is retracted by the anterior fibres of the genio-glossus aided by the hyo-glossus (both these muscles serve to draw the palatine part of the tongue towards the hyoid bone) and the stylo-glossus.

The stylo-glossus and palato-glossus serve to draw the tongue up and back, and hence pull the whole larynx, including the hyoid bone, in the same direction providing there is no opposing tension.

The position of the tongue is dependent on the position of the hyoid bone at its base. This is determined partly by the extrinsic muscles of the tongue and partly by the muscles from the hyoid bone to other parts of the head and neck as described below.

THE RESONATORS

MUSCLES OF THE NECK

Apart from the muscles of the vertebral column and the muscles of the tongue and pharynx already described, the muscles which lie wholly or chiefly in the neck are the *sterno-mastoid* and the *muscles of the hyoid bone*.

The *sterno-mastoid* muscle lies obliquely in the side of the neck and stands out prominently when thrown into action. It arises from the breast bone and collar bone and is inserted into the mastoid bone. When in tension, it presses against the larynx, thereby providing a most efficient conduction of sound to the inner ear. The greater the tension on these muscles, the more efficiently they will act as conductors of sound directly to the ear and also the more they will press against the larynx.

The muscles of the hyoid bone may be divided into two antagonistic groups—the supra-hyoid and the infra-hyoid.

Supra-hyoid Muscles

(1) *Muscles from the hyoid bone to tongue—genio-glossus and hyo-glossus.* These muscles have already been described above. The genio-glossus when in tension, pulls the hyoid bone upwards and forwards.

(2) *Muscles from hyoid bone to chin—genio-hyoid and mylo-hyoid.* The mylo-hyoid muscles are a layer connecting the hyoid bone to the lower jaw round about, forming a diaphragm in the floor of the mouth. The *genio-hyoid* muscles, just above the mylo-hyoid muscles and near the middle, connect the hyoid bone to the point of the jaw. Like the genio-glossus to which it is parallel, it draws the hyoid bone upwards and forwards. One can feel their tension if the thumbs are pressed under the chin and 'ee' is pronounced. This can be compared with pronunciation of 'ah', when their relaxation is noticeable.

(3) *Muscles from hyoid bone to chin and cranium—digastric.* The digastric muscles run from the front part of the lower jaw, partly to a loop on the side of the hyoid and partly through it to the mastoid bone at the side of the cranium.

(4) *Muscles from hyoid bone to cranium—stylo-hyoid.* The stylo-hyoid muscle connects the front side of the hyoid bone directly to the styloid process.

Infra-hyoid Muscles

(5) *Muscles from hyoid bone to skeleton—sterno-hyoid and omo-hyoid.*
The sterno-hyoid muscles connect the hyoid bone to the breast
bone, while the omo-hyoid muscles connect the hyoid bone to the
collar bone and shoulder blade. They function to lower the hyoid
bone and drop the whole larynx, thus elongating the pharynx.

(6) *Muscles from larynx to hyoid bone and skeleton—sterno-thyroid,
thyro-hyoid.* Both the sterno-thyroid and thyro-hyoid are attached
to the thyroid cartilage of the larynx, the former passes downwards
to the breast bone (sternum); the latter passes upwards to attach
to the edges of the hyoid bone, serving thus to control the relationship between the two. The influence of these muscles on the
hyoid bone and larynx depend on whether or not the hyoid bone
is held firmly in a fixed position by the supra-hyoid muscles. If
the hyoid bone is not fixed, the sterno-thyroid (although not
attached to the hyoid bone) acts in concert with the thyro-hyoid
to depress the hyoid bone. When the hyoid bone is fixed by the
appropriate muscles, the thyro-hyoid muscle pulls the larynx
upwards in the production of high notes; while the sterno-
thyroid pulls the larynx markedly down when low notes are produced.

The hyoid bone is steaded by the supra-hyoid and infra-hyoid
muscles, as a ship rides when anchored fore and aft. The hyoid
bone, through its muscles, provides a fulcrum for the action of
the tongue. The supra-hyoid and infra-hyoid groups act in concert, and, whether the bone is being raised by the former group or
lowered by the latter, the opposing group steadies the bone like
a guy-rope.

Action of Muscles Concerned in Shaping Resonators and Positioning Larynx and Hyoid Bone

Before discussing the co-ordinated action of the various tongue
and neck muscles described above which shape the resonators and
position the larynx, the muscles concerned will be summarized
below, grouped roughly according to their function in enlarging or
reducing the size of the oral and laryngeal pharynx (opening and
closing the throat).

THE RESONATORS

(1) *Muscles which pull head and skeleton together*—
    sterno-mastoid

(2) *Muscles which pull hyoid bone* DOWN *towards*
    skeleton—sterno-hyoid, omo-hyoid (infra-hyoid)

(3) *Muscles which raise base of tongue* UP *and* BACK—
    palato-glossus, stylo-glossus (tongue muscles)

(4) *Muscles which pull hyoid bone* UP *and* BACK—
    stylo-hyoid, digastric (supra-hyoid)

active in closing throat

(5) *Muscles which raise hyoid bone* UPWARDS *and*
    FORWARDS—genio-hyoid, mylo-hyoid, posterior
    genio-glossus (supra-hyoid)

(6) *Muscles which draw tongue towards hyoid bone*—
    anterior genio-glossus, hyo-glossus (supra-hyoid)

co-ordinated action opens throat

(7) *Muscles directly affecting larynx*
    thyro-hyoid—draws hyoid bone and larynx together } infra-
    sterno-thyroid—draws larynx down towards sternum } hyoid.

stylo-pharyngeus
palato-pharyngeus
{ muscles of the inner pharyngeal wall: they serve to raise the larynx and diminish the pharynx. The stylo-pharyngeus may also serve to rotate the thyroid on the cricoid cartilage.

It will be seen that the supra-hyoid muscles can be divided into (*a*) those which raise the hyoid bone up and back and are active in closing the throat (stylo-hyoid and digastric) and (*b*) those which raise the hyoid bone and draw it forward thus opening the throat (genio-hyoid, genio-glossus, mylo-hyoid, hyo-glossus). The infra-hyoid are active in closing the throat.

POSITION OF REST

In the position of rest, although the muscles of the neck, hyoid bone and tongue have their normal tone, no attempt is being made to voluntarily tense them. The larynx is fairly low and the base of the tongue lies low and close to the posterior wall of the pharynx (Fig. 40).

SWALLOWING

In the first stages of swallowing, the mylo-hyoid and genio-hyoid, assisted by the digastric and stylo-hyoid (groups 4 and 5 above).

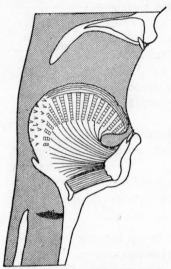

FIG. 40. *Tongue in Relaxed Position*
The tongue may be set in this position
in throaty singing

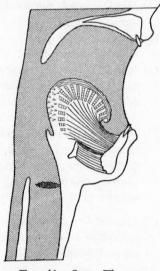

FIG. 41. *Open Throat*
Note distance between base of
tongue and back wall of pharynx

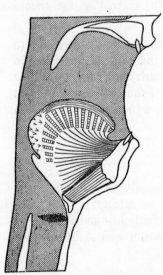

FIG. 42. *Closed Throat I*
Hyoid bone pulled down towards
larynx

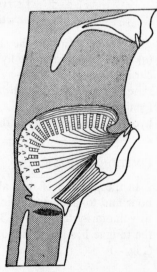

FIG. 43. *Closed Throat II*
Tongue flattened but not pulled
forward, epiglottis constricting larynx
from above

raise the hyoid bone and the floor of the mouth, and the tongue is pressed against the palate, while the infra-hyoid group steadies the hyoid bone.

Note that in swallowing, the genio-glossus and hyo-glossus are relaxed. This allows the palatine part of the tongue to be pushed up against the palate as the hyoid bone is raised, while the base of the tongue is drawn backwards. If the genio-glossus and genio-hyoid are tensed simultaneously, then the tongue is not pushed up against the palate but assumes a position as in Fig. 41 (hyoid bone raised forwards and palatine part of tongue drawn down towards hyoid bone).

PROTRUDING THE TONGUE

When the tongue is protruded the genio-hyoid is relaxed and the posterior fibres of the genio-glossus are tensed.

'OPEN THROAT' POSITION

To open the throat and enlarge its capacity, i.e. to pull the base of the tongue forwards and away from the posterior wall of the pharynx (Fig. 41), it is necessary to bring into simultaneous tension the genio-hyoid, hyo-glossus and both the posterior and anterior fibres of the genio-glossus, while at the same time relaxing all the antagonistic neck and tongue muscles in groups 1–4 (page 125). This is brought about as explained in Chapter XII and also by making an effort to pull the base of the tongue forwards, making sure that there is no tension directed to the neck, jaw or lips.[1]

Note that it is possible to tense either the genio-hyoid or the genio-glossus separately in conjunction with tension on the neck muscles (as in swallowing or protrusion of the tongue), but it is not possible to tense both these muscles simultaneously while such tension on the neck muscles exists.

It becomes more difficult to keep the throat open when singing high notes and extra effort may be needed in these circumstances. Apart from conscious effort to keep the throat open whilst singing, exercises may be undertaken to strengthen the genio-glossus and

[1] An important exception to this is the lip position shown in Fig. 51 where the upper lip is raised towards the nose, making the upper teeth visible. This action actually assists in opening the throat and is therefore an essential part of good technique.

genio-hyoid which will enable the base of the tongue to be drawn further forward.

'CLOSED THROAT' POSITIONS

While there is only one way of opening the throat, there are many ways of closing it. The singer must be aware of these as well as the manner of opening the throat, otherwise he may make many mistakes. Without this knowledge, the singer may have a completely false idea of the position of his tongue. Russell[1] took X-ray photographs of numerous singers, none of whom thought he was taking the tongue position X-rayed. One was so positive that he was not convinced after having seen ten different exposures made on two different days.

The throat is opened by conscious effort to tense the throat-opening muscles. It remains closed as a result of failure to tense the throat-opening muscles while the closure is increased if tension is placed on any of the throat-closing muscles. These latter actions may be achieved either deliberately or unwittingly if the actions of the muscles are not understood.

'Closed Throat'—Incorrect Tongue Tensions

1. *Tongue flattened—base of tongue back and down.* One of the most common errors is to think that merely flattening of the tongue opens the throat. What actually happens, unless effort is also made to pull the base of the tongue forwards, can be seen in Fig. 43. Such flattening of the tongue enlarges the mouth cavity and the oropharyngeal isthmus, but the base of the tongue is pushed right into the throat cavity towards the back wall of the pharynx, thus constricting the throat cavity. In this case, the hyo-glossus and anterior fibres of the genio-glossus are tensed but the posterior fibres and the genio-hyoid are relaxed.

2. *Tongue against teeth—base of tongue back and up.* The throat is also closed as a result of the often-heard injunction to press the tongue against the lower teeth, but, in this case, the base will be pulled back and *up*. The muscular action is similar to protrusion of the tongue, i.e. the posterior fibres of the genio-glossus are tensed but the anterior fibres, the genio-hyoid and the hyo-glossus are relaxed. Meanwhile the palato-glossus and stylo-glossus are unhindered in their action of raising the base of the tongue up and back.

[1] *Speech and Voice*, p. 141 (Macmillan, New York 1931).

3. *Tongue tensed in resting position.* Another type of constriction of the throat occurs when the tongue relaxes as in the position of rest (Fig. 40) and is then tensed in this position.

It must not be thought, however, that a flat tongue or a tongue touching the teeth is a sign of a closed throat. The throat will close only if the action of flattening the tongue or placing it against the teeth is not accompanied by an effort to open the throat and pull forward the base of the tongue. The front part of the tongue may assume almost any position while the back part is pulled forwards, and in fact, does so in the production of the different vowels when the technique is correct, but positioning the front part of the tongue alone will not ensure an open throat.

'Closed Throat'—Neck Muscles Tensed

Any tension on the neck muscles (sterno-mastoid, infra-hyoid group) makes it impossible to maintain correct throat-opening tensions, it draws the hyoid bone and base of the tongue down and back, diminishes the length of the pharynx, squeezes the larynx and constricts the throat to a greater or lesser degree depending on the extent of the tensions applied.

SECTION FOUR

Control of the Vocal Mechanism

IX

Principles of Breath Control
in Singing

CONTROL OF INTRA-THORACIC PRESSURE

Air flows from a region of higher pressure to one of lower pressure. During inspiration, the thorax is enlarged by muscular force, the pressure of the same quantity of air in the larger space drops so that the air outside at atmospheric pressure flows in through the glottis to equalize the pressure. During inspiration, the pressure of air in the lungs is below atmospheric because the thorax is normally enlarged more quickly than air can enter. On completion of inspiration, the pressure of air in the lungs is the same as atmospheric.

If now, the size of the thorax is reduced, the pressure will be raised accordingly as the air is compressed into a smaller space. If, however, air escapes from the thorax as in expiration, this will tend to reduce the pressure according to the rate of the airflow. The pressure of air in the lungs during expiration depends, therefore, on two factors—the rate of reduction of thoracic capacity and the rate of air flow.

The rate of air flow is influenced by the size of the opening of the glottis. If the capacity of the thorax is reduced at the same rate as air flows out, the pressure will be maintained. If contraction of the thorax is too slight in relation to the airflow, pressure will be reduced and vice versa. If the glottis is smaller, a higher pressure can be maintained with slower reduction of thoracic capacity.

In *normal breathing*, when the voice is not being used, the reduction of thoracic capacity by elastic forces is faster than the rate of air escape through the glottis so that pressure is raised during expiration. The force exerted by elastic recoil in reducing the capacity of the thorax depends on the volume of air in the lungs; the greater the volume the greater the force of elastic recoil. Therefore, the rate of reduction of thoracic capacity is greatest at the beginning of expiration and grows less as expiration continues.[1] The opening of the

[1] See page 90.

glottis does not vary, however, as expiration proceeds. These facts explain why it is that intra-thoracic pressure is greatest at the beginning of expiration and gradually decreases as expiration proceeds.[1] When muscular effort is employed during expiration, the reasons for the further increase in breath pressure involve both factors, i.e. faster reduction of thoracic capacity as well as narrowing of the glottis (see below).

In *singing*, the rate of reduction of thoracic capacity can be carefully controlled as described in Chapter VI, but in order to understand the control of breath pressure in singing, it is necessary to know more about the state of the glottis in these circumstances. Is vibration of the cords achieved by increasing the pressure of breath against the cords by more rapid reduction of thoracic capacity? In practice, we find that extremely powerful tones can be produced with the use of less breath than that used in the production of less powerful tones. How can this be?

CO-ORDINATION BETWEEN ABDOMINAL TENSION AND GLOTTAL OPENING

(a) *During Ordinary Breathing*

The opening between the vocal cords, i.e. the glottis, is controlled directly by two groups of muscles—the abductors which separate the vocal cords and widen the lumen of the glottis, and the adductors which draw the vocal cords closer together and narrow the glottis.

In normal quiet respiration, the action of the muscles controlling the glottis is carried out unconsciously. During inspiration, the glottis is wide open to facilitate air intake; during expiration, it closes slightly. There are several theories why this closure takes place. It slows down the speed of expiration and thus prevents too sudden deflation of the lungs, a factor which may be necessary to the rhythm of breathing best suited to man. It is possible that contraction of the adductor muscles may help to maintain infra-glottal airways in a state of opening. Negus[2] has suggested that the closure of the glottis during expiration may, by raising the intra-thoracic pressure, put back pressure on the venous circulation and slow down the entrance of venous blood to the lungs during expiration when oxygenization cannot be carried out effectively.

Negus has also demonstrated the direct relationship which exists

[1] See page 91.
[2] *Comparative Anatomy and Physiology of the Larynx*, p. 67 (Heinemann, London 1949).

between movements of the glottis and the movements of the anterior abdominal wall and his experiments indicate that *the greater the tension on the abdominal muscles, the greater the closure of the glottis.*

The following diagram indicates the degree of movement of the thyro-arytenoid fold in a cat. The tracing shows the increase in opening and closure of the glottis during forced breathing and the decrease in the amplitude when the trachea is opened and breathing becomes normal. The increased magnitude of vocal cord movement does not appear to be dependent on the amount of air flow or air pressure (in this case, it would actually be less because of closure of the trachea) but is more directly related to the degree of tension on the abdominal muscles during the expiratory phase. In Man, who has a much greater capacity for controlling muscular tensions, these movements may be even more pronounced.

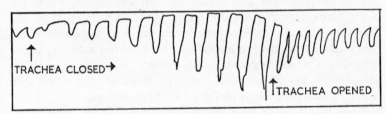

Upward stroke—inspiratory opening of glottis. Downward stroke—expiratory closing of glottis.

FIG. 44. *Movements of Thyro-arytenoid Fold in a Cat* (*based on* Comparative Anatomy of the Larynx, *Negus, p. 61, Fig. 72*)

Another example of the association between abdominal tension and closure of the glottis is at the end of maximum inspiration when simultaneous contraction of the abdominal muscles and adduction of the vocal cords is one of the factors limiting inspiration.[1]

(b) *During Whispering*

The relationship between the action of the respiratory muscles and vocal cord action in ordinary breathing has been described above. The observations of J. J. Pressman[2] below give us reason to believe

[1] E. J. M. Campbell and J. H. Green, 'The variations in intra-abdominal pressure and the activity of the abdominal muscles during breathing; a study in man', *J. Physiol.* (London 1953) 122, pp. 282–90.

[2] J. J. Pressman, 'Physiology of the vocal cords in phonation and respiration', *Arch. Otolaryng,* 35:355, 1942.

that *a similar mechanism operates during whispering and phonation.*[1]

In whispering, the vocal cords come closer together but not as closely as they do in phonation. There remains a wide triangular gap through which air escapes, giving the whisper its breathy quality, while the vocal cords are sufficiently taut to vibrate at low intensity. However, when attempts are made to whisper more forcefully greater tension is automatically exerted on the abdominal muscles and it is found that this *increased abdominal tension is again associated with further narrowing of the glottal opening.*

(c) *During Phonation*

In phonation, the will to phonate and mental concepts of pitch adduct the vocal cords at a certain length and tension *before phonation commences* (Pressman) and the movements of the vocal cords become more complex.

J. J. Pressman has shown that the vibratory movements of the vocal cords during phonation are in two directions, vertical and horizontal. He has pointed out that increases in amplitude of the vibrations during the production of more powerful tones are repre-sented by a greater horizontal swing towards the midline, i.e. *a more complete closure* of the vocal cords, He has also shown that they remain closed for a longer period on higher intensities.

From this it would seem that the greater amplitude of the vibra-tions is not simply a result of ever-increasing quantity of breath or pressure of breath against the vocal cords but is a matter of changes in tension of the cords themselves. According to the above theory, this increased amplitude of the vocal cord vibrations is an indirect result of increased tension on the abdominal muscles, similar to the action in normal respiration and whispering when tension on these muscles is increased; if greater amplitude of the vibrations was a result simply of greater quantity or greater pressure of breath against the vocal cords, we should expect to see an increase in the vertical displacement of the cords or a greater horizontal swing of the vocal cords *away* from the midline, causing wider opening of the glottis.[2]

---

[1] This reinforces the argument of Negus that the larynx was primarily evolved for the protection of the lungs and modified to include other functions essential to the survival of the species as a result of changes in environment, its suitability for the production of sound being only incidental so that man, by his gradual intellectual rise, acquired the power of speech by making the best use of a mechanism already at his disposal for other purposes.

[2] There is at present no complete confirmation that respiratory tensions affect the vocal cord movements as suggested here. This, however, is the logical con-clusion of the facts which are known to us at present, and must be accepted or rejected as such until further work is done, bearing in mind the practical con-siderations in this and the following chapters.

It must be stressed that, as in forced expiration and more intense whispering, this increased amplitude and closer adduction of the vocal cords during more intense phonation is not a result of conscious control of the larynx, but occurs in association with increased tension on the abdominal muscles.

VERTICAL DISPLACEMENT OF VOCAL CORD VIBRATIONS

What then are the factors affecting the vertical displacement of the vocal cords? As suggested above, once the size of the glottis has been set according to mental concepts of tone, the amplitude of vocal cord vibrations in a horizontal direction is dependent on the degree of abdominal tension rather than on the pressure of breath. As the

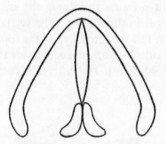 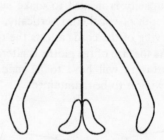

Open phase as in vertical movements 2 and 3.

Closed phase corresponding to vertical movements 1 and 4.

FIG. 45. *Horizontal Movement of Vocal Cords*

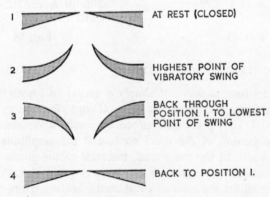

1   AT REST (CLOSED)

2   HIGHEST POINT OF VIBRATORY SWING

3   BACK THROUGH POSITION I. TO LOWEST POINT OF SWING

4   BACK TO POSITION I.

FIG. 46. *Vertical Movement of Vocal Cords*

amplitude of vocal cord vibration increases in phonation and the glottis narrows accordingly, a higher breath pressure will be maintained even with slower reduction of thoracic capacity. I suggest that the breath pressure so created by inward movement of the thoracic cage then affects the *vertical* swing of the tensed cords whose horizontal movement has already been determined by the degree of abdominal tension exerted.

The extent of the vertical swing, and thus the depth of vocal cord in action, will depend on changes in intra-thoracic pressure. These pressure changes arise when the rate of reduction of thoracic capacity is varied in relation to breath flow through the glottis which, as explained above, is a result of independent control of the diaphragm and intercostal muscles (see page 102), Figs. 47 and 48. The greater the adduction of the vocal cords, the less reduction of thoracic capacity is needed to make sufficient pressure to vibrate the same depth of vocal cord vertically. Changes in the extent of the vertical swing of the cords affects the quality, not the intensity, of the tone. As the size of the glottis is altered by other factors, changes in breath pressure will have to be made accordingly if the correct vertical swing is to be maintained.

LESS BREATH VIBRATES
LESS DEPTH OF VOCAL
CORD IN A VERTICAL
DIRECTION

MORE BREATH VIBRATES
GREATER DEPTH OF VOCAL
CORD IN A VERTICAL .
DIRECTION

FIG. 47   FIG. 48

DUAL CONTROL OF BREATHING

Laryngeal tone is thus not simply a matter of breath or breath pressure affecting the amplitude of vocal cord vibration as is generally believed. It is a complex process whereby abdominal tension affects the tension of the vocal cords and the amplitude of their vibration while, at the same time, the state of the glottis resulting from such abdominal tension in turn helps to control breath pressure which then affects the mass of vocal cord vibrating. Thus, as Negus points out, the vocal cords have a function in *controlling* breath pressure as well as being in turn controlled by it. Breath pressure in phonation is not a simple one-way process as it is when the breath is held or as it would be if the glottis remained unaltered.

It is, of course, easily demonstrated that increase of tension on the breathing muscles is accompanied by more powerful tone and many teachers believe that this is due to increased pressure of air in the lungs vibrating the cords more strongly. This, of course, is an over-simplification which does not really explain how breath pressure is increased and decreased. It is an over-simplification in which the dualism of breath control is not recognized, a dualism arising from the fact that pressure of air in a container may be raised either by increasing the rate of compression or reducing the size of the opening. It is an over-simplification which does not explain how increased power is accompanied by the flow of less, not more, breath because intensity is related not to breath flow but to abdominal tension, and its effect on the vocal cord vibrations.

In practice, the difference between these two concepts is that in the one case, breath control implies dual control with independent use of the diaphragm and abdominal muscles, while in the second case, the logical result of an incomplete, one-way conception of breath pressure is a single, one-way control of the breath which cannot produce effective results. (This statement must be qualified only in that the amount of independent control is not unlimited; a certain interdependence exists which will be explained below.)

The preceding theory as to the co-ordination between the respiratory muscles and vocal cord action will now be discussed in relation to practical problems of voice production. First, however, let us summarize this theory briefly in the following rules which form the basis of a practical means of breath control, and which are but different ways of expressing the same principles. The reader is reminded that the vocal cords vibrate horizontally as well as vertically and that increased amplitude of the vibrations is represented by a greater horizontal swing towards the midline, i.e. a more complete closure of the glottis. The vocal cords are not, as is commonly thought, forced wider apart as the power of the tone is increased. Increased pressure affects rather the quality of the tone as the increased vertical swing of the cords results in a greater mass of vocal cord in action.

1. **The greater the tension on the abdominal muscles:**
   (a) the greater the amplitude of the vibrations;

(b) the greater the power of the tone;

(c) the greater the closure of the glottis; and therefore

(d) *the higher the breath pressure* (if, as the size of the glottal opening is reduced, thoracic capacity continues to decrease at the same rate).

2. **The greater the tension on the diaphragm:**
    (a) the less the inward movement of the thorax;
    (b) the lower the rate of breath expulsion; and therefore
    (c) the smaller the mass of vocal cord in vibration;
    (b) *the lower the breath pressure* (assuming abdominal tension remains .constant) because of the slower reduction of thoracic capacity against a glottis of the same size.

Conversely, **the greater the relaxation of the diaphragm:**
    (a) the greater the contraction of the chest cavity;
    (b) the higher the rate of breath expulsion; and therefore
    (c) the greater the mass of vocal cord in vibration;
    (d) *the higher the breath pressure* because of the faster reduction of thoracic capacity against a glottis of the same size.

Whether tension on the respiratory muscles makes more or less breath pressure depends, then, on which of the respiratory muscles are concerned. Thus:

If tension is added only to the abdominal muscles, pressure is increased.

If tension is added only to the diaphragm, pressure is reduced.

It follows therefore that *if tension is added simultaneously to both the abdominal muscles and diaphragm*, increase of pressure due to further closure of the glottal opening is cancelled out by decrease of pressure due to slower reduction of thoracic capacity. *In this case, the pressure will tend to remain constant*. The same will happen in reverse if tensions are reduced simultaneously on both sets of muscles, i.e. decrease of pressure due to widening of the glottal opening as the abdominal muscles relax is cancelled out by increase of pressure due to faster reduction of thoracic capacity as the diaphragm relaxes.

Or, to put it another way, the smaller the glottis resulting from increased abdominal tension, the slower the rate of reduction of thoracic capacity needed to make the same pressure, and this is achieved automatically by the natural tendency to increase tension on the diaphragm at the same time as it is being increased on the abdominal muscles—and vice versa if the tensions are reduced.

It will be noted from the above rules that it is possible to increase breath pressure in two ways—(a) by increasing the tension only on the abdominal muscles and (b) by reducing tension only on the diaphragm. If the first method of raising breath pressure is chosen, the amplitude of the vibrations, and thus the power of the tone, is increased. If the second method is chosen, the mass of vocal cord in vibration is increased and the quality of the tone is altered, the volume of breath expelled will increase but any increase in power will be negligible.

LIMITATION OF DUAL CONTROL

If it were possible to continue increasing abdominal tension and reducing diaphragmic tension at the same time, it would mean that the pressure could be raised simultaneously by both methods with disastrous results. Fortunately, there is a limit to the extent of the dual control described above and thus a limit to the extent to which this can occur. In practice, we find that the will to phonate is accompanied by sufficient tension on the respiratory muscles to slow down the reduction of thoracic capacity so that, as the glottis becomes smaller, the breath pressure does not become too great. Then, during phonation, the natural tendency is to increase or decrease tension of both sets of muscles *simultaneously* when making changes in intensity. This co-ordinated action has the effect on breath pressure described above which provides a natural check against its being raised to a harmful level.[1]

As tensions on the respiratory muscles are increased or reduced simultaneously in this way, the breath pressure is maintained generally on a suitable level as the increase in pressure by one method is compensated by a corresponding decrease in the other.

As a general rule, therefore, it is correct to say that the tension on the respiratory muscles should be increased or decreased simultaneously. This rule, however, must be modified somewhat as the setting of the vocal cords alters in relation to changing concepts of pitch, dynamics and colour. In practice, therefore, it is essential to

[1] Further evidence for the connection between the respiratory muscles and vocal cord action during controlled phonation is not available. However, if such a connection did not exist and if the vocal cords could be controlled quite independently of respiratory action, it could be very easy to force the vocal cords considerably by pushing out great quantities of air through a very small glottis.

operate the dual control outlined above to the extent necessary for the establishment of appropriate vocal tones.

EXTENT OF DUAL CONTROL

In normal speech, the tensions on the abdominal muscles and diaphragm co-ordinate as above with each other and with laryngeal movements in such a manner that breath pressure and breath flow are correctly adjusted to produce the sounds desired. This natural co-ordination ensures that the breath pressure does not become so high that too much depth of vocal cord is vibrated, or so low that too little cord is vibrated. This is a co-ordination learnt in early childhood.

In singing, the fine co-ordinations required are not natural and must be acquired. A similar general co-ordination applies but it is not so accurate that it ensures production of the best tone quality over the much greater pitch and intensity range used. The breath pressures can be and usually are, either too high or too low on different notes for the most satisfying vocal tone and can be so high as to harm the vocal cords. In some cases too much depth of vocal cord is vibrated and in other cases, too little.[1] *This cannot be corrected or adjusted by trying to control the vocal cords but only by altering the ratio between abdominal tension and the rate of reduction of thoracic capacity.* Fortunately, as described above, while the tensions on the respiratory muscles are related to each other, there is sufficient possible independence of movement to correct this state of affairs and this is something of which the singer must learn to take full advantage in order to make the greatest possible improvement to the tone, on any frequency and at whatever intensity is chosen.

APPLICATION OF DUAL CONTROL

Thus, development of a singer's breathing involves two main objectives—(*a*) increase of tension on the abdominal muscles in order to increase the amplitude of the vibrations and the power of the voice; and (*b*) careful control over the relationship of diaphragmic tension to abdominal tension at all stages and on all notes so that the most beautiful vocal tone is obtained with no harm to the vocal cords.

The tension on both sets of muscles (diaphragm and abdominal)

[1] The results can be heard in the tone produced, according to the laws of vibrating strings, pages 48–51. See also pages 138–41 and 149–50.

must be in the correct ratio for every tone sung. On certain notes, the natural co-ordination may provide the tones required. On other notes, the singer may need to depart considerably from the natural co-ordination just as a skier has to overcome a natural, instinctive muscular co-ordination in order to execute a skilful turn. This is one reason why pianissimo is a real test of a singer's technique; *the co-ordination required for pianissimo departs furthest from the natural co-ordination*. Similarly, greater control is needed for the higher and lower notes of a singer's range than for the middle notes, where the natural muscular co-ordinations are much nearer to those which produce the correct ratio of breath flow to glottal opening.

If the teacher understands the principles of correct co-ordination between breathing and vocal cord action, no harm can come to the vocal cords as a result of increased tension on the breathing muscles. This is because as the increased amplitude of the vibrations reduces the size of the glottis, the volume of breath is decreased accordingly. As indicated above, this is achieved automatically to a great extent, but must be carefully controlled to obtain absolute results. Careful control of breath volume is necessary because the greater the mass of vocal cord in action, the greater the tension needed on the laryngeal muscles to maintain pitch.[1] Thus, if the diaphragm is too relaxed and too much breath is used, the muscles controlling the vocal cords may be placed under too much strain and there may be poor intonation.

Incorrect co-ordination may occur on any note at any intensity *if the diaphragm is too relaxed* in relation to abdominal tension. If this occurs, even when the power is low the tone will be, and will sound forced, as the greater volume of air under compression will vibrate too much mass of the vocal cords. This state tends to occur particularly on high notes where the ratio of diaphragmic tension to abdominal tension must be greatest.[2] If the diaphragm is tightened up so that less breath is used, it may be possible to use even greater abdominal tension with no forcing of the intrinsic muscles of the larynx. Incorrect co-ordination of this type may not harm the vocal mechanism on the lower notes and lower intensities as it most certainly will on the higher notes and higher intensities, but even on the lower notes and lower intensities it can have far-reaching consequences.[3]

Many people will be surprised to learn that forcing can be caused by too much relaxation, but this is indeed the case if the diaphragm is too relaxed in relation to the tension on the abdominal muscles; and

[1] See page 50. [2] See Fig. 496. [3] See Chapter XV

it can be easily proved by the immediate improvement in tone if the diaphragm is put under greater tension while the abdominal tension remains constant.

On the other hand, *if the tension on the diaphragm is too great* in relation to abdominal tension, the pressure will be too low to vibrate sufficient mass of the vocal cord to make good tone and it will be necessary to relax the diaphragm or increase the tension on the abdominal muscles, depending on the intensity and colour of the tone required. There is a tendency for this state to occur in the lower part of a singer's range, as this is where most breath is needed.

Thus, it is not the tension on any one of these groups of muscles that is important. It is the ratio of tension between the two that must be correctly controlled for every type of tone on every pitch.

What happens when the action of these two muscle groups is not understood can now be easily imagined. The great majority of teachers and writers on singing speak only of the diaphragm and say little or nothing of the abdominal muscles. In ignorance of the above facts a student, when asked by his teacher to 'tighten the diaphragm', usually adds tension indiscriminately to both sets of muscles (diaphragm and abdominal) and is quite incapable of exercising independent control.[1]

Before concluding this chapter, it should be noted that tension may be added to muscles either directly, as a result of an effort of will to produce tension in the muscles concerned; or indirectly, as a result of desire to perform an action or produce a certain type of tone. Apart from being more accurate for all but the very advanced singer,[2] the first method makes possible the production of a greater degree of tension in the respiratory muscles than that which results indirectly from trying to sing more powerfully.

SUPPORT

To simplify instructions and further explanations we shall use the well-known term 'support' to indicate the general level of tension in both groups of antagonistic respiratory muscles—diaphragm and abdominal. We shall also speak of more or less breath flow in relation to the amount of 'support'—to be obtained, of course, by exercising independent control of the two muscle groups.

[1] At the commencement of training, it is very difficult for a student to localize tension. There is a tendency for him to tense or relax everywhere but this is only a passing phase in his development. With proper training, which implies that the student is given a clear understanding of what is required, the necessary tensions can be applied with great accuracy.   [2] See pages 246-9.

X

Control of the Laryngeal Mechanism

Once the principles of breath control are understood, a practical set of breathing rules cannot be evolved, however, without detailed knowledge of the working of the larynx and resonators. One could experiment with various ratios of diaphragmic tension to abdominal tension on different notes but in order to judge the results one must be able to relate these to knowledge of the effect on the tone of all other factors in the production of the voice. Our knowledge of the larynx is still by no means complete but it is sufficient to be of great practical assistance; whereas in former times, a teacher had to work almost entirely in the dark as far as knowledge of the laryngeal mechanism was concerned, he now has definite pointers and signposts which enable him to work with much greater efficiency and saving of valuable time. The method of trial and error indicated above is still necessary to a degree and will never be entirely ruled out in practice[1] but our present knowledge of the working of the larynx enables us to gain a much deeper theoretical understanding of the vocal mechanism which is an essential prerequisite to improving our training technique.

We have seen in Chapter IX the relationship between the respiratory mechanism and the amplitude and depth of vocal cord vibrations on a single note in which other factors remain constant. It is now necessary to relate this information to the changes that occur in the vocal cords as a result of changing mental concepts which adduct the vocal cords accordingly at a certain length and tension before phonation commences, or which alter the setting of the vocal cords during phonation independently of any changes which may occur in control of the breathing mechanism. These are:

(a) Changes in the state of the vocal cords as the concept of the pitch of the note is altered; these changes have been described in detail in Chapter VII.[2]

(b) Changes in dynamic concepts and concepts of colour.[3]

[1] See page 28. [2] Pressman. [3] See pages 150–60 and 164–7.

CONTROL OF THE LARYNGEAL MECHANISM

The Larynx in Relation to Pitch Changes

The significant changes occurring in the larynx on an ascending scale may be summarized as follows:

1. The tension of the muscles controlling the vocal cords, including the thyro-arytenoid muscles within the cords themselves, *gradually* increases.
2. The size of the glottis (the opening between the vocal cords) *gradually* decreases.

Now, how do these facts help in the formulation of a set of breathing rules applicable to singing? How should the respiratory muscles be controlled in the singing of an evenly-rising scale?

The most important lesson to be learnt from the researches of French, Pressman and others is that the changes that take place in the vocal cords in relation to pitch are gradual and we may assume from this that changes in the use of the breath should also be gradual. *If we find the pattern of gradual change in breath control to accord with the gradual changes in the vocal cords as the pitch rises, we will have come a long way in the understanding of vocal technique.*

The second assumption we can make is that, if as the pitch rises, the opening of the glottis becomes smaller, it follows that the amount of breath required will gradually decrease. In other words, a greater amount of breath flow will be needed to make the vocal cords vibrate at sufficient thickness on a low note where the glottis is very wide than on a high note where the glottis is very small. In practice, we find that this assumption is correct and breath volume must be decreased as the scale is ascended, by increasing the tension on the diaphragm.

As abdominal tension usually increases simultaneously with increased diaphragmic tension, and as an evenly-rising scale requires greater intensity on the higher notes, we can also assume that greater abdominal tension is required as the pitch ascends. In practice, we find that this assumption is also correct.

It can therefore be taken as a rule that the higher the pitch the greater the abdominal tension and the greater the diaphragmic tension required.

Any experienced teacher knows that in most cases an untrained singer does instinctively endeavour to increase tension on the breathing muscles in this way as the pitch rises but is this increase sufficient for the requirements of an evenly-rising scale? And is the automatic increase of diaphragmic tension in relation to abdominal tension sufficiently accurate or is it necessary for the singer to exercise independent control over these two muscle groups?

The answer to the first question is that the untrained singer rarely increases these tensions sufficiently. He may be able to produce good tone in the middle of his range but this will become thinner and weaker as he ascends the scale until he reaches a point where he can no longer produce the notes. Full extension of the range will require a great deal of experience in control of the larynx and the breathing, but it is not unusual for several notes to be added to a beginner's range merely by his learning to take in the breath correctly and to increase the tensions generally on the abdominal muscles and diaphragm as he sings an ascending scale.

The answer to the second question posed above is that even when the general level of tension on the breathing muscles is increased sufficiently during the production of an evenly-rising scale, the natural co-ordination between diaphragm and abdominal muscles is not such as to produce uniform fullness of tone. (If it were, the task of the teacher would be much simpler!) It is therefore essential to use a certain amount of independent control and teachers fail who do not understand the nature of this independent control.

In many years of experience I have found that the following basic pattern of gradual change applies to all singers, the only variation lying in the degree to which each singer attains naturally to the correct pattern before training.

If we take Fig. 49A[1] as showing diagramatically the average natural co-ordination between abdominal and diaphragmic tension when ascending a scale, and Fig. 49B as showing the increased abdominal tension necessary for an evenly-rising scale (with automatic natural increase of diaphragmic tension), Fig. 49C (heavy lines) will give an idea of the adjustment that is necessary to sing a scale of evenly rising intensity with fullness of tone maintained throughout and without forcing the vocal mechanism.

If we compare Figs. 49B and C we can see that it is necessary to reduce diaphragmic tension on the lower notes in relation to the same abdominal tension and to increase it on the higher notes. This

---

[1] It must be stressed that these diagrams are intended to show the amount of tension on the various muscles *as conceived by the singer*. They are not intended to show the actual tensions on the muscles. Even if these were measured, it does not follow that such measurements would reflect exactly the tensions which must be conceived by the singer. All we can hope to do here is to describe the concepts by which maximum control of the mechanism is obtained and indicate the ratios by which it is possible to produce the desired tones.

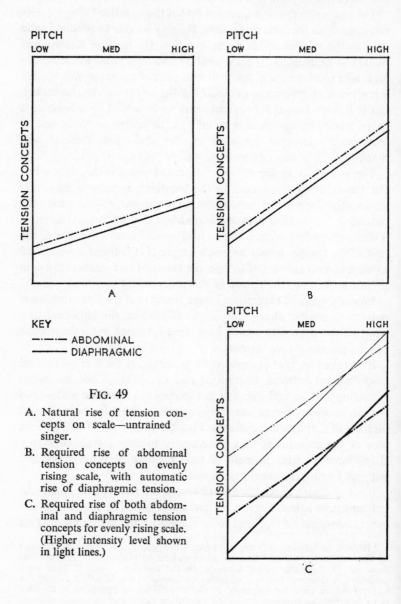

FIG. 49

A. Natural rise of tension concepts on scale—untrained singer.

B. Required rise of abdominal tension concepts on evenly rising scale, with automatic rise of diaphragmic tension.

C. Required rise of both abdominal and diaphragmic tension concepts for evenly rising scale. (Higher intensity level shown in light lines.)

is because (*a*) in most cases, the natural co-ordination provides too little volume of breath on lower notes where the vocal cords are less tense because of pitch requirements and where the glottis is consequently wider, and (*b*) on high notes the natural co-ordination does not reduce sufficiently the amount of breath volume to accord with the shortening and increased tension of the vocal cords which reduces the size of the opening of the glottis. *Thus, if the natural co-ordination is allowed to take place, the tone will be thin on the bottom through insufficient breath, and too dark and heavy on the higher notes through too much breath.*

THE LARYNX IN RELATION TO PITCH AND INTENSITY CHANGES

It is now a simple matter to relate the breathing rules concerning amplitude of the vibrations on a single frequency (see page 139–41) to the changing requirements of pitch.

As we learnt in Chapter IX increase in amplitude is simply a matter of increasing the general level of tensions on the respiratory muscles, during which the breath flow decreases accordingly. We can relate this rule to the breathing requirements of notes of varying frequency by studying the following examples:

If we wish to increase the intensity of a low note (less abdominal tension and higher breath flow required than on higher notes) it will be necessary to increase the abdominal tension and reduce the breath flow accordingly, so that the amounts used are more like those of a middle note sung at the original intensity.

Similarly, the breathing requirements of a middle note of high intensity will be closer to those of a higher note at medium intensity.

An increase in intensity thus tends towards cancelling out the adjustments required for a lowering of pitch; a decrease of intensity tends towards cancelling out the adjustments required for a raising of pitch as follows:

Raising the intensity calls for *less* breath and *more* support.

Lowering the pitch calls for *more* breath and *less* support.

Thus, if the singer lowers the pitch and raises the intensity at the same time, he will have to make little or no adjustment to his breathing. (There is not a great deal of latitude for changes of intensity on the very high and very low notes.)

In our attempts to put the above theories into practice our knowledge of the effect of different respiratory tensions on the vocal cords is of considerable assistance. If we know that increased amplitude is obtained by increased abdominal tension, and that greater thickness of vocal cord is vibrated with greater diaphragmic relaxation and a consequently greater breath flow, we can immediately (provided we have acquired the necessary skill) rectify thinness of tone caused by too small a mass of vocal cord, or dullness of tone caused by too great a mass of vocal cord, vibrating on any intensity.

CONTROL OF DYNAMICS

The above, however, is not all there is to the question of vocal strength, and adding tension to the breathing muscles is not the only means of increasing power. Nor is it all there is to control of the vocal cords. Unfortunately, our knowledge of the working of the larynx is more limited scientifically here than it is in relation to pitch. Statements on amplitude, such as that of Pressman above, show how much interesting work remains to be done in this field. For example, Pressman talks about increases in breath pressure but does not distinguish between the two different methods of raising intra-thoracic pressure and does not make this distinction in his observations of the vocal cords in action. Also he does not consider whether the vocal cords are affected directly by changing dynamic concepts and concepts of colour in a manner similar to the way they are affected by changing concepts of pitch, i.e. not as a result of respiratory action.

To fully appreciate the problem, the reader must understand that increase or decrease in amplitude of the vibrations as described above is not the same thing as changing the dynamics with all the variations between double pianissimo and double fortissimo. If the singer has no means of altering the dynamics other than by varying the tension on the abdominal muscles, his dynamic range will be very limited and, when using a small amount of support, the result will not be pianissimo but an ineffective sound with little carrying power. Any singer with an effective pianissimo will testify to the fact that it requires even greater tension on the abdominal muscles than a fortissimo tone and this is puzzling until we realize that dynamics is also the function of a little-understood control of the vocal cords. When this control is thoroughly understood and consciously operated there is a different setting of the vocal cords for every variation in dynamics. On a certain setting, e.g. for pianissimo, if the abdominal tension is low, we shall have a pianissimo of low intensity; if the tension is increased we shall have a pianissimo of a higher intensity.

Although the amplitude of the actual sound waves is affected both by change in the dynamic concept controlling the vocal cords directly, *as well as* by increase in respiratory tensions controlling the vocal cords indirectly, **to avoid confusion throughout this book the word 'intensity' will always relate to the amount of abdominal tension (support). Changes in the dynamic concepts—pianissimo to fortissimo—will relate to the direct mental control over the vocal cords we are about to consider.**

Unfortunately, in musical notation, the terms pianissimo, mezzo forte and fortissimo sometimes require a change of intensity and at other times a change in the setting of the vocal cords mentioned above, or both. Furthermore, the term 'intensity' is usually applied in connection with both these phenomena which, as can be expected, results in a great deal of confusion. When the setting of the vocal cords can be controlled for dynamic effects, the singer must use his discretion at all times in deciding whether to use this control or to employ a change of intensity in order to produce the most appropriate effect.

When this is not understood, the instruction to sing a note pianissimo more often than not results in a drop of intensity (and a decrease in effectiveness) while the instruction to sing fortissimo will not produce a thrilling, resounding note no matter how much breath support is given, and no matter how correct the resonance, unless the necessary adjustment to the vocal cord setting is made. Similarly (and this may help to illuminate the point) if one has the mental concept of a whisper, increase of tension on the abdominal muscles will increase the intensity of the whisper, but a whisper it will remain and no amount of additional tension on the abdominal muscles will make it anything but a whisper unless the mental concept controlling the setting of the vocal cords is altered.

The control I am about to describe is used to some extent by every singer but because it has never, to my knowledge, been clearly analysed and isolated, and because he uses it instinctively and unconsciously, its full potential to the singer as a means of controlling his tone is rarely achieved. Most untrained singers do not use this control at all but adhere to a setting somewhere along the possible range between pianissimo and fortissimo and try for dynamic effects mainly by altering the respiratory tensions. They may find it very difficult psychologically to accept the sound of a different setting. Trained singers who may have good breath control may alter the setting as a result of musical 'instinct' but, unfortunately, not with the accuracy possible when one has greater understanding of the technique. They may be encouraged by various indirect means to alter the setting of their vocal cords but the amount of variation obtained by traditional methods of training is very limited.

CONTROL OF THE VOCAL CORDS AND DEFINITION OF THE TERM 'EDGE'

We have described above the differences in the state of the vocal cords between breathing and a whisper and between a whisper and a phonated sound, and have pointed out that these differences result solely from changes in the mental concepts from that of merely breathing to that of whispering or phonation, the vocal cords becoming progressively closer together as one changes the concept from that of breathing, first to that of whispering and then to that of phonating. Similar differences in the distance between the vocal cords, and in the strength of their vibration, can be obtained solely as a result of different concepts of tone during phonation.

The student should place his hand lightly on his neck, breathe without making any sound, and then whisper a vowel such as 'ah' which does not require any adjustment of the resonators. He will not feel any tensing of the muscles in the neck but will be conscious of exactly where the whisper is being produced. He should then phonate lightly, taking care not to place any tension on the muscles of the neck or jaw. A soft sounding tone will be produced and he will be able to feel an intensification of the same muscular action that produced the whisper. Again, without placing tension on any of the neck or jaw muscles, but as a result of an intensification of the same muscular action that came into play when changing from a whisper to a softly phonated tone, other tones can be produced which are much harder and steelier and in which the vocal cords come together more strongly still. All these sounds, provided they are produced without any tension on the neck or jaw muscles, are the sounds on which the mature voice is built; the soft sounds when supported sufficiently by the breathing will become the vibrant, floating pianissimo tones, the harder sounding tones will be the fortissimo tones and in between we will have the mezzo forte.

To think in terms of pianissimo or fortissimo are concepts too vague for the student to take hold of and will not automatically produce the correct degree of hardness or what we term 'edge'—that characteristic of a well-produced voice that the teachers of the old Italian school called the metal or the steel of the voice. This is particularly so as the degree of hardness or edge required for dynamics will vary on different frequencies and this makes it very difficult for a student to realize just how much edge he should hear in the tone in these very varied circumstances in order to satisfy the audience. Much more satisfactory progress is made by letting the student concentrate on being able to vary his edge at will. When he has mastered the technique—when he has had practice in varying the tension on the muscles that increase the strength of the 'edge' and is familiar with the sounds that result—the singer will be able to reverse the process and bring the muscles under the required tension merely by conceiving of the type of tone desired; he must then learn to judge the degree of edge required in relation to the musical and interpretative requirements of the score.

Another method of localizing the point at which muscular tension should be intensified to produce a stronger edge tone is to note the area which is affected by changing the mental concept of the pitch of the note. It will be found that it is in the same area in which is felt physiological changes resulting from changing the mental concept from that of breathing to that of whispering and phonation.

It must be stressed that edge or hard edge refers to the sound the singer hears and the amount of tension on the muscles described in the preceding paragraphs; it does not refer to the sound the audience hears. We do not intend any tone that is harsh or unpleasant to the listener. What will be experienced by the singer himself as a hard edge tone will be heard by the audience as a bright, resonant, unforced tone provided, that is, that the hard edge tone is produced in accordance with the technical considerations given.

A simple experiment should make this quite clear. A student should ask a friend to stand a foot away from him while he sings with a strong hard edge on a middle note at medium or high intensity. The friend will hear a sound very similar to the sound the singer himself is hearing. This will be a harsh, thin sound. Now the friend should move to a position nine or ten feet away while the singer reproduces the same kind of tone. The sound as heard by the singer will of course be the same, but the sound as heard by the listener will be softened and modified by the acoustics of the room or hall, and more so if he moves still further away although the singer is still hearing the same harsh sound.

If, however, the singer now produces the same hard edge on a high note and the experiment is repeated, it will be all too painfully clear that if he uses in another part of his range the same kind of tone that produced such excellent results in the first experiment, he will not necessarily have the same success. He must learn, therefore, to recognize those circumstances where a hard edge is appropriate and those circumstances where it will produce a tone which is unacceptable to his audience and harmful to the voice. This intensification of the sound by altering the vocal cord setting directly is in contrast to the action of the average untrained singer (and many 'trained' singers) who, when asked for more power, increase tension on the neck muscles or simply open the mouth wider and yell with an uncontrolled too 'open' sound. Both these latter actions are harmful to the voice, whereas additional power gained by increase of edge will not harm the vocal cords when introduced in accordance with the rules given below.

If the reader wishes to hear what is meant by hard and soft edge tone, he can do no better than to get Dietrich Fischer-Dieskau's recording of a Schubert Lieder Recital No. 4, ALP 1827 and, on Side 2, Band 3, listen to 'Greisengesang', where very clearly defined hard and soft edges are used. One hearing of these tones is worth pages of description but it must, of course, be remembered that these tones are as heard by the audience and not by the singer in performance. However, on this particular recording, because of the lie of the song and the particularly clear definition, it will be possible for the student to get a good idea of what is required of him in his internal technique.

Many singers before training naturally use a hard edge without realizing they are doing so because its use is so habitual and natural to them (and they are usually the ones people describe as having good natural voices). On the other hand, we find singers who begin their training without using any appreciable amount of edge, who are averse to or frightened of using an edge, and who find it difficult to realize that the difference between their 'smaller' voices and the envied singer with 'the fine natural voice' lies not in any great physical difference in the vocal organs but in different habits of vocal production which have developed for many and varied reasons since childhood, partly psychological and temperamental and partly environmental.[1]

[1] Many teachers of course are also unaware of such factors and are therefore unable to properly assess the potential of an untrained singer with a soft edge. It is this more than anything else that accounts for the many stories that can

The following quotation from a general outline of phonetic theory written for Nuttall's Standard Dictionary under the direction of Professor Daniel Jones, M.A., D.Phil., is of interest as it describes how these differences are expressed in the fabric of language.

'All vowel sounds are voiced sounds; consonants may be voiced or voiceless. Languages vary among themselves as to the degree of vocal vibration they use in the articulation of their voiced sounds. As a general rule it may be observed that Romance languages use a greater amount of vocal vibration than Teutonic languages; the former making use of fully voiced consonants, the latter of partially voiced and devoiced consonants. English seems to show a preference for the partially voiced variety.'

It is often just as difficult to persuade a natural hard edge singer to sing with less edge, especially on the top of his range, as it may be to overcome the inhibitions and fears of a natural soft edge singer who finds difficulty in producing a hard edge tone. The former problem applies more so in the case of male singers, the latter more so in the case of female singers.

Many teachers also fail for similar reasons; having always had a strong edge voice, or having developed it as a result of indirect methods over a great many years, they do not understand that a student who is not used to producing his voice in this way will be unable to do so until he develops concepts of a much stronger edge than the teacher himself, because of his different vocal influences, has ever had to conceive of. Edge is thus a very relative, subjective concept in the minds of different people. In order to get two students to sing an identically produced note, it may be necessary to ask one to use a stronger edge and the other to use a weaker edge.

When making such adjustments, however, it is essential that they are made to the setting of the vocal cords only, as described above, and not to other parts of the vocal mechanism. Perhaps the greatest harm to the voice is caused when a singer who is unable to consciously control the amount of edge and who, when asked to produce a more mellow tone, will instead of using less edge, close down the resonators while the vocal cords are still vibrating strongly. The resulting tone may be what is often called 'covered' but if it is produced in this way it can harm the vocal cords if persisted in. A sign of this production will be tension of the muscles of the neck and jaw,

---

be quoted of successful opera singers who had been told earlier in their careers that they would never sing on an operatic stage. Caruso is perhaps the most famous case in point. Like an iceberg, a soft edge voice is many parts submerged.

and the stronger the edge *in these circumstances*, the more potentially harmful to the vocal cords.

It should also be realized that when a singer has learned to increase the amount of edge in circumstances where a stronger edge is required, he may tend to want to use a similar amount in other circumstances where this is not desirable and this temptation must of course be resisted and controlled.

It is easier at first for the student to produce a stronger edge with the mouth more closed but, with more experience, this will be no longer necessary.

The most useful exercise for increasing the 'edge' and for gaining control over the vocal cord vibrations is staccato. It is through these staccato exercises, however, that eventually a stronger legato line may be achieved.

TECHNIQUE OF DYNAMIC CONTROL

When a soft edge tone (pianissimo) is employed, the vocal cords are more relaxed and more breath flow and more support is required than when a stronger edge is used in mezzo forte. When the edge is increased further for fortissimo, the vocal cords are more tense, less breath flow and less support is required than for pianissimo singing, although more than for mezzo forte, in order to obtain the required crescendo effect.

If a high support is used, it will be unlikely that the singer will use too much edge. On the other hand, if there is insufficient support, there is a temptation to use more edge than is desirable in an attempt to sing with sufficient power. In this case, the voice will sound hard and strained to the listener. This is especially so, of course, on the higher notes. Greater care must therefore be exercised on this account when singing with a low support than when the support is high.

When the support is high, there may on the other hand be a tendency to use too little edge and it is a pity if this is allowed to happen as the potential quality of the voice will not be fully realized.

The technique of dynamic control may be summarized in the following rules from which it will be seen that a 'plus' amount of edge is reserved for fortissimo passages. Apart from this, it will be required only occasionally for special effects as indicated on pages 164 to 167, and for the lower notes in the lower-pitched voices.[1]

[1] See page 159–60.

Edge, support and breath flow in relation to dynamic requirements

	Degree Concepts of		
	Edge	Support	Breath Flow
MF	1	1	1
P	-1	++1	++1
F	+1	+1	+1

Thus, if we go from m.f. to p. the rule is:

The softer the edge, the more support, and the greater the breath flow.

If we go from m.f. to f. the rule is:

When the edge is increased, support and breath flow are increased accordingly but not as much as for pianissimo.

The increased breath flow in each case above is largely automatic and no attempt need be made by the singer in general to augment it although he must make sure, particularly in pianissimo, that he has sufficient capacity (see Fig. 50).

Thus, in dynamic deviations from the normal m.f. level, either towards fortissimo for a crescendo or towards pianissimo for a decrescendo, one increases the support and breath flow in both cases according to the above rules; in the former effect, however, the edge will be increased while in the latter it will be decreased.

Of course, one must expect the voice to tire after it has been used a great deal, just as one's body tires after exercise or activity. But this is natural and the more edge one uses the more quickly the voice will tire. However, the greater the support at the singer's command, and the more skilful he is, the less edge will it be necessary for him to use in order to give a satisfying performance, and when rehearsing a role he should of course conserve his voice not so much by reducing the support as by taking care to use less edge.

Similarly, the more support the singer uses, the more his body will tire and in planning an exacting operatic role or recital the singer must take both these factors into consideration so that he is not exhausted either physically or vocally before he has completed his performance. If the production is correct, he is more likely to find himself exhausted physically than vocally, and vice versa, and he should bear this fact in mind when husbanding his resources.

Physically speaking, a singer can very quickly learn to use as much edge as will ever be required of him, although psychological factors may make this process more difficult for him. Building up of adequate support, however, requires considerably greater time, effort and will-power. He should therefore regard the edge as the steel of the voice which gives it vibrancy and life but not power. His power-house is his support. Thus, when there is sufficient edge in the tone, he must not attempt to increase this further but must get all the additional power from his breathing muscles. As his support increases, the range of tones at his command increases and so must his skill in relating support, breath flow and edge to every note in his range and every dynamic effect within his scope.

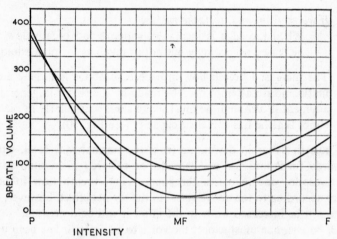

FIG. 50. *'Breath-intensity' Curves of a well-produced Voice from Douglas Stanley's* Your Voice (*Pitman*)

This figure shows a curve of the breath expulsion plotted against intensity for a middle tone sung by a well-produced voice.
Notice that the maximum expulsion is at pianissimo, and that it drops progressively until M.F. (a full free tone) is reached, when it starts to rise until the maximum loudness—F. is reached. Notice also that the drop between P. and M.F. is far greater than is the rise from M.F. to F.

PITCH QUALITY AND DYNAMICS

Just as the breathing ratios must be related to pitch, the amount of edge must be in correct relationship not only to dynamic requirements but also both to pitch and to the breathing ratios employed. All the most important elements of singing technique are summed up in this one sentence which should dominate the singer's attitude to every note he utters.

CONTROL OF THE LARYNGEAL MECHANISM

On the lower notes, where the vocal cords are more relaxed and wider apart, a comparatively strong edge tone is essential if the voice is going to be fully effective even when the marking is m.f. On high notes, however, a strong edge is unnecessary if there is sufficient support and can be harmful to the voice if employed because of the greater tension of the vocal cords in this part of the range. A high note, up to about Ab, when sung fortissimo will of course require a stronger edge than when sung pianissimo but it will certainly be less than that required for a fortissimo note of lower frequency. (Above Ab there is not much latitude for changes of intensity or edge.) The foregoing may be summarized in the following rule:

Edge, support and breath flow in relation to pitch

1	2
The higher the pitch	*The lower the pitch*
the *more* support,	the *less* support,
the *less* breath flow,	the *more* breath flow,
the *less* edge.	the *stronger* the edge.

When the above rule is studied in conjunction with those on page 157, it will be apparent that *the amount of edge for any dynamic effect will vary according to the pitch of the note.* Mezzo forte on a low note will therefore require a stronger edge than mezzo forte on higher note. Pianissimo on a low note will require a slightly stronger edge than pianissimo on a middle note.

It will also be apparent why top notes and pianissimo are such a test of a singer's technique and skill. On top notes, he needs the highest support and the confidence that this support will vibrate the vocal cords without need to supplement the tone by use of the same edge as he employs on the lower notes. And on pianissimo, he needs the greatest breath capacity, a very high support as for top notes and the least amount of edge.

The reader should now understand why it is that a singer may have strong, fully developed top notes with weak low notes. This will of course be due to the fact that this singer has a preference for soft edge tones which, with adequate support, will give good top notes, but which is insufficient for effective lower notes. On the other hand, a singer with a good lower range and no top will be one who uses a strong edge on lower notes, but has insufficient support for the greater demands of his high notes and inability to phase out the edge as the pitch rises, so that his only resort is to falsetto when the strain of this production becomes too great to continue. (This will not apply, of course, to a female singer whose voice will simply come to a full stop many notes below her potential range.) He may instinctively reduce the amount of edge on the top but, without adequate support, it is more likely that he will employ the panic measures of trying to keep the edge and counteracting what would be the resulting difficulty by closing the throat with all the evils of this production described below.

The above rules are most important when it comes to the training of voices of differing ranges. A bass, for example, because of his lower tessitura, will need to use a greater amount of edge than a baritone, who in turn will need more than a tenor, in order to develop the full potential quality of the voice. Because of the greater relaxation of the vocal cords on the lower frequencies, the lower pitched voices may use somewhat more edge without fear of harm to the voice than can the higher pitched voices.

ADVANTAGES OF USING 'EDGE' AS A CONTROL FACTOR

It may be helpful and interesting at this stage, especially for the singer who has had some experience, to describe some of the methods employed traditionally to try to achieve the same results which can be achieved so much more positively by means of the above controls. The most usual technique is to ask the singer for more head tone when a softer edge is required or for more chest tone in circumstances where a stronger edge is required. These concepts may indirectly result in decreasing or augmenting the amount of edge the singer in fact produces but not usually with sufficient accuracy and not usually without upsetting other factors such as breathing or resonation. Such concepts are too vague to cover all the technical problems that have to be tackled simultaneously and of which the singer remains unaware while trying to improve his technique with these inadequate concepts.

Instead of trying to achieve a balance between head and chest, our singers learn to achieve a balance between support, breath flow and edge on every note and can vary this according to any dynamic requirement. After a certain amount of experience one of these three controls takes care of itself in most circumstances, namely breath flow. In practice, therefore, our advanced singer achieves all his dynamic effects on any frequency with only *two* positive controls: (1) support, and (2) edge.

Finally, a most important consideration is that concepts of degrees of edge are much more easily remembered by the singer and do not alter in unfamiliar acoustic conditions. A singer is easily deflected from his production if he thinks in terms of tone which may be radically modified in unfamiliar conditions and this is a source of considerable difficulty to most singers. It gives no cause for concern, however, to a singer who has learnt to control his tone by varying the edge as concepts in these terms remain stable in all conditions. This consideration applies as much to control of dynamics as it does to control of tone colour described below.

THE LARYNX IN RELATION TO TENSION, RELAXATION AND CONSTRICTION

Before considering colour, however, there remains the very vexed question of tension and relaxation in relation to the laryngeal mechanism. The reader is referred to a general discussion of this problem in Section 5 and I hope that he has sufficient understanding to be able to recognize, for example, that it is quite illogical to ask a singer to relax in the area of the throat and at the same time ask him to keep it open; he will not be able to keep it open if the throat opening muscles are relaxed! Furthermore, the reader of this section will also understand that when an action is habitual, the performer is often quite unconscious of the muscular tensions he is using in order to carry it out. A teacher who tells his pupils to keep his throat relaxed has simply not been able to analyse the tensions that he must be employing in order to make any sound at all, as against simply breathing. Paradoxically, when the correct tensions are understood and applied, the singer will experience localized tension where they are employed but a feeling of general relaxation in the area of the throat. On the other hand, the more the singer is told simply to relax, the less likely he is to use these correctly localized tensions and the more he tends to tense muscles which are harmful to the vocal cords; he may or may not be consciously aware of these harmful tensions. Until he learns to employ the correct tensions, no amount of exhortation to relax will enable him to remove these harmful tensions if he is to sing at all.

When employing an edge, the singer will of course be placing tension on the muscles of the larynx and if he wishes to avoid this he should not sing at all, or speak! The important thing to realize and remember when increasing edge is that it is an intensification of the same action that produces a whisper or a softer edge, just as when one wishes to lift heavier and heavier objects one increases the effort made by the lifting muscles; one does not bring in muscles which would be used, say for pushing. In a habitual visible action like lifting, this is of course obvious, but when learning a new action like increasing the amount of edge, the singer must beware of unconsciously increasing tensions on muscles nearby which have nothing to do with the edge and which should remain out of action, namely muscles of the neck and those which lock the jaw.

It is relaxation of these neck and jaw muscles that is really meant by those teachers who employ this production themselves but who speak only of relaxation in the area of the throat. Such teachers vary their edge in relation to the required tones so unconsciously that they are no more aware of it than a cyclist is of the muscles which enable him to keep his balance. The more such advice results in stopping the student from employing a strong enough edge, the more he will tend to tense his neck muscles in spite of the instruction to relax (a) because it is the only other way open to him of producing a sound of reasonable size, and (b) because while the vibrant sound of an edge gives the singer an indication of the tension he may be placing on the vocal cords, it is more difficult for him to realize just how much tension he is using when he places it on the neck muscles and he is usually quite unaware that he is doing so at all, although it could be easily felt if he simply placed his hands on his neck before he began to sing.

When using a strong edge, the muscles of the neck can still be so relaxed that there is complete freedom of the movement of the head. If the singer cannot do this, he may be sure that his technique is incorrect. When the neck muscles are tensed or if the jaw is locked, this vibrant strong edge tone is difficult if not impossible to obtain. Instead we have a forced sound described by Douglas Stanley[1] as throat whistling in which sound is formed by breath being forced through a constriction. It is not possible to call such singing relaxed even though the singer may be far less conscious of employing tension at the throat than the singer with the freely moving head, and the richly flowing tone who is exerting conscious effort to produce a strong edge.

What happens when the neck and jaw muscles are tensed? The actions of the vocal cords described above are dependent on their correct elongation. It is therefore necessary that there be no forward

[1] *Your Voice* (Pitman, London 1945).

displacement of the cricoid cartilage and arytenoid cartilages and no backward displacement of the thyroid cartilage. When the neck muscles are tensed, such displacement is allowed to occur, the vocal cords become foreshortened and flaccid instead of lengthened and tensed. In these circumstances, pitch can only be maintained by certain adjustments in the action of the thyro-arytenoid muscles but in this way, as stated above, the vocal cords become 'bunched up' and the conditions are established for the formation of nodules and destruction of the voice. Apart from the use of incorrect tensions described above, there is another answer to the question of how such conditions occur and how they can be prevented—a question which has baffled singers for a great many years. It is really quite simple and lies in an understanding of the sphincter action of the larynx. The foreshortening of the vocal cords described above, which has a harmful effect whilst singing, serves a useful function in sphincteric closure of the glottis as when swallowing, or when 'holding the breath'. This sphincteric closure is necessary to thoracic fixation and elevation of intra-abdominal pressure which is an essential part of many physiological functions as in lifting heavy objects or swinging from branches for which purposes it was originally evolved.[1]

If foreshortening of the vocal cords is to be prevented whilst singing, all muscular action connected with holding the breath at the level of the throat must be relaxed as soon as singing is commenced. This is usually difficult for an untrained or badly trained singer to achieve because his respiratory muscles are incapable of maintaining sufficient tension to sing with power in the correct manner; the abdominal muscles are too weak to cause the vocal cords to vibrate at a great amplitude and the inspiratory muscles are too weak to inhibit relaxation of the thorax. So, partly because in this state he finds he can get greater power by constricting, and partly because he is simply frightened of losing control of his breath, he instinctively continues the action of 'holding the breath' at the throat even though he has commenced to sing. The will to phonate results in partial relaxation of the sphincter mechanism but this is not sufficient to allow the vocal cords to elongate and tense in the correct manner. Instead of vibrating freely in the manner of a stringed instrument (even though, of course, it is only the edges of muscular sheets that vibrate and not strings as such) the vocal cords are bunched up and breath is forced through them. The correct formation of partials of

---

[1] J. J. Pressman, 'Sphincter Action of the Larynx', *Arch. Otolaryng.* 33:351, 1941.

tone by segmentation of the vibrations is not possible in these circumstances and it is impossible to produce the type of vibration essential to good vocal tone.

This state can be easily observed because the neck muscles remain very tense and prominent and there is general tension and rigidity in the region of the throat. It can be remedied by establishing correct functioning of the breathing muscles and by ensuring that the singer has sufficient understanding and confidence in the correct method of breathing to relax this hold on those muscles of the throat which affect the larynx in this way. Apart from establishing correct tensions on the vocal cords as a result of concepts of edge, the only tension desirable at the throat should be directed to keeping it open—not to holding it tightly shut.

Whenever in phonation, the breathing mechanism is used as in normal respiration, i.e. in a relaxed manner or with tension only on the expiratory muscles, relaxation of the intrinsic adductor (closing) muscles of the larynx occurs reflexly as in the normal breathing act and the necessity arises for other means of closure if sound is to be produced.

If correct tensions are established on the breathing muscles, the singer need have no fear of excessive loss of breath even though the throat is held open because, in this case, the glottis is effectively approximated reflexly by the intrinsic muscles as a result of abdominal tension and breath expulsion is controlled by tension on the inspiratory muscles. There is no need for any additional sphincter action.

The sphincter action described above is brought about partly by incorrect tensions on the muscles of the tongue, neck and jaw. These incorrect tensions can also be brought about as a result of incorrect conceptions of resonance.

CONTROL OF TONE COLOUR

It may surprise many readers to find the question of colour discussed in this chapter and not in resonance. Variations in the quality of the tone, e.g. bright, dark, warm, etc., have traditionally been regarded as a function of the resonators. However, the more closely one studies the human voice, the more one realizes that this is not so. The resonators can be varied only in so far as there is one setting for efficient resonation, and a number of other settings which provide inefficient resonation and cutting off of the tone.

We should look on the resonators from the point of view of amplification of the tone as the loudspeaker of a radio. In the pre-electronic age (and the voice is not electronically amplified) we bought the biggest speaker we could afford and similarly, the vocal resonators should be as large as we can make them in order to resonate with greatest efficiency. The tone control on a radio was an advantage because of the very wide range of frequencies for example in orchestral music (and a similar consideration applies in the voice on the higher notes[1]) but, apart from tuning in for bass or treble, one did not continually fiddle with the tone control of the radio, the tremendous range of sounds heard in an average radio programme being a result of the infinite variety of colour in the original stimulus of the electrical vibrations reaching the instrument before they were amplified by the speakers. As in a violin variations in tone colour are obtained by differences in bowing and fingering of the strings, not by manipulation of the box while playing, tone colour in a voice is obtained by similarly varying the composition of the tone coming from the vocal cords and this is achieved by subtle variations in the same three factors given above for dynamic control:

(1) Edge   (2) Support   (3) Breath flow.

On any particular dynamic setting, these may be balanced in such proportions as to give a uniform quality throughout the voice in the sense that each note will be sung, say, in the middle of its colour range between bright and dark, so that the only variations heard will be those in accordance with the pitch quality attributes of each frequency; or, on this basic tone colour, enormous variation is possible by varying the ratio of edge to support and breath flow, and the singer is thus given a tremendous scope for colouring and effects.

If a note sounds too hard and edgy or forced to the audience, it will be necessary to soften the edge if the same intensity is to be maintained. Alternatively, the singer may maintain the same degree of edge and lower the support, which will result in a good quality tone at a lower intensity.

If the support is kept constant, a hard edge note will sound louder than a soft edge. It will also sound brighter. If it is desired to make the tone sound brighter without making it sound louder, the only change necessary will be to reduce the support; if it is desired to make it sound darker without making it sound quieter, it will be

---

[1] See page 172.

necessary to increase the breath flow while keeping the same edge and support.

By these means, the colour may be subtly and positively varied on any dynamic setting and on any intensity or pitch. However, it must be understood that the scope is not unlimited because a certain minimum edge and support is required for each frequency. If the edge is too low for a given pitch, the note will tend to be sung flat. Similarly, if the support is insufficient in relation to a given edge. On the higher and lower pitches, the singer has less opportunity for making variations in tone colour and intensity than in the middle of his range. Here colour and intensity are much more determined by pitch and it is up to the composer to write the vocal line with this in mind, and the greatest composers have of course done this. Other composers without the same understanding of the voice make impossible demands upon the singer completely outside his vocal limits.

Because of these limitations, a soprano and tenor have fewer opportunities than the lower voices to vary tone colour in their interpretations. It is, in fact, in the latter categories of voice that we find the most successful lieder singers.

It is possible to maintain a suitable edge throughout one's singing and get louder and softer by increasing or decreasing the intensity and the great majority of singers do this. It is much more plain sailing but, even though a good tone may be obtained, it becomes very monotonous and it is impossible by this means to do full justice to the emotional depth of a work. If, for example, a hard edge is used with a comparatively low breath pressure, a pianissimo of sorts results, thin and without the emotional content of a soft edge pianissimo with greater support. The former pianissimo is most commonly heard today. While it may be desirable in certain circumstances, in most cases it has very little value. As musical markings give very little indication of colour, a singer who automically relaxes his support every time he sees a decrescendo is obviously unaware of the difference between this type of pianissimo and one in which a pianissimo effect is obtained by keeping up a high support against more relaxed vocal cords. To introduce colour changes by altering the settings of the vocal cords requires understanding and skill. However, there is nothing mysterious about it. The rules are very straightforward and it requires only knowledge and understanding of them, practice, adequate muscular development and sound artistic judgment.

Of course, many singers do achieve some of these effects without the above technical knowledge, through musical instinct and sensitivity after long experience but, unless the principles are fully understood, the results will tend to be broad rather than subtle; many mistakes will be made and many opportunities lost.

The most commonly used method of colouring the tone is, of course, for the singer to think in terms of bright and dark tones rather than in the above technical terms. But here again, although some results in terms of colour may be obtained, it is rather difficult by these means to obtain consistent results because the technical constituents of tone are lost sight of while the singer is thinking in terms of tone, either as he himself wants to hear it or as he thinks the audience should hear it, and not as it must be *manufactured*.

It is too difficult, for example, to think in terms of dynamics and colour simultaneously, e.g. the concept of, say, 'dark pianissimo' is very unlikely to produce the desired quality on the correct intensity but if this is translated, as can be easily done after a little experience in the above technique, into 'very soft edge, high support, greatly increased breath flow', every one of the singer's technical requirements are taken care of with great accuracy. If the pitch rises, he merely decreases the breath flow and raises the support—if the jump is sufficiently great to warrant this adjustment. If a lighter, gayer mood develops, he increases the edge and reduces the support and breath flow.

With experience, the singer learns to read all the musical and interpretative requirements of the score in terms of these three controls just as a linguist learns to think in another language without having to go through the process of translating. With greater experience and technical command, control of breath flow will be achieved more or less automatically. The advanced singer thus has only two controls (edge and support) to consider and calculate consciously for the greater part of the time. Because of this simplification, he can concentrate on applying them with great precision and subtlety.

Before concluding this chapter, it should be pointed out that when speaking of colour in relation to the larynx, we mean instrumental quality or colour as defined on page 64, and not vowel colour which, of course, is a function of the resonators. The reader might also refer again to the discussion on page 63 of the respective roles of the vibrator and resonator in the dynamics of tone.

XI

The Vocal Resonance System

Comparison of the vocal cords with the vibrator of a stringed instrument and understanding of their function in voice production is perhaps simpler than understanding of the vocal resonance system, although this does not necessarily mean that the latter is correspondingly more difficult to control.

The resonance system of the human voice is more complex than the mechanical instruments. In the piano and violin, the pitch of the note is determined by the frequency of the vibrator and all notes are resonated by a general resonance system whose tuning remains the same whatever the pitch of the note. In a mechanical wind instrument, it is the resonator which is responsible for determining the pitch of the note, the vibrator serving only to agitate the body of air in the resonating tube more or less powerfully. Most wind instruments have only one resonating tube, the frequency of which is altered mechanically to correspond to the pitch of the desired note. In an organ, of course, there is an individual resonator for each note of the instrument. In an instrument having more than one string or, as in the organ, more than one tube it is possible to play two or more notes simultaneously, but it is not possible to vary the frequency of the resonator concerned in the amplification of any one note. In other mechanical wind instruments having only one tube, it is possible to play only one note at a time.

In the voice, too, only one note may be sung at a time and the frequency of this note is determined by the frequency of the vibrator (vocal cords); as in the piano and violin, the frequency of the vocal cord vibrations is not overpowered by the resonance system. The voice is unique, however, in having several resonance cavities reinforcing the same vocal note simultaneously of which two may be modulated to different frequencies without altering the frequency of the vocal note.

THE VOCAL RESONANCE SYSTEM

Harmonic analysis of a large number of voices singing over a wide range shows a consistent pattern comprising one resonance which remains fairly constant in pitch on any vowel sound no matter what the frequency of the vocal note, and two resonances which vary in pitch as the vowel alters. These resonances, one unvariable in frequency and two variable, correspond to the three main resonating systems of the voice, one of which is untunable and two being capable of modulation to different frequencies.

When a tone is sung, it is thus resonated (*a*) by the untunable resonance system emphasizing the high frequency band, (*b*) by one of the tunable cavities tuned to the frequency of the upper vowel component, and (*c*) by the remaining tunable cavity tuned to the frequency of the lower vowel component. Each cavity picks out and resonates more strongly than other partials of the vocal note those which most closely correspond or relate to its own frequency, the neighbouring partials within the range of the cavity receiving comparatively less emphasis than the partial to which the cavity is tuned.

It is in control of these three resonating systems, and these only, wherein lies our ability to affect the resonation of the tone. Our study of vocal resonance is concerned with the role of these three systems in enhancement of tone quality and articulation of the vowels. The possibility of employing the resonators for colour control will also be considered. They are as follows:

UNTUNABLE RESONANCE SYSTEM

There is much disagreement among scientists as to the source of the high-pitched resonance found in all voices and specially prominent in those of good quality. Bartholomew,[1] who made a special study of the male voice, attributed it to a part of the larynx, but as it is relatively unvarying in pitch (between e^4 (2640 c.p.s.) and g^4 (3168 c.p.s.) in male voices) it seems more likely to be due to the untunable cavities of the head. The structure of these cavities, particularly the maxillary sinuses, would seem to make them a most likely source of this type of resonance although, according to Bartholomew, they persist with undiminished strength when the air entrance to the nasopharynx from the throat is closed by the soft palate. On the other hand, it has been suggested that the head cavities may be stimulated into resonance through the vibrations of the hard palate.

Whatever the sources of these higher resonances, they play no part

[1] *Journ. Acous. Soc. Amer.*, vol. 6 (1934), p. 25.

in vowel production. Their role in enhancement of tone quality will, however, be appreciated by referring to Figs. 52 and 53. From these diagrams it will be seen that while the lower notes in the bass range can be quite adequately reinforced in the throat and mouth cavities (the upper limit of which is about e^4 (2640 c.p.s.) in the male voice), the tone will be deprived of more and more of its upper harmonics if, as the pitch of the vocal note rises, resonance is confined to these two cavities. Whereas the low F (88 c.p.s.) in the bass range has approximately 30 partials within the range of these cavities, c^1 (264 c.p.s.) in the middle of the tenor voice has only 9; e^2 (660 c.p.s.) in the middle of the soprano range has only 4 partials within the range of the throat and mouth cavities, the upper limit of which is about g^4 (3168 c.p.s.) in the female voice. As the pitch rises, therefore, the higher resonances of the untunable cavities become more and more important.

The presence of the upper formants of the untunable system, however, is not limited to high notes. According to Bartholomew, a marked high formant is one of the characteristics of good vocal quality throughout a singer's range and not only on the higher notes which are traditionally accepted as being produced 'in the head' or with 'head tone' as these resonances are popularly termed. Only on notes lower than about C 132, does it become no longer possible to augment these resonances. There is a change of quality at this point when a bass or baritone, who normally uses head tone, descends below this note. The tenor rarely sings below C 132 and and it is well below the compass of the female voice, so that these singers can use head tone throughout their ranges.

When the high formant of the head tone is present, it has been universally noted that it is possible to sing for longer periods without tiring the voice and it is possible to use much higher intensities without damaging the vocal cords. Sustained singing without head tone, particularly on high intensities, is very likely to result in vocal deterioration. The presence of head tone in the voice is, in fact, a sign that the production is correct. If any factor in the production of the voice is incorrect, it will be impossible to produce a head tone.

Correct pitch quality also, needless to say, is dependent on having the correct proportion of head tone to other resonances in the voice and this varies according to pitch, the higher the note the more head tone being required.

A good idea of the amount of head tone necessary on any pitch can be gauged by humming on the various frequencies throughout the range of the voice at intensities similar to those employed in singing. The singer will be aware of vibrations across the bridge of the nose as described by great singers of the past and present; these vibrations are an indication to the singer himself of the presence of the untunable resonances. The proportionate amount of head tone experienced on each note while humming indicates the proportion which should be present while singing with very little edge, and it will be noted that this increases as the hum rises in pitch. It will be noted also that the higher the intensity, the stronger the head tone present in the hum and consequently the greater the amount which should be present when singing if the technique is correct. (The head tone vibrations are more strongly felt by the singer in the hum than during singing, but the proportions remain applicable.) It should be remembered that head tone is absent on notes lower than C132.

TUNABLE RESONANCES (Mouth and Throat Cavities)

These comprise the throat and mouth cavities, each of which can be modulated to a range of different frequencies. It is this feature of the voice that enables the vowel sounds to be produced as each cavity is tuned to one of the formants of the desired vowel. Models have been constructed by Paget in which there are two coupled, tuned resonators and by the use of these it has been possible to reproduce the vowel sounds by mechanical means.

The singer is unable to alter the frequency of these tunable resonators without altering the vowel. Control therefore consists only in being able to alter the size and selectivity of these resonators. This is possible because the cavities may assume various shapes without the tuning being affected. Russell[1] with his X-rays and Paget[2] with his vowel models have demonstrated that the exact shape, cross-section or length of the cavities is immaterial and that these may alter considerably without altering the tuning. If one modification of shape or size raises the frequency of one or both cavities, another modification takes place to lower it.

Changes in selectivity in order to enhance the quality of the tone apply particularly to the throat cavity. In its resting state some of the surfaces of the throat cavity are soft and fleshy and therefore more highly damped. Increase in the size of the cavity, which alone would result in more efficient resonation of the tone, is accompanied by a stretching and tightening of these surfaces, in particular the palatine

[1] Russell, op. cit.   [2] Paget, op. cit., p. 60.

arches, and this reduces the damping. This is of particular importance on high notes which are absorbed by soft surfaces, and a special effort to increase the size of the throat cavity still further is required here (see page 64).

If greater damping is required, this can be obtained without reducing the size of the throat cavity, but rather by increasing the breath flow which also has a damping effect. The latter is always preferable in singing as any reduction of throat capacity—'closing the throat' as it is called, or failure to open it—results in deterioration of vocal quality and destruction of the vocal line.

(a) because the amount of damping resulting from the soft surfaces of the closed throat is greater than that which can be accomplished by increased breath flow, and too much for proper amplification of the tone;

(b) because the muscles which enlarge the pharyngeal cavities also hold the larynx steady. When the throat is not open every change of vowel shape allows the larynx to change position, each change affecting the stringing of the vocal cords and the nature of the tone; and

(c) if the throat is kept open, little change in damping is effected when the various vowels are formed. If the throat is allowed to close, each change of vowel results in a considerable change of shape and selectivity of this resonator. A greater proportion of the energy of the note will lie in the vowel components rather than in the instrumental resonance of the vocal note, and the tone will be dominated by the colour of the constantly changing vowel, each of which has a distinctive quality determined by its harmonic structure, just as each note of the scale has a distinctive quality. Differences in pitch quality, do not disturb the vocal line as these are expected and accepted. However, differences occurring when the vowel colour is dominant are unmusical and disturbing, unless required for a deliberate effect. It is therefore essential that the selectivity of this cavity is kept stable and this can only be achieved by maintaining the throat in an open position. Under these circumstances, the changes of shape necessary to ensure the production of recognizable vowels must not be such as to destroy the desired relationship between the instrumental and vowel resonances. In this way, the vowel colour will be subordinate to the instrumental quality and the vocal line will be assured by the proportionately greater strength of the instrumental resonance; the vowel formants will give colour and variety to the tone without interfering with the musical line. If a smooth vocal line is desired, it may also be necessary to modify the vowel shapes as in Chapter XIII.

Need for sufficient breath flow to increase the damping of the resonators will be understood when it is realized that a very selective resonator will amplify very strongly the component to which it is tuned, other partials of the note receiving much less emphasis, while a less selective, more damped resonator will amplify adjacent partials to a much greater degree. The greater number of partials emphasized in the second case, when the resonator is more damped by the breath, will result in a greater richness of quality, while the lack of supporting partials in the more selective resonator will be heard as thinner, less resonant tone.[1] Thus, even if the throat is fully open, if there is insufficient breath flow, the tone will still be lacking in quality. The voice will not be under strain while the throat is open but the tone may not have its potential richness in all circumstances unless the breath flow is correct. It can be and will sound forced however, even when the throat is open, if too much edge is employed.

As the damping of the mouth cavity is not so altered by change of shape, the mouth cavity can be tuned much more selectively than the throat cavity to ensure adequate articulation of the vowels. Clarity of diction is improved by fullest possible use of all factors affecting the shape of the mouth cavity but only in so far as they do not inhibit the opening of the throat. To achieve best results, therefore, the student must pay fullest attention to the instrumental resonance of the note and then articulate as clearly as possible without disturbing the instrumental resonance already established. Some effect on tone quality can be achieved by maintaining tension on the upper lip which must be raised as high as possible towards the nose at all times so that the upper teeth are visible. This position of the upper lip as shown in Fig. 51 has been generally found to have a beneficial effect on the tone.

ROLE OF THE RESONATORS IN CONTROL OF TONE COLOUR

Apart from modification of the tone by the vowel colours as described above and utilization of the very limited scope for tone control of the mouth cavity, any attempt to use the resonators as a means of controlling tone colour can only result in diminishing the stability and degree of opening of the throat cavity and this, of

---

[1] See Chapter IV.

course, is not permissible, nor is it necessary. Adequate scope for colour variation is possible by suitable control of the vocal cords as given above. The closest analogy is that of a stringed instrument where tone colour is obtained by variations in the bowing and fingering of the strings and not by altering the dimensions of the box while playing.

The role of the vocal cords in tone colour control has never been at all clearly understood. In the absence of such understanding, teaching methods have always sought instead to achieve such control by a variety of methods designed in attempts to adjust the resonators, elaborate focusing and placing systems which are extremely difficult for the singer to follow and which cannot give a really positive control no matter how conscientiously they are attempted. The student is instructed to think the tone forward or back, up or down, in the head or in the chest. Or he may be asked to focus or direct the tone towards different parts of the mouth and face, or to feel certain sensations, e.g. a tingling behind the teeth. Unfortunately, such methods leave much to be desired and the reason for this should now be apparent.

The theories on which such methods are based do not bear scientific investigation; *it is impossible to focus the tone as it is borne by sound waves which radiate in all directions and not by an air stream; and* the direction in which the breath travels a few feet from the mouth has no effect on the sound waves which are travelling out at the speed of 1,100 feet per second. In any case, the breath pressure has already been converted into sound waves at the vocal cords before it reaches the mouth.

What happens when a singer tries to focus the tone or the breath or place the voice is that these attempts to carry out a mental conception result indirectly in physical changes in the shape and size of the resonators which affect the quality of the tone. Thus, in practice, all attempts to focus or place the voice are really no more than different empirical attempts to control the resonators by altering one's mental concepts and, as such, can only be judged by results. And one cannot deny that these methods do enable us to alter the dimensions of the resonators, but only in a very limited and inefficient manner.[1]

[1] Apart from this inefficiency in altering the dimensions of the resonator, these methods have one very serious disadvantage in that they do not encourage the singer to open his throat—in fact, they definitely inhibit such opening. A type of throaty, covered tone is achieved which is more acceptable to this type of teacher than a shouty, white tone, but which is unacceptable to a teacher who knows how to obtain a correctly covered, mellowed but still bright tone, in which the throat is maintained in a fully open position.

They are more likely to confuse than help the student. 'Forward' and 'back' and 'in the head' by themselves are too nebulous and vague and not clearly enough defined conceptions. If there is a difference in breath volume, the singer is at a loss to adjust closely enough. A certain amount of success is possible by such methods with a talented singer over a period of time, particularly if the breath volumes and pressures are kept fairly constant. It is obvious, however, that by these particular concepts it is virtually impossible to gain sufficient mastery over tone control to be able to subtly alter the tone colour at will. Conceptions giving a much more positive control are needed. When such control is acquired no elaborate focusing is necessary.

Pianissimo singing has perhaps suffered most of all, for, unless the singer can, either through knowledge or instinct, reduce his edge to a minimum and hold his throat cavity at its maximum capacity, the natural tendency is to close the throat for this effect which is, of course, the very reverse of what is required. It must be stressed, however, that the above technique is possible only when the singer has adequate breath capacity and support. The reason for particular stress on the open throat in pianissimo singing is to counter the damping effect of the increased breath flow through the comparatively more relaxed soft edge setting of the vocal cords. This kind of pianissimo is, in effect, all but a complete whisper, relying for its quality and carrying power on high support, greatly increased breath flow (in order to vibrate sufficient mass of vocal cord) and extremely efficient resonation (see page 64).

Although the rules given for control of colour are easy to understand, the singer requires great skill in order to put them into practice; just as car-driving efficiency depends not on the complexity of the controls but on the skill and judgement of the driver in the use and co-ordination of the few simple controls at his command. In learning to drive a car, one knows exactly the controls one has and failure to do well is rightly attributed to lack of skill. With the voice, one must be sure that one has all the controls that are necessary and then be prepared to study and practice until skill is acquired. Students must not be misled into a search for complex controls which do not exist.

ROLE OF THE THROAT AND MOUTH CAVITIES IN VOWEL FORMATION

The differences which we hear between various vowels, as explained above, are due to differences in the harmonic structure of the sounds. In each vowel sound, two harmonic components are emphasized, the pitch and probably the relative intensity of which determines the shape of the vowel. These harmonic differences give to each vowel not only its distinguishing sound but also a distinctive tone quality or colour, from ee the brightest, to oo the darkest.

If we sing the different vowels to the same vocal note, the instrumental quality of the note will be modified in each case by the colour of the vowel. The degree to which the vowel colour affects the instrumental quality of the tone depends, as explained above, on the proportionate strength of the vowel components to other partials of the note.

Vowel formation may be observed in its simplest form in whispering where there is no vocal note. Instead, the two cavities are stirred into resonance by an intensified current of air, each cavity being tuned to one of the two components of the required vowel sound.[1]

In speech and song, the cavities are stirred into resonation not by an unmodulated airstream as in whispering, but by sound waves set up by the regular vibrations of the vocal cords. Whereas in whispering, the pitch of the vowel components is the only consideration, in speech and song the resonators can only amplify partials of the vocal note.

Those partials of the vocal note corresponding to the frequencies of the vowel resonances to which the cavities are tuned will be reinforced most strongly. Other partials within the range of the respective cavities will also be reinforced but not to the same degree. If the partials of the vocal note lie outside the range of one or other of the vowel resonances, it becomes difficult to produce the vowel sound as conceived. The greater the discrepancy, the less possibility for producing the desired vowel.

The question that now arises is which cavity is responsible for the higher and which for the lower formants of the vowels. In whispered speech, Paget concluded that in all vowels from ah to oo inclusive the lower formant is produced in the mouth cavity and the upper formant in the throat, while, in all other vowels, the lower formant is produced in the throat cavity. He has constructed models of these vowels with the higher resonances in the back resonator, next to the vibrator. Whether the same changeover occurs in speech and song has not been demonstrated. Theoretically, there seems to be no reason why this should not be so but, on the other hand, when the capacity of the throat is increased there is marked improvement of tone quality whatever the vowel being sung.

[1] See page 65.

The range of the vowel resonances in the male voice extends from about e^1 (330 c.p.s.) which is reached by the deepest of the lower formants, to an upper limit of about e^4 (2640 c.p.s.), above which the male head resonance extends from e^4 to g^4. According to most observers, the vowel formants in the female voice are slightly higher than in the male voice but the range of her resonance cavities is also higher, extending upwards to about g^4 (3168 c.p.s.) which is, of course, the upper limit of the male head resonance. Presumably, head resonance in the female voice commences at this point.

The highest lower vowel formant produced appears to be that of uh (cup) which extends upwards to a^2 sharp although Aiken suggested an extreme upper limit of f^2 (704 c.p.s.) for the lower vowel resonances of the male voice and a^{2b} (approx. 880 c.p.s.) in the female voice.

Reference to Fig. 53 will show that the lower the pitch of the vocal note, the more partials there are available in both cavities not only for reinforcement of instrumental resonance but also for vowel differentiation. In speech, the frequency range used by both men and women is comparatively low and furthermore, the frequencies of the spoken sounds are unconsciously varied so that they lie on the most suitable frequency for the formation of the desired vowel. In song, not only is the range much higher, but the frequency of the note cannot, obviously, be varied to correspond with vowel requirements. If, on the lower notes, the partials resonated in the lower pitched cavity do not correspond to vowel requirements, there are usually sufficient in the higher pitched cavity to produce the upper formant.

In the higher ranges of the female voice, however, where the vocal note rises above the normal compass of the lower pitched cavity and where the higher pitched cavity also begins to run short of partials, adequate reproduction of the vowel sounds becomes progressively more difficult and finally impossible. (Where the vocal note does thus rise above the normal compass of the lower pitched cavity, it has been assumed that in these cases, notwithstanding, the fundamental continues to be resonated in that cavity.)

From the information given in Fig. 53, the vowels one would expect to give most difficulty are ee and oo in which the lower vowel formants descend furthest and in practice this is found to be the case. Here the singer should modify towards the vowel with a higher pitched lower formant—ee towards i (hit), and oo towards u (put).

XII

Control of the Resonators

This chapter is concerned with control of the resonators in so far as they affect the quality and amplification of the tone. Control of the resonators from the point of view of articulation is discussed in the following chapter.

THE OPEN THROAT

Enlargement of the pharyngeal cavities during singing—the 'open throat' as it is called—is an essential part of singing technique for two reasons. Firstly, because the tauter surfaces of the open throat are more efficient in amplification of the tone. Secondly, when the throat is open the hyoid bone is raised in a forward position and the larynx is suspended from the hyoid bone in a mid-position which enables the vocal cords to vibrate at maximum length for a given pitch. This of course becomes more important as the singer learns to use higher intensities.

What happens when the throat is closed? The hyoid bone drops and no longer provides an effective point of fixation by which the thyro-hyoid muscles can raise the larynx. The larynx and its glottis are squeezed by the epiglottis as the tongue goes back into the throat and further closure may be effected by tension on the neck muscles. It becomes impossible for the extrinsic muscles to elongate the vocal cords correctly and, in order to establish the tensions required for maintenance of pitch on these shortened cords, they become bunched up. 'Any such external closure brings the vocal cords together unevenly, so that they are more tightly pressed together at one point of their length than at another because of this external pressure. Therefore, they are more or less bound to rub together at one or more points. This friction of the unevenly approximated vocal cords often brings about the formation of nodules which are actually corn-like

178

growths. The greater the development of the neck muscles, the greater the danger of the formation of nodules becomes.'[1]

The neck muscles active in closing the throat are described on pages 123 to 125. They may be brought into action in a number of ways and for a number of reasons.

Most of the muscles concerned pass from the skeleton to the head and jaw and may be brought into tension from above or below, or both. Any movement which draws the head closer to the body involves the neck muscles, as does raising of the chest and shoulders. Pulling in the chin towards the neck is another efficient means of tensing the neck muscles. Again, tension may be directed to the muscles of the neck without any specific effort to bring the head or chin closer to the body. In this action, the sterno-mastoid muscles will be seen to stand out markedly and, of course, it will be impossible to tense the opposing throat-opening muscles.

The singer will tend to bring these neck muscles into tension if his breathing muscles are not sufficiently developed, because it enables him to produce a more powerful tone than he would otherwise be capable of producing. Unfortunately, this method of producing a more powerful sound has too many drawbacks: the tone produced is not a pleasant one, the amount of extra power to be obtained is very limited and, worst of all, it interferes with the correct action of the larynx and results in eventual destruction of the voice.

When the neck muscles are so used, the sound is conducted to the ear by the sterno-mastoid muscles which, in this production, press against the larynx and then pass up to the mastoid bone. Thus the untrained or badly trained singer prefers using his neck muscles because the sound which he hears when singing in this way is much richer and more satisfying to himself than the sound which he hears when singing without this inner conduction of sound direct to his own ears. He must be made to realize that a method of singing which gives him most satisfaction may not necessarily be that which produces the most desirable sound to his audience.

There is one further reason why the singer instinctively desires to use his neck muscles and this is because he feels that it helps him to check excessive breath expulsion. When the neck muscles are out of action, excessive breath expulsion is prevented by tension of the inspiratory muscles and correct approximation of the vocal cords. The right way to check excessive breath expulsion is by proper development of the laryngeal muscles and development and correct

[1] Douglas Stanley, *Your Voice* (Pitman, London 1945), p. 134.

use of the breathing muscles, not by bringing in the neck muscles. Even when the laryngeal and breathing muscles are correctly developed and correctly used, the singer may not have sufficient confidence in their ability to check breath, and he must be made to overcome this instinctive desire to check his breath expulsion by use of the neck muscles.

If the throat closing muscles described above are kept out of action the throat will not, however, be 'open' until the throat opening actions are performed. Before describing these, however, it must be stressed that it is impossible to put them into effect unless they are given priority. Any resonatory concept which is given preference over the opening of the throat cavity immediately limits or prevents the possibility of such opening. Thus, if the throat is enlarged, it is possible to produce the various vowel sounds while maintaining this opening. If the singer thinks of the vowel shape first and foremost, or of any focusing or placing concept or of any other control which he may be given over the resonators, he will be the less able to open the throat and establish the condition for a strong throat resonance.

If opening the throat is subordinate in any way to such concepts or to shaping of the mouth, no great improvement can be made to the tone and there is very little scope for control. If the throat cavity is kept open, a very noticeable difference is made to the tone and the mouth still has sufficient freedom of movement to shape itself to the vowel component so that the vowels are produced as accurately as possible.

The throat cavity is of course opened and enlarged by pulling the base of the tongue forwards and away from the back wall of the pharynx as explained in Chapter VIII. In practice, however, the ability to maintain an open throat lies not so much in trying to control the throat cavity physically as in gaining an entirely new conception of the way in which the vowels are formed.

Tied and Free Resonation

In speech, the tunable cavities adjust their shape and size in order to raise or lower their respective frequencies according to the components of the desired vowels. It is easily demonstrated, however, that if these cavity shapes are adhered to while using the breath pressures and frequencies needed in singing, the tones produced are not satisfactory. Physical attempts to open the throat are not enough. The history of developments in training technique, in so far as resonance is concerned, has consisted also of various attempts to provide a system of focusing and/or positioning of the vowels or the tone aimed at altering these cavity shapes in such a way as to improve the tone while still maintaining clear and recognizable vowels.

It is not sufficiently understood, however, that there are fundamentally only two different ways of producing vowel sounds, one giving almost no scope to the singer for improvement of the tone no matter how hard he may try to focus or carry out any of the various directions evolved over the years in attempts to control the resonators. If we wish to have control over the size of the pharyngeal cavities on which efficient amplification of the tone mainly depends, the second method of producing the vowel sounds must be employed.

These two methods of vowel production are: (*a*) with the throat cavity subordinate to the shape the mouth has been made to assume, with the resonating cavities 'tied' and functioning as a single unit, in which there is one, and only one setting of the cavities for each vowel, an alteration of shape giving a different vowel sound, and (b) with the throat cavity left free to alter its dimensions to a very great extent while the vowel shape is maintained by reflex adjustments of the tongue and mouth.[1]

We may term these two types of vowel production *Tied* and *Free*. As we know, the mouth and pharyngeal cavities share a common boundary in the oro-pharyngeal isthmus. Very briefly, the difference between the tied and free production is that in the tied production, both orifices of the mouth (oro-pharyngeal isthmus and oral fissure) adjust jointly in a certain position when the vowel is formed; in the free production, the singer has greater control over the oro-pharyngeal isthmus.

In the free production, the vowel sounds are not produced by shaping the resonators according to any preconceived shape. They are produced by reflex adjustments of the tongue in response to a mental concept of the vowel shape. If those dimensions of the throat over which we have physical control are altered or predetermined, reflex adjustments are made so that the vowel conceived is produced without substantial alteration. The more supple the muscles of the tongue, the less modification to the vowel is perceived. The free production, in an extreme way, is used by the ventriloquist who relies solely upon the inter-adjustability of the pharyngeal cavities and

[1] The X-ray photographs taken by Oscar Russell show clearly that 'there is a striking lack of uniformity in cavities. It apparently cannot be said that all individuals take the same position for a given cavity in order to produce a given vowel, although there are some characteristics which are fairly outstanding.' (op. cit., p. 39.)

movements of the tongue to produce all sounds: the jaw and lips do not move at all but this restriction of his mouth movements does not prevent him from being able to produce clearly articulated vowel sounds.

In normal speech some people move their jaw and lips very little and, in fact, use their pharyngeal cavities freely, with the mouth movements helping to make the articulation distinct.

In clearly enunciated, traditional elocution speech, however, the speaker sets the jaw and lips more deliberately in conventional positions, which results in a tie of both orifices of the mouth and an inability to control them separately. Many teachers of singing think that clear diction in singing should be obtained in the same manner and do not realize that all control over the pharyngeal cavities is thus lost.

Such deliberate setting of the mouth produces somewhat stilted, unnatural sounds and modern elocutionary trends are tending correctly to the view that it is not necessary to clear articulation and improvement of tone quality. In natural speech there are two elements in vowel and tone control—the use of the pharyngeal cavities and the use of the jaw and lips and front part of the tongue. In order to increase the scope of our control, in speech and singing alike, both these aspects must be exploited. Old-fashioned methods aimed at giving the student more efficient use of his mouth while the pharyngeal cavities were ignored and even constricted. A comprehensive natural development takes both aspects into consideration; the student's control over his pharyngeal cavities is increased and the mouth used as much as possible to assist in achieving the desired results—clear diction and enhancement of tone quality. *The mouth must not be used in such a way as to restrict the efficiency of the pharyngeal cavities, particularly as it is here that harmonics most important to tone quality are produced.*

Resonator tie thus occurs if the setting of the jaw, tongue and lips in a preconceived position is given preference over shaping of the pharyngeal cavities so as to prevent control being exercised over these cavities for the purposes of enhancement of tone quality. Even if no attempt is made to set the mouth in a preconceived position, *adherence to habits of vowel formation used in ordinary speech will have a similar deleterious effect.* Furthermore, resonator tie is associated with inability to tense the throat-opening muscles and therefore in a closed throat. When any feature of voice production is not being carried out correctly attempts are usually made to compensate for the resulting deficiency by employing harmful substitute procedures. Thus, resonator tie is usually also associated with tension on the neck muscles and cramping of the larynx with the harmful consequences described above.

I would like to draw attention to the word 'setting'. 'Setting' the mouth cavity is a very different matter to shaping it, as it can still be shaped when the tone is resonated primarily by the pharyngeal cavities.

The difference between shaping and setting may be clarified by an analogy with the arm. The arm may be moved up or down simply by alternately tensing and relaxing the muscles which raise it. On the other hand, the arm may be tensed or 'set' prior to moving it by placing equal tension simultaneously on the muscles which raise the arm and on those which lower it against resistance. In this case, raising of the arm requires added tension to the raising muscles so that they exert more force than the lowering muscles. The action involves both the raising *and* lowering muscles, whereas in the simple action before the arm was set, only the raising muscles were involved. Similarly, the jaw may be dropped by relaxation of the muscles which keep it in its normal closed position, or it may be opened against resistance, which brings into action the neck muscles.

This increased tension on the neck muscles can be easily felt by placing one hand on the neck whilst opening the jaw against resistance. The association between the setting of the jaw and tension on the neck muscles can also be felt if the reader sets his mouth in the conventional position for any vowel and then increases the tension on the mouth without altering its shape—just as he would increase the tension on the arm without moving it; he will feel the neck muscles increase their tension at the same time.

A similar result is obtained when the jaw is 'set' in a pre-determined midway position for singing, irrespective of the vowel to be formed. Again both the lowering and raising muscles are in balanced antagonism to hold the position.

When the mouth is so set, the tension on the neck muscles determines the position of the hyoid bone and the shape of the back resonator which cannot be altered while this tension on the neck muscles exists. A different setting of the jaw will result in a difference in the extent and degree of the neck tension and a corresponding difference in the shape of the oro-pharyngeal isthmus and the back resonator, each position giving a different vowel.

In these circumstances, the shape of the pharynx is almost entirely dependent on the shape the mouth is made to assume. If the mouth is 'set', we have, for all practical purposes, only one tunable resonator. This resonator is made up of the pharyngeal cavities and the mouth, but they are tied to each other and must be considered as a single resonator because the separate parts cannot be individually adjusted without altering the frequency of the adjoining cavity; when the mouth cavity alters the other cavities follow suit.

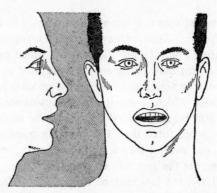

FIG. 51. *Correct lip position* (*see note on page* 127; *also page,* 173 *Chapter XI*)

On the other hand, if shaping of the pharyngeal cavities is given preference, then there remains sufficient adjustability of the tongue and mouth to ensure accurate production of the vowels without destroying the efficiency of the pharyngeal resonation already established. In order therefore to maintain adequate inter-adjustability of the resonators, the shaping of the pharyngeal resonators—opening of the throat—must come first and foremost in the mind of the singer.

In a nutshell: if the pharynx is first shaped as required for amplification of the tone, reflex adjustability of the tongue for accurate vowel differentiation is retained; if attention is paid first of all to articulation of the vowels, adjustability of the pharynx is then beyond the control of the singer.

The difference between the tied and the free resonation can be experienced by anyone in ordinary speech. First, drop the jaw in a completely relaxed position and then form the vowels, using the tongue alone, and without altering the shape of the mouth. Control over the pharynx will be experienced and the student will have the feeling that the vowels are being formed in a low position; *if the vowels are not produced in this same low position during singing one*

184

may be sure that the throat is not open. Next, form the mouth and lips in the conventional positions for each vowel and it will be seen that all possibility of control over the tongue and pharynx is lost. Any attempt to exercise this control under these circumstances only results in distortion and failure to achieve the desired improvement in tone quality and amplification.

When the neck muscles are relaxed and the throat opening muscles tensed, the desired vowel is produced merely by conceiving of the vowel required and without thought of any further shaping of the resonators apart from making use of the limited extent to which the mouth may still be adjusted to improve the diction. The lips, of course, must be kept as far as possible in the position shown in Fig. 51. A feeling of enlargement of the pharynx and a lowering of the vowel position is experienced as soon as this position of the lips is adopted. Any modification of the vowel that may be caused by enlargement of the throat cavity is compensated by ear as a result of which the shape of the tongue is altered reflexly to correct the tuning.

Briefly then, if the singer wishes to maintain an open throat, he should think of the pharynx as the main resonator of the tone and of the mouth mainly as an aid to good diction. He should practice trying to produce the vowel sounds with the pharynx alone and without the use of the mouth, as does a ventriloquist, and then learn to enhance the tone and the diction by varying the extent of the mouth opening, i.e. the vertical movements of the jaw. He must abandon the normal positions for vowel formation used in speech and substitute for these the low position described above in which the mouth is of secondary importance and the pharynx becomes the main resonator of the tone. Any deviation from this low position or a return to the normal use of the mouth as in speech will result in closing of the throat no matter how hard the singer tries to make it 'feel' open or how hard he tries to pull the base of the tongue forward. Similarly any other focusing or placing concept—forward, high or back—if applied to vowel position will have the same unsatisfactory result. Forward, high or in the head are concepts that have a place in singing to be discussed below but not as far as positioning of the vowel is concerned.

Importance of the Open Throat

Although the need for an open throat is very widely recognized amongst singing teachers, its very great importance in singing is not always sufficiently stressed even by those teachers who understand its necessity. The opening of the throat cannot, in fact, be over-emphasized. Even when visual examination shows the base of the tongue to be well away from the posterior wall of the pharynx, exercise should not be discontinued *as even slight increases in the capacity of the throat may make a considerable difference to the amount of resonance obtained.*

Exercises must be designed to strengthen the genio-hyoid and genio-glossus muscles but under no circumstances to develop the antagonistic neck muscles. At the same time, the muscles which alter the shape of the tongue (after the position of the hyoid bone has been established by the genio-hyoid and genio-glossus) must be made as flexible as possible in order that they may be able to assume any position needed by the singer.

If a student has been singing for some time with a throaty produc-tion using the neck muscles, it may take some time before they lose tone and will relax sufficiently. Meanwhile the singer will have to develop the genio-hyoid and genio-glossus which will have remained undeveloped while the singer was using a neck-muscle production.

While the muscles concerned are not under the complete command of the singer's will, either in strength or flexibility, there is little likelihood of achieving an open throat or proper shaping of the resonators.

Throat 'Openings'

As the voice is trained and muscles become more responsive, as the throat becomes more open and the breathing muscles stronger, the breathing ratios and the amount of edge must be continually checked and corrected and the pupil must adjust to new ideas of the sonority of the tone. An increase in the resonant capacity of the throat may occur gradually or in sudden, quite noticeable stages after a period of stability, particualrly with undeveloped voices. Each of these resonator 'openings' and every increase in the strength of the breathing muscles must be met with a further adjustment in technique. The greater the strength of the breathing muscles, and the greater the capacity of the throat, the less edge is required in order to produce a tone of good quality at high intensity.

The above adjustments may be fairly considerable and before they are made, there may be a temporary loss of control due to incorrect balancing between the resonators and other parts of the vocal mechanism. A correct diagnosis is essential. If a teacher does not understand these openings, he will be at a loss to explain what has happened and if he does not understand the adjustments which are necessary in order to take full advantage of the extra throat capacity, the singer may suffer a serious setback instead of being able to benefit almost immediately from the extra resonant capacity of the throat.

The more efficient the resonance, the more confidence the singer can have in the ability of the tone to carry and the less likely he is to bring unwanted inhibiting tensions into play.

HEAD TONE

The term 'head tone' has been used throughout the history of singing in many ways and with many meanings, and usually grossly mishandled so that it has come in for a great deal of criticism from many sources. It is associated with attempts to sing 'in the head' and with numerous unfounded theories on resonation with the idea of focusing the tone into the skull and various parts of the head in some of which it is impossible for the tone to be resonated.

On the other hand, it is generally associated with a certain desirable vocal quality in which the higher harmonics of tone are emphasized. In describing such tones, it would be an advantage to use a term which does not have the undesirable associations described above. There are other terms such as higher partial quality, or upper pitch quality tones, which might be more accurate but, in practice, they are far too clumsy and do not evoke a sympathetic response from the student. For this reason, we shall continue to use the term 'head tone' for that vocal quality in which the higher harmonics are emphasized by the untunable resonance system, but it must be clearly understood that this term has no reference to the way in which such tone is produced. *It is merely a term which conveys to the student, better than any other, the type of tone under consideration providing he understands that he must not try to sing in the head or focus the tone in any way.*

When used thus, the term 'head tone' is no more than a kind of shorthand by which to convey very briefly to a properly trained and informed singer a wealth of technical information. Used as it usually is, without this technical background, it is practically meaningless, if not actually harmful.

It must be said, however, that although the source of the high frequency resonance of the human voice has not been indisputably established, it is a fact that when present, the singer is conscious of vibrations across the bridge of the nose as described by many great singers. The mistake made is in thinking that these vibrations can be produced by singing 'in the head', focusing towards that position or by other similar methods traditionally assoicated with head tone. *A strong head tone can in fact be produced without employing any such methods but solely by ensuring that all aspects of voice production already described are thoroughly understood and are being put into practice and correctly co-ordinated.*

Those who expect instruction on head tone to include elaborate focusing or placing directions will not find any here and those who expect a super new method will also be disappointed. Head tone quite simply is present when all factors in technique described above are established in correct proportions and absent if any factor is not being carried out correctly or is out of proportion to the other factors: it is not something extra which the singer has to do over and above taking care of his breathing, the setting of his vocal cords and maintenance of an open throat. In some circumstances, therefore, head tone may be augmented by opening the throat, in others by increasing the breath flow or edge or, again, by adding to the support.

From the point of view of control, head tone should be regarded merely as a gauge for checking purposes, a means by which the singer can tell whether or not his technique is correct. If he is not aware of the presence of head tone, he can be sure that an adjustment in technique is required and he must get to know the amount of head tone to be expected on the various frequencies as he changes the edge and support in accordance with the musical and artistic requirements of his score.

If the student fails to produce a head tone and set up the vibrations across the bridge of the nose already described, there is little or nothing to be gained by exhortation to sing in the head or focus into the mask other than in exceptional cases where such exhortation may cause a particular student to respond by making those adjustments in technique necessary for the production of a stronger head tone. Such a roundabout method of producing a head tone cannot be relied upon for accuracy or consistency. In most cases, however, instructions to focus or sing in the head merely succeed in making it impossible for the singer to keep the vowel in the low position necessary for maintenance of the open throat.

If a student attempts to 'cover' a tone that is too harsh and edgy, by employing the above method, thereby closing the throat, this will succeed in damping down the resonance but the resulting 'covered' tone will be a dull and lifeless sound that is extremely harmful to the mechanism, particularly if used on a high intensity; it is very different from the mellow, but vibrant sound characteristic of the proper head tone.

A vocal coach may use the terms head tone and open or chest tone in trying to describe various tones required. A properly trained singer must be able to translate these requests into terms which relate to the methods of producing such tones. When requested to use more head tone, he does not do this by trying to put the voice deeper or higher in the head but by adjusting the amount of edge and/or support and making sure the throat is open. The request for less head tone or a more open tone must be translated by the singer into corresponding terms. A teacher who has been trained in this technique will know exactly what adjustment is necesary in the particular circumstances but, in the absence of such a teacher and when working with a coach or repetiteur who has no knowledge of the techniques of voice production, it may be necessary for the student to try several alternative adjustments before he is able to provide the tones required of him.

A correctly trained singer, according to Bartholomew,[1] will keep the head tone throughout his range and not only on the higher notes which are traditionally accepted as being produced 'in the head' or with head tone. Why, then, do so many teachers state that head tone or head register is needed only on the higher notes? To understand this, it must be realized firstly that control of the higher harmonics cannot be fully appreciated or exercised until the throat is open and secondly that, without the techniques given above, it has always been a difficult matter to keep the head tone at the same time as one is using an open tone resonated strongly in the throat and mouth cavities. It has therefore been easier to concentrate on the open tones for the lower notes and switch to the head tone or something resembling it on the higher notes even though this has meant, particularly if lack of head tone is paralleled by incorrect breathing habits, the existence of distinct and awkward quality changes in a voice and the need for smoothing-out techniques which do not really solve the problem and which are unnecessary if head tone is employed throughout the range in correct proportion to the open sounding components of the tone resonated in the lower-pitched cavities, the presence of which is also due to correct control of the

[1] See page 170.

vibration of the vocal cords. If the voice is used in this manner, there should be no registers or points of sudden change where a smoothing out technique is required, but a gradual change in pitch quality as the tone ascends. Attempts to eliminate quality changes except on these lines result in a great variety of vocal distortions.

The actual amount of head tone heard will depend on the type of voice, the lower pitched voices having less head tone than the higher pitched voices. The difference in the amount of head tone apparent in the various voices is not due to a difference in technique but to a difference in the physical make-up of the voice, and the fact that they are singing on a different tessitura with different pitch qualities. Where the range of a male voice overlaps that of the female, a similar amount of higher resonance emphasis should be heard, even though it may be a high note in the male voice and a comparatively low note in the female voice.

These differences will give rise to different sensations in each singer and if a teacher tries to analyse these sensations to pass on to others, he can only describe the sensations that apply to a particular type of voice. This is perhaps why some teachers have success only with students who have the same type of voice as themselves, and why voices of all categories are often produced in the same mould as that of the teacher.

The usual division of all voices into three zones—chest, middle and head—is very misleading in that it gives the impression that one does not have to augment the higher resonances on one's lower notes and only to a limited extent in the middle of one's range. There are of course many teachers who say that a female singer should use the 'head voice' throughout her range and who may succeed in teaching their female students to do so. However, such teachers are unlikely to encourage these students to use sufficient edge, particularly on the lower notes, as they are concentrating on the like-sounding properties of the notes. Only when the individual properties of each note (due to differences in pitch quality) are taken into account together with those properties which are common to all notes when head tone is present is there the possibility of a positive voice control, and only when head tone or head voice is discussed and considered in relation to the other components of the tone and the concept of pitch quality does it have any real meaning.

Because of the higher pitches used by the female singer, more higher pitch quality will normally be heard even when she is not deliberately augmenting her head tone, and the need to augment this resonance further may not be so apparent to a teacher who is not fully conversant with this problem. An idea of the amount of head tone required can be gauged from the hum as already described on pages 170–1.

Nasal Resonance

The reader may also come across the term 'nasal resonance'. This term is used by some teachers instead of head tone and is based on the theory that these tones are produced in the nasal cavities and sinuses. It should be understood as a concept synonymous with head tone and not confused with nasality or nasal twang—an unpleasant quality achieved, not by opening the entrance to the nasal cavities, but by penning the sound in a cul-de-sac. Such a cul-de-sac may be formed in the nasal cavities if, as in a cold, the turbinates are congested so that the sound which enters the nose is prevented from escaping at the nostrils. In the production of an m or n, it is at the palatal cavity where such a cul-de-sac is formed, and not in the nose. It is not so well known, however, that a similar cul-de-sac may be formed in the lower pharyngeal cavities by constriction produced by the epiglottis, by the interior larynx, or between the tongue and the walls of the pharynx when the throat is closed. There is then given off a tonal quality which the ear recognizes as being somewhat analogous to that produced by swollen turbinates. It is only in this latter manner that nasality can be produced in a singing voice—providing, of course, that the singer does not have a cold.

It is very easy to determine whether the entrance to the nasal cavities is open or shut, either with a stethoscope held to either nostril or by closing both nostrils while using the voice. If the passage is open, the closure of the nostril produces a marked change in vocal quality. In speech, the nasal cavities are employed by some people on certain vowels and not by others. The presence or absence of this resonance does not make any appreciable difference to the audible vowel or consonant character of most of the speech sounds. In song too, similar experiments by Paget[1] with a few well-known singers showed that none of them were using the nasal cavities in the resonance of their tone. As the higher resonances of the head tone are present in all voices to a greater or lesser extent, these experiments would seem to indicate without doubt that they are not made by opening the entrance to the nasal cavities.

[1] *Human Speech* (Kegan Paul, London 1930), p. 215.

CONTROL OF THE RESONATORS

FORWARD PRODUCTION

Before concluding, a word should be said about forward production, much of which is heard in singing circles. A free sounding tone is associated with a frontal position from which it is imagined that the tone may issue forth without obstruction and, conversely, a forced or inhibited tone conjures up the image of the sound being blocked or bottled up in a back position where it is prevented from issuing freely. However, these are only subjective images and have nothing to do with where the vocal action takes place. In fact, when the production is correct, all laryngeal and resonatory control lies low in the throat. It is here that changes resulting from differences in pitch concepts are felt to take place, here that 'edge' is controlled and it is also in this low position that the vowel sounds are articulated when the throat is open and pharyngeal resonance is employed.[1]

Confusion arises because at the same time as this action is taking place in the larynx and low in the pharynx, vibrations may be felt across the bridge of the nose as described[2] and the singer may also feel a tingling behind the upper teeth. When these factors are not analysed clearly some singers will be more conscious of the actual muscular tensions being exerted, while others will be more aware of the resulting sensations. Thus, in an article by Richard Merryman[3] which appeared as this book was going to press, Joan Sutherland states, 'You ask two singers how they get a particular note, and they'll describe exactly opposite feelings—and what they're doing may be exactly the same thing.' In the same article Marilyn Horne says, 'Or the teacher will say, "Wonderful! That's a great, free tone. That's it. What did you do?" and you'll say, "I don't know." What happens is that over a long period of time and practice you find the sensations that work—and that's what a teacher and student are doing over the years: discovering what works, and then putting a name to it that means something to the singer, then they can return to it. It's all terribly hit-or-miss. It took my husband and me three years before we both understood what he meant when he said, "It sounds more forward." I'd say, "But I'm not singing forward." And then I finally realized that that meant I was singing deeper in the throat while resonating in the mask.'

[1] See pages 184–5.   [2] See page 188
[3] *Life International*, Vol. 49, No. 9, October 26, 1970.

XIII

Articulation

CLASSIFICATION OF SOUNDS

All speech sounds may be divided into two classes, viz.:

(*a*) *Voiceless or breathed sounds* (aspirated) in which the vocal cords are silent. Consonants in this category require in their formation a definite intensified expulsion of breath and consequently a cessation of vocal tone.

(*b*) *Voiced sounds*, in which the vocal cords vibrate to form voice and which do not require any intensification of breath pressure in speech. In this group are all the vowel sounds, b, d, hard g, j, th in thou, z, j (vision), v, r, m, n, ng, l.

The voiced sounds are divided into *fully voiced* and *partially voiced* depending on whether the vibration of the vocal cords persists throughout the period of articulation of the sound (as in vowels and continuants) or throughout a part of the period of articulation (plosives); and thirdly, *devoiced sounds*. The vibration of the vocal cords may be entirely absent throughout the period of articulation of a devoiced sound but it is not the same as a voiceless sound, as can be seen when the b in bat is devoiced; it is not the same as the voiceless p in pat. There is a difference in each case in the force of exhalation.

Consonants. Sounds, whether voiced or voiceless, that arise from partial or complete obstruction in the mouth are known as consonant sounds. They are sometimes classified according to the place of obstruction or articulation, but shall be classified here according to the nature of the obstruction or articulation. Every voiced consonant in the first three groups has its voiceless counterpart, thus z (the buzzing sound) and s (the hissing sound) form a pair, as also do d and t, hard g and k or hard c.

(*a*) *Plosive consonants*, when the obstruction is complete and the

193

outflow of breath is completely blocked for an instant so that it issues explosively when released. These may be subdivided as follows:

Aspirated or voiceless plosives. In these consonants, the outflow of breath is intensified so that there is an audible puff of breath following the explosion, p, t, k.

Unaspirated or voiced plosives. The passage of the mouth is completely blocked at the same place as above, but the outflow of breath is not intensified so that there is hardly any explosion when it is released, and the ensuing vowel follows instantaneously. These consonants can be voiced but only for a brief moment, or may be devoiced. They are b, d, hard g.

(*b*) *Affricate consonants.* These are similar to the plosives except that the explosion is followed by a slow audible release. The voiceless affricate is ch as in church, its voiced counterpart is j as in judge.

(All following categories are also known as continuants because they can be voiced for an indefinite period as long as the breath lasts.)

(*c*) *Fricative consonants*, when there is no complete obstruction, but only a constriction that gives rise to audible friction.

Aspirates or voiceless fricatives: h, th (thousand), s, sh, f.

Unaspirated or voiced fricatives: th (thou), z, j (pleasure), v, English r.

(*d*) *Nasal consonants*, when the mouth is completely obstructed, and the nose passage is open, m, n, ng (sing), gn (agneau—French).

(*e*) *Rolled consonants* (*continuant*), when there is rapid intermittent contact, as in Scottish r, Spanish rr, Italian r, and one type of French r.

(*f*) *Lateral consonants* (*continuant*), when the obstruction is along the middle of the mouth, one or both sides being free. L is a lateral consonant, also Spanish ll, Italian gl, and the Welsh ll which is a variety of breathed l.

CONSONANTS

The beauty of the voice and the expression of emotion is heard in the vowel sounds, the intensity and colour of which can be varied to a very great extent. Clear enunciation of the consonants, however, is essential to intelligibility of the sung words.

Vowels are formed with the mouth open, while the consonants are a result of an obstruction of the cavity of the mouth at one point or another, interrupting the vocal tone altogether or confining it to a

hum or buzz. Great care must, of course, be taken so that the formation of the consonants does not cause the singer to interfere with the
proper resonation of the vowels or interrupt the flow of tone in such
a way as to destroy the vocal line.

At the same time, the consonants should not be thought of only as
a destructive element or a necessary evil to be got over as quickly as
possible. Each consonant has its own distinctive character which may
be used in singing with great dramatic effect just as it can in speech.
To take no note of these distinctive consonantal qualities is to ignore
a fundamental aspect of the expression of language, no less important in interpretation than the vowels.

EFFECT OF CONSONANTS ON LEGATO

It is misleading to state, as many books do, that the maintenance
of a legato line depends on rapid articulation of the consonants. A
legato line depends on a rapid movement from the vowel position on
to the following consonant so that the preceding vowel is not influenced by it, and on a rapid movement to the resonance position
of the next vowel after the consonant has been articulated. The consonant may then be dwelt on if desired for dramatic effect without
affecting the vocal line. But if there is no proper movement from the
preceding vowel to the consonant position and then to the position
of the following vowel, no matter how briefly the consonant is
actually sounded, a smooth line will not result. The rapid movement
from vowel to consonant position and vice versa depends on flexibility of the mouth, lips and tongue. The major mistake in making
consonants is that the mouth, lips and tongue are not sufficiently
supple so that the time lag in opening the mouth and getting the
tongue into position for the vowel is too great. One often hears that
the mouth must be loose but there is a great difference between relaxed, lazy muscles and flexible muscles which can be relaxed when
required but which are also capable of rapid movements, and a certain amount of tension and muscle tonus is required to effect such
rapid changes of shape.

To simply state that the consonants must be articulated rapidly
does not ensure that vowel resonance both before and after the consonant will be effected correctly, but it may discourage the singer
from placing sufficient emphasis on the consonants to make them
audible and prevent the singer from using them intelligently for
dramatic effect.

ARTICULATION

In articulation, one of the commonest faults is the inaudibility of the consonants. Sir Richard Paget conducted experiments on the audibility of vowels and consonants in which he found that the effect of voicing consonants in speech increased their range of audibility from two to four times as compared with the ten to twenty-fold increase of range which was found between whispered and voiced vowels, which makes the carrying power of a voiced vowel very much greater than that of a consonant, as follows:[1]

Phonetic Symbol	As in Key Word	Carrying Distance in yards		Increase of Range
		Unvoiced	Voiced	
u	who	26	363	14 times
e	men	51	950	19
ou	know	57	960	17
ei	hay	69	960	14
i	eat	93	740	8
f		45	75	2
th	thigh	79	220	4
s		123	470	3
sh		320	470	2

Further intensification of the vowels as required in singing is welcomed by the student who hears this as an improvement in the power of the voice. Similar intensification of the consonants, however, feels exaggerated and affected and a beginner tends to use the same intensity for sung consonants as in ordinary speech. It is possible for a singer to use his voice at full power in a studio as far as vowel tone is concerned but with normal unintensified consonants, and the listener will not be conscious of any great difference in audibility—the diction will be clear and intelligible. But if the same production of consonants is used in a large hall, then their lack of carrying power is immediately evident.

Similarly, if the singer intensifies his consonants in a small room

---

[1] Paget, op. cit., pp. 38, 124.

as he needs to in a large hall, this may sound exaggerated to the listener as well as to the singer. The teacher must, of course, be aware of this, and the pupil must overcome his psychological aversion to making a consonant of seemingly greater relative intensity than a vowel. The pupil must learn to judge correctly the relative intensities required in all circumstances.

The audibility of the voiced consonants may be increased by intensifying the vocal cord action. *All consonants which may be either voiced, devoiced, or whispered are stronger, if voiced.* Whispered consonants can only be intensified by increasing the breath pressure, and by careful control of tongue and lip tensions and timing in the case of whispered plosives. It will also be seen that certain consonants do not carry as far as others. These need to be paid particular attention if they are to be heard.

In practice, the main fault causing inaudibility of consonants is insufficient tension on the lips and tongue.

DRAMATIC USE OF CONSONANTS

All consonants can be used effectively from a dramatic point of view, but some are more difficult to control than others. The same factors which need to be voluntarily controlled to make the consonants audible can also be exploited for dramatic effect. Thus, the degree of vocal cord action or breath pressure may be intensified beyond the amount needed for audibility in order to give added emphasis, *while skill in timing, either the release in the case of the plosives or the duration in the case of continuants, becomes one of the most important factors in dramatic use of the consonants.* Control over these factors must be carried out with precision if the vocal and musical line is not to be disturbed.

Consonants in each classification have their own distinctive character. The voiced sounds are more dominant than the unvoiced and the dramatic nature of the plosives is expressed in their explosive release, the force of which may be varied by controlling the breath pressure or vocal cord action, the tension of the lips or pressure of the tongue as the case may be, and the timing of the release. A very rapid release heightens the dramatic effect. The voiced plosives in particular, are amongst the most powerful of the consonants where great dramatic effects can be produced. A beginner tends to underestimate the tension on the lips and the pressure of the tongue and miscalculates the timing, and so gets a very insipid effect.

ARTICULATION

Complete understanding of the nature of the various consonants and of the factors involved in audibility are essential to the singer if he is to modify the consonants skilfully according to the nature of the music he is interpreting.

NOTES ON INDIVIDUAL CONSONANTS

We will now consider some special problems involved in the production of individual consonants.

One group which must be carefully watched are those consonants in which it is necessary to close the lips completely or almost so— b, p, f, v, m. The lips must be very supple and capable of rapid movement and must, in fact, be moved rapidly at the beginning and end of each consonant so that the preceding and following vowels are not modified by the consonant.

The other consonants in which the lips play no part, and which depend on the position of the tongue and teeth, should be articulated with the mind already concentrating on the following vowel.

Two consonants which require particular flexibility of the tongue are th (think) and l. There is a tendency to sound the l longer than is necessary and the delay in the return of the tongue to the vowel position can have a drawling effect on the articulation. This is caused mainly by a tendency to laziness of the muscles of the tongue and can be overcome by its extensive use as a tongue exercise.

Then there are such consonants as h, k and v in which the throat opening muscles are more likely to relax. If the throat closes while forming the consonant, it makes an open-throated attack on the following vowel more difficult. Care must be taken at all times to ensure that the throat does not close, but particular concentration on this aspect is required in the case of the above consonants.

Apart from this tendency to close the throat, h is one of the simplest consonants to form and it can be uttered with the mouth in any vowel position which makes it one of the easiest of preludes to a vowel attack. For this reason, it has been misused a great deal, even by many famous singers and it has to be carefully handled so that it does not become habitual in its use in the wrong places. The temptation to insert it between two notes on the same vowel and in a series of notes in a cadenza as a means to clear attack of pitch is sometimes overpowering.

The aspirated consonants, particularly the aspirated fricatives h, th, s, sh, and f, can be somewhat troublesome by being exceedingly wasteful of breath. It is necessary to control the breath very carefully whilst forming these consonants. They can be very helpful when used in exercises for a student who tends to use insufficient breath as they encourage him to use more breath than that to which he is accustomed.

M is formed by opening up a passage from the throat to the nose; the mouth is entirely closed. Concentration on the timing of the release is essential as this can be done with a quick or with a slow, gliding release, each being effective for its purpose but destructive if used unskilfully.

Ng, formed by the back of the tongue and the hard palate, is usually an extremely easy consonant to form and this extreme easiness causes it to be made too soon at the expense of the preceding vowel.

ARTICULATION OF VOWELS

Instrumental resonation of the vocal tone requires the vowels to be formed in a manner different from that employed in speech. However, this should not give rise to any distortion of the vowel as reflex adjustments enable the singer to produce the vowel as conceived even when the needs of instrumental resonation are taken into account. If he has good speech models and imitates them conscientiously, he should produce correct sung vowels except in the circumstances outlined below. If the voice is not produced correctly as far as instrumental resonance is concerned, the vowel shapes may be modified and distorted no matter how accurately he conceives of them.

For the reasons given in Chapter XI, the vowels become more and more difficult to produce as conceived as the vocal note rises in pitch. In order to sing the vowels as clearly and as accurately as possible on the higher notes, certain modifications are found to be necessary. The first modification given below is based on the fact that as the frequencies of the resonating cavities alter in the formation of naturally produced vowels, each vowel feels as though it is being formed in a different position in the mouth, ranging from ee (heed) in the most forward position to oo (hoot) in the most backward position. The most common English vowels in order of position, from front to back, are as follows. Ee (heed), i (hit), ey (tape), e (ten), a (tap), er (pert), uh (hut), ah, o (not), aw, oh (tone), u (put), oo (hoot). These feelings of position arise from the tendency of the tongue to hump itself progressively forwards in the vowels of the er to ee series so as to reduce the mouth cavity and enlarge the throat cavity, with a reversal of the process in the uh to oo series.

The first modification consists of conceiving of the vowel as it should be heard but singing it in the position of the adjacent vowel in the scale, back vowels being modified to a more forward position and vice versa.

If correctly produced, with proper resonance and breathing co-ordinations, this is the only modification that should be necessary in the male voice. It allows all vowels to be pronounced clearly without undesirable modification of the singing tone, a modification which can occur if no attempt is made to modify the vowel position on the higher notes.

A similar modification is required in the female voice as the vocal note rises above the frequency of the lower vowel formants, such modification being needed on ee, i, oh (tone), u (put) and oo (hood) before the vowels with the higher pitched lower formants. As the vocal note rises still further in the female voice, it becomes no longer possible to conceive of some of the vowels as written. Attempts to do so only result in deterioration of the instrumental quality of the note as the pitch of the vibrator rises higher and higher above the frequency of the resonator. Here, to a certain extent, one can modify the conception as well as the position by thinking of the sound of the adjacent vowel, always modifying towards the vowel with the higher pitched lower formant. Thus ee is modified towards the i sound and the oh vowel modified towards aw, etc. In this way the frequency of the cavity is raised to correspond a little more closely to the pitch of the vibrator. On extremely high notes when such modification of the vowel shape no longer succeeds, it is best to make no attempt to pronounce the vowel correctly, but to concentrate on producing correct pitch quality on the neutral er or uh (hut) sounds. These are the easiest to produce and in a central position with high lower formants.

In all cases, the instrumental resonance of the sound must be given priority over vowel differentiation. On the highest notes of the soprano range, accurate pronunciation of the words is seldom essential. Where possible, one must rely on the consonants to make the words intelligible, and many singers quite often alter the words so as to provide on their high notes, vowels which are easier to produce.

XIV

Intensity, Dynamics and Colour in the Art of Singing

The application of the rules of voice production to performance of a musical composition requires very careful thought and understanding.

If the question of pitch quality is understood, it is realized that every note of the singer's range has its own special colour. Composers, particularly the greatest composers, are aware of this and make use of these colours in their compositions, choosing notes whose colours have a direct relationship to the emotion expressed in the words. If the words of a song are poetically written, the colour of the vowels and nature of the consonants will also have a direct relationship to the meaning.

Where there is a perfect relationship between pitch quality, language and the emotions and thoughts of the poet and composer, the singer has little to do except establish the intensity and the basic colour to be used and then produce every note perfectly to allow the composer's palette to shine forth. Perfect production will automatically lead to perfect interpretation, and the colours inherent in the pitch of the notes will be the colours of the song, enhanced by the colours of the vowels which, in a correctly produced voice, do not disturb the vocal line.

This marriage of words and pitch quality applies much more to lieder than to opera, partly because the composers of lieder were more concerned with expressing the subtleties of poetic thought in song, and partly because the differences of pitch quality are more apparent when singing at the intensities usual in the more intimate circumstances of the concert hall.

Many singers fail not only because they cannot produce their voices correctly but also because they are unnecessarily fussy, picking and choosing tones and obscuring the colours already provided by the composer. Thus, in some circumstances, a conscientious, earnest student who is genuinely interested in interpreting the song may fail where the singer who is only interested in singing the musical line will succeed, provided the latter's voice is correctly produced. The singer must learn to discriminate between those compositions, or passages within a composition, where there is a need for tonal emphasis or modification of words or phrases and those in which the music must be allowed to speak for itself.

When studying a composition, therefore, one must first ascertain whether the required colours are already inherent in the pitch quality of the notes when sung at the intensities and with the dynamics required by the various passages. Only where the colours needed are felt to be different from those provided in the music will a singer need to use his ability to vary the tone colour within the limits allowed by correct technique, in order to produce a more suitable colour than that indicated by the pitch of the note in the composition. This is particularly so in translations where the words may be no longer so intimately bound to the musical notes as in the original version. If this is the case, the singer will need to be much more of a colourist in order to convey the intentions of the composer.

Often, the best results are obtained when the singer emphasizes rather than modifies the existing colours. At other times, he must provide his own colours to a much greater extent. He must in all circumstances be very sensitive to the colours already present in the music before he decides how and where they should be altered.

If there is no understanding of pitch quality, all colours in a voice are virtually eliminated in an attempt to make every note sound alike. If the possessor of such a colourless voice then tries to colour a song, it is no wonder that the results are disastrous.

It is usually believed that lieder calls for the greatest skill in the art of colouring and that opera is a less subtle form in which the ability to vary colour of the tone is not so essential. However, as with many other aspects of singing, what the listener hears does not quite correspond with what the singer actually does. In fact, the opera singer must use his ability to colour quite as much as, if not more than, the concert singer, even though the listener may be aware of much more subtle colour effects in a good concert performance than when he visits the opera. This is because there is a basic difference between operatic and concert singing which should be noted. In opera, because of the need for greater carrying power, the need to be heard in a large opera house above the volume of the orchestra, the singer must maintain a very high intensity and in general, a stronger edge.

In the seventeenth and eighteenth centuries, because the singers were more concerned with a beautiful vocal line than with dramatic effects, they tended to maintain such relatively stable intensity naturally. Today people are much more conscious of the need for colour and dramatic effect and approach singing more intellectually. While the greatest of present-day singers are able to invest the great works of the past with much more colour and drama than they received at the time they were written and still maintain the impeccable vocal line demanded, particularly in the works of the Bel Canto school, most singers today try to be expressive in quite the wrong way. They try to obtain dramatic contrasts by varying the intensity and do not understand how limited the opera singer is in this respect. By this means, the only contrast obtained is between effective singing when the intensity is high and ineffective singing when the intensity is dropped.

In opera, the maintenance of an extremely high intensity is required not only because of the need for the voice to carry in a large opera house but also because of the artistic needs of the operatic form based as it is on the combination of voice and orchestra. For an opera singer to drop the intensity below a certain point, even if he can still be heard, is to step out of the unified form created by the composer.

It is the concert singer, not the opera singer, who achieves his best effects by the use of intensity changes as well as by variations in colour and dynamics. Although it is true that the heightened intensity used by the opera singer excites the emotions of the listener, the concert singer would sound dull if his intensity range were similarly limited. Sometimes, as in song cycles such as the *Liederkreise*, *Dichterliebe* or *Winterreise*, one obtains intensity variations by the juxtaposition of songs in which the intensities differ; sometimes contrasts are achieved in the same song as, for example, in 'In questa tomba oscura' by Beethoven, or 'Frühlingstraum' and 'Der Doppelgänger' by Schubert.

The opera singer must realize that the operatic form is best served by a comparatively steady intensity line and dramatic variation of dynamics. If used intelligently, the colours inherent in the pitch qualities can also be emphasized or modified to enhance the results. Singing on a high intensity, however, presents its problems. In the first place, the differences in vowel and pitch quality tend to be minimized and the singer must therefore work much harder in order to make apparent to his audience the tonal variations necessary to his interpretation. In the second place, the voice is much more difficult to control when used at a high intensity and, although the permutations of tone available to the opera singer are not as great as those at the command of the concert singer, those that are within his scope are much more difficult to achieve because of the greater demands on skill and endurance imposed by the higher intensity of the operatic form.

When a singer has an understanding of pitch quality and can produce the various vowel shapes without disturbing the vocal line, he approaches a new work in quite a different manner. He makes the surprising discovery, perhaps, that works as widely divergent as an aria from a Richard Strauss opera, the 'Erlkönig' by Schubert, the 'Credo' in Verdi's *Otello* and Gounod's 'Ave Maria' are alike in that the colours desired by the composer are already written clearly note by note in the music and words and can be sung on correct pitch quality with very little conscious attempt at colouring. If the Strauss sounds more colourful than the other works mentioned, it is not because the singer has adopted a more aggressively colourful technique but because the composer has created these colours in his more colourfully written music.

In songs like Schubert's 'Lindenbaum' and 'Frühlingstraum', and in operas like *Lucia di Lammermoor*, the colour is only sketched in and the singer must be much more creative in his use of colour. In songs like 'Der Doppelgänger' on the other hand, colouring is not simply a matter of putting in colours suggested by the composer. Here there is scope for individual interpretation of the composer's intentions. Is it the eeriness, the emptiness or the loneliness in the opening passage of 'Der Doppelgänger' that the singer feels should be conveyed in his interpretation? Whatever he decides will affect his choice of colour dynamics and intensity and the effect upon the audience.

Bound up with these questions is the ability of the singer to convey emotion. Sincere expression of emotion cannot, of course, be reduced simply to a matter of colour and dynamics. Unless the singer himself feels the emotions he wishes to convey there will be a very important element missing from the performance. *He must realize, however, that he can give reign to his emotions only when his technical command is so firmly established that his emotions enhance the performance and do not detract from it.* He must be able to 'feel' and at the same time be in complete command of every technical aspect of his art. To 'feel' before he has attained this command may actually destroy much of the technical proficiency he has acquired, and this destruction of vocal technique will reduce rather than enhance his power to convey his emotion and the composer's intentions to the audience.

XV

Registers

The next question we must ask is what effect, if any, has resonance and the action of the vocal cords on what are known as register changes and breaks in the voice.

The question of registers is one on which much discussion has taken place over the years, and on which many opposing theories have been advanced. In fact, this question is the basis of one of the greatest controversies ever raised in the whole history of singing. Fierce conflicts of opinion have raged around this word. But whatever the theory, the cause of the inquiry is always an attempt to eliminate marked changes of quality that, with hardly an exception, appear in untrained, badly or partly trained voices. Obviously there can be no smoothness of line if there are continual changes of power and quality and it is up to the singing teacher to know the causes of these quality changes and how they may be eliminated.

There may be a distinct quality change between c^1 and g^1 but a number of less distinct quality changes may be present in an untrained or badly trained voice. Some writers say that there are two, three or even five registers in a voice.

There are, of course, some voices that even without training do not have such sudden breaks at all. Are these 'no break' voices fundamentally different from the normal in some way? Do the owners of such voices use them more skilfully, or are their muscles more developed allowing them to sing without a break? All these questions must be answered.

The belief most widely held as to the reason for these quality changes is that they are inevitably caused by changes in the mechanism of the larynx, changes in the quality of the tones produced corresponding with changes in the appearance and functioning of the larynx. Hence, the normally accepted definition of a vocal register is a series of tones made by the same mechanism. What foundation is there for this belief?

REGISTERS

That certain changes do occur in the larynx while singing up the scale has been demonstrated by many investigators. As explained in an earlier chapter, the appearance of the larynx shows three main aspects and superficially they may appear to coincide with three distinct quality characteristics of a given voice. Yet more detailed investigation shows many inconsistencies. First of all, the changes in the appearance of the larynx have been shown by Pressman and others to be almost always gradual, a slight change occurring with *every* change of pitch, whereas the quality changes under discussion are quite sudden ones and usually occur after a series of notes. Furthermore, the same three aspects of laryngeal change are present in the larynx even in voices which do not have these quality changes. Slight sudden changes in tension of the vocal cords on certain notes have been detected in several subjects whose voices had not been trained, these changes coinciding with a distinct break in the voice. However, these sudden changes do not necessarily coincide with the merging of one laryngeal aspect into another.

Pressman says[1] that although the term 'falsetto' is often given to tones produced by the third laryngeal aspect, this is not a good term, 'as it denotes an entirely artificial distinction and gives the impression of a false, unreal or unnatural state of affairs, whereas the mechanism actually represents a perfectly normal, logical step in the production of tones of a gradually ascending scale'.

No, register changes are no more inherent in the anatomy of the vocal cords than they are in the construction of a violin where higher frequencies are obtained by fingering and shortening the length of that part of the string which is free to vibrate, or in the piano where a number of different types of covered and uncovered wires may be used on the one instrument. If there are marked changes of quality in a voice, there must be some other reason.

The answer lies in the fact that it is possible to sing a series of notes of the same pitch but with great differences in quality and with corresponding differences in the tension of the vocal cords. Although they may be varied infinitely by altering breath pressure and breath volume in relation to the amount of 'edge', these differences in quality may be divided fundamentally into two different qualities, popularly termed 'head' and 'chest', either of which may be employed on almost any note of the singer's range. In other words, there is no evidence for a change of register or mechanism in the vocal cords at a particular

[1] 'Physiology of the vocal cords in phonation and respiration', *Arch. Otolaryng.* 35:355, 1942.

pitch as one ascends the scale, but there is evidence of a change of appearance, which may be called a change of register, when the quality of a note is fundamentally altered.[1]

The foundation for the widespread theory of two registers in a voice—one for the upper and one for the lower notes—lies in the fact that an untrained singer, or a singer who for any reason has an inadequate technique, tends to use one quality for the upper notes and another quality of voice for the lower notes and does not produce his voice in accordance with correct pitch quality as described on pages 47–50. This may be due to ignorance or to emotional factors discussed below.

INCORRECT PITCH QUALITY CONCEPTS AND REGISTER CHANGES

Incorrect concepts of pitch quality can cause a singer to have sudden quality changes on ascending the scale even though there is no physical reason why this should be so if the voice were produced correctly.

If a singer tries to, or is taught to attempt to, produce notes having too much of the lower pitch quality attributes on the higher notes, the laryngeal mechanism will be placed under too much strain until the muscles must 'give' and assume another ratio between length, tension and mass in order to maintain pitch with a corresponding sudden change in tone quality.

If, on the other hand, he has a preference for upper pitch quality tones and uses too high a proportion of these tones as he goes down the scale, his quality becomes so thin that he cannot avoid a change to a more appropriate quality at some point.

The singer must understand that on going up the scale, there should be a gradual change in quality from dark, mellow tone to brilliant tone as in a piano.[2] The note may be louder or softer but its essential

---

[1] Oscar Russell, *Speech and Voice* (Macmillan, 1931), p. 93.

[2] It should be understood that although the quality of the tone alters on every note according to pitch, a voice should keep the same character throughout, just as in a piano the pitch quality alters but every note retains the essential character of the instrument. Thus, one describes a piano as having a certain 'tone' and may prefer the 'tone' of one piano to that of another even though every note of each piano differs according to pitch. This is because, while the strings vary according to pitch, they possess a definite mathematical relationship to each other and there are other factors which remain constant and unchanging and affect every note similarly, e.g. in a piano, the wood, felting and sound-board. In the voice, the comparable factors can be varied if the production is not

quality should remain unaltered except for legitimate modifications in order to produce interpretative variations in colour. Only if the correct pitch quality is maintained can the power of any note be increased without fear of undesirable consequences. Luisa Tetrazzinni understood this point when she said that if you ensure that each individual note is correct, the problem of the registers need not trouble one.

Unfortunately, it is not only the student who errs in these ways. Teachers often display the same lack of understanding of the physical properties of a voice. Ignorance of the concept of pitch quality is one of the main reasons for conflicting opinions that occur again and again over the classification of voices. One teacher, on hearing a singer produce rich notes on certain pitches may immediately classify him as a baritone, not realizing that the same richness on those particular notes should be present even in the voice of a tenor. Another teacher may realize that while the singer possesses beautiful, rich quality on those particular notes, he is also capable of producing the ringing top notes of a tenor and will rightly classify him as such and develop his voice accordingly.

This ignorance of pitch quality explains how controversy could arise even over the classification of a voice such as that of Caruso. Many people claim that Caruso should have kept to the lower tessitura of a baritone and cite his rich lower notes as evidence for this contention. These people, if they had had their way, would have made Caruso carry up the quality of his lower notes as high as he could, albeit by forcing his voice, and would not have allowed him to develop his high notes as he did, even if they knew how to do so, as their conception of how a voice should sound is completely wrong.

It is well known that many distinguished tenors began their careers as baritones and would have remained possibly good but undistinguished performers in that range if they had not learnt to understand the true nature of their higher notes. Caruso sang and studied for many long years before being able to produce his top notes properly. With correct teaching, he should have been able to do this much earlier.

The tones of all the great singers of the past are in accord with this concept of pitch quality as reference to available records indicate. It also applies to the best singers of today. All efforts to eliminate breaks by misguided attempts to produce the voice in accordance

---

correct, but this must not be allowed to happen. They should be kept in a certain relationship if the voice is to retain its essential character throughout.

with an artificial concept of unchanging quality throughout a singer's range have resulted in mediocre singing and even destruction of fine voices. Such ignorance of pitch quality concepts in relation to singing is demonstrated in the following quotation from a well-known book on singing by Madame Kate Emil Behnke.[1]

'While it is quite correctly stated that the voice must *sound* the same from top to bottom, it will *not* sound so if the same mechanism be adhered to . . . whereas if the changes are made at the proper places, with the right breath pressure, and so forth, the notes will, after due practice, *sound alike*.'

It is possible that Madame Behnke may have had correct pitch quality concepts herself, in spite of the above statement, if her mind was dwelling on certain like-sounding properties of all correctly produced notes—vibrancy, freedom from strain and emphasis of the higher harmonics of the 'head tone'. If this is so, her words certainly give a very wrong impression and a very incomplete and misleading picture of how a voice should sound.

EMOTIONAL BASIS FOR QUALITY CHANGES

Apart from the physical and mental factors which cause quality changes in a voice, i.e. ignorance of pitch quality and lack of technique, there are emotional factors as well. Most singers have a preference for one or other of the two pitch quality attributes that should be present in a voice and have a dislike of producing the other. When a teacher attempts to eliminate forced tone on higher notes when too great a proportion of lower pitch quality attributes are present, he is met with resistance on the part of the student for emotional reasons. This resistance is caused by greed for tone when the student is ignorant of the true nature of the voice, an attempt to produce a bigger tone than he is entitled to, particularly on high notes. This greed for tone can also make the singer produce his voice in such a way on the lower notes that a break becomes inevitable as he ascends a scale. On the other hand, if a singer prefers the sweeter, more refined tones, he may not have a break but will not produce the lower pitch quality attributes in sufficient strength to add the required virility to the tone, particularly on the lower notes.

Of course, one reason why the student tries to enrich his tone incorrectly as above is that it is much easier for him. He can produce strong lower and middle notes with comparatively little skill if he has

[1] *Singer's Difficulties* (Chappel, London, 1926).

a strong 'edge' and, even if when using too strong an edge in relation to the pitch, they sound forced to his audience, they will not seem unpleasant to his own ears. On the other hand, to produce legitimate high notes that will satisfy the singer as well as the audience by their power and brilliance, knowledge, skill and development of appropriate muscles are necessary. Until this is achieved, he will derive little or no satisfaction from his top notes as they will be very much thinner and weaker than his lower notes. So, instead of developing the equally exciting but rather different qualities of the high notes in a proper manner, he tries to invest them with the properties of the lower notes from which he already derives such satisfaction and which he find much easier to produce.

Even if a singer has very modest ideas as to the size and tone of his own voice, he may come up against this problem as a voice, when correctly produced, will always sound different to the singer than to his audience. A tape recorder is very useful in demonstrating to the student the difference between the tone as he hears it whilst singing, and the same tone as it sounds to a listener.

While middle and lower notes may be wrongly sung because of greed for a bigger tone than one can legitimately produce, there is resistance—more so on top notes—of a rather different kind—caused by fear. As explained above, greater tension is required on the breathing muscles on the higher notes in a properly produced voice. But many people associate tension on the breathing muscles with strain on the vocal cords and are reluctant to use tension because they do not really understand how it can be used without harm. It is also because the correct tone produced on these very high notes, because of the increasing thinness of the vocal cords, sounds strange to the singer himself when he is not used to producing them with power. There are two instinctive reactions against producing this type of tone. The first is to simply reduce the power and go into 'falsetto'. On the other hand, if the singer does sing these notes with power, he tries to eliminate this unfamiliar tone by employing certain resonance adjustments which will modify it. These resonance adjustments, however, are very harmful to the vocal cords and make the tone sound squeezed and throaty to the listener. Here again, a tape recorder is useful in demonstrating to the student that the tone which he rejects sounds pleasing to an outsider. Until this is rectified, an undesirable quality change will be apparent unless, of course, the voice is unnaturally forced into a similar mould on the lower notes to match.

REGISTERS

Difference between Male and Female Voices—the Fallacy of the Weak Lower Register

Whether or not there is a marked break in a voice, an untrained male voice is usually stronger on the bottom while a female voice is stronger on the top of the range. However, this is not due, as many people think, to a corresponding weakness or strength in the vocal cord mechanism. As previously explained, the muscles of the larynx are at their highest tension on the higher notes. It follows, therefore, that if there should be any weakness in the muscles, it would be more apparent, not on the lower notes, but on the higher notes where the laryngeal muscles are at their greatest tension. It is inconceivable that the low notes could be weaker than high notes because of this reason. If the lower notes are weaker there must be a reason other than weakness of the laryngeal muscles.

The reason for the greater strength of the male voice on the lower notes of his range is that (a) he is usually capable of employing a stronger edge than a female singer and (b) is more likely to have a greater breath capacity needed in this part of his range.

Because the tessitura of the female voice is higher, her most effective notes in the middle of her range, even without training, are much higher than in the male voice. As her lower notes are generally weak because of inadequate breath capacity and inability to produce a strong enough edge, it is usually believed that whereas a male voice is naturally stronger in the 'lower register', the female voice is naturally stronger in the 'upper register'. In practice, a female singer has the same difficulties in extending the upper limits of her range as does the male singer, in so far as increasing the support is concerned. In fact, she may have more difficulty as she is less used to exerting physical tension.

In other words, the vocal mechanism in male and female voices, apart from the octave difference in pitch, is similarly constructed and subject to exactly the same rules of voice production. The only difference lies (a) in the extent to which the muscles concerned have been developed before training is commenced, and (b) in different concepts of tone acquired as a result of different environmental factors. In a fully developed voice of either sex, both male and female characteristics must be present. The female singer may have greater difficulty than the male in learning to employ a robust technique necessary to the development of her voice. The male singer may have more difficulty in accepting the necessity for a phasing out of the vocal cord 'edge' on higher notes and for softer passages.

In singing, no less than in other activities, the opposing negative and positive forces, expressed in Eastern philosophy by the terms 'yin' and 'yang', must be in a state of equilibrium for a harmonious creation. Any one-sided development, whether it be of the male or female attributes, will not result in a powerful and beautifully produced voice.

LARYNGEAL WEAKNESS AND RESTRICTION OF RANGE

In developing a voice, the strength of the laryngeal mechanism is something which must be taken into account, not only as far as development of power and quality is concerned, but also in regard to extension of range. The teacher must know how far limitation of range is due to weakness of the laryngeal mechanism and how far it is due to other factors, e.g. insufficient support and inadequate technique.

In fact, immaturity of the laryngeal mechanism is not in any way responsible for restriction of range. If the laryngeal mechanism is immature, the whole of the range is restricted in power but the singer should not be prevented from singing every note in his potential range (without resorting to falsetto in the male voice) providing he has an adequate technique. The concept that the weak top notes of an otherwise strong voice must be developed slowly, note by note, because of weakness of the larynx is quite incorrect.

Unfortunately, most people have a very limited conception of the true range of a voice. The normal untrained singer uses a range of about one and three-quarter octaves. Most singing teachers believe that the range of the normal trained singing voice is about two octaves. Therefore, they proceed until the singer can produce two octaves and think that they have accomplished all that is required of them. Two octaves may be achieved by forcing the voice on the top. If the extra notes are added by forcing, the student soon reaches a point beyond which he cannot proceed, whereas if his top notes were developed legitimately he would be able to go much higher. Of course, the range can be restricted on the bottom as well as the top if the technique is not correct.

Anyone who attempts seriously to develop the voice without forcing the tone or to extend the range fully without lightening the voice, must fully understand the problems of voice production.

213

If a teacher does not know how to develop a student's top notes he simply tells the student that he has reached the end of his range and probably believes it himself. This is one of the major reasons why so many first-class tenors are today singing as baritones. Many of these so-called baritones are actually robust tenors but, as this problem is not understood by their teachers, they have learnt to sing their lower notes in such a way that makes it impossible for them to attain their true range. In this way, the world is being robbed of many magnificent tenors and is one reason why we are so short of this type of singer today.

Unfortunately, the student also has a very inaccurate idea of what a singer's range should be. Because he has no proof to the contrary, he must simply accept the teacher's word when he is told that two octaves is the limit of his range. Yet the potential range in which good quality can be obtained by the male singer (i.e. excluding falsetto) with a properly trained voice is around two and a half octaves and about three octaves in the case of a female singer. Many of these notes lie outside the range that these singers would normally use in public. The reason for developing the voice to such an extent is not necessarily so that the whole of this extensive range can be used in performance but in order to give the singer greater beauty and power and greater freedom of movement within the required range than if the voice is only developed to two octaves. The greater the development of the voice in range and power, the greater the command of the singer in the control of his voice and in his range of artistic expression.

EXPLANATION OF TRADITIONAL TERMS

Now, let us examine the various beliefs and practices of teachers who are ignorant of these facts. When viewed against the background outlined above, we will find the reason behind many apparent contradictions and will be able to see a gleam of logic underlying the confusion and controversy with which this question is surrounded. Also it may be helpful to the student to gain a general idea of what is meant by some of the terms commonly used by teachers of singing and vocal coaches, terms whose meanings are usually most obscure.

Some teachers use the term 'falsetto' for the high-pitched effeminate quality in a male voice not normally used in performance and divide the remainder of the voice into three registers—'chest', 'middle' and 'head'. Other teachers use the term 'falsetto' for the highest legitimate tones in both the male and female voice. Thus this term may be synonymous with the term 'head' when used by another teacher. Other terms are 'thick' and 'thin', 'upper' and 'lower'. These divisions are not usually based on observation or understanding of the larynx but on what is heard to happen in a voice, it being assumed that the changes are a result of different registers or mechanisms in the larynx. In some cases, attempts have been made to connect quality changes with physical changes in the larynx but these attempts are not convincing.

The following statement by Hemery[1] illustrates very well the confusion of terminology on this subject.

'The high note produced by the normal dramatic voice is the correct aim. Expert singers rarely, if ever, use the falsetto (head register). Being two distinct physiological actions, the normal range (chest) and the falsetto (head) where they do overlap do not blend.'

However, the terms most commonly used, and the ones we shall adopt in this discussion, are as stated in italics in the second paragraph of this chapter section.

'Mixing or Blending the Registers'

Because teachers have not really understood the voice, nor known how to control breath pressure and vocal cord action correctly to get the type of tone they desire, they can only try to correct faults in production by the very back-to-front method of trying to describe the tone they want the student to produce without being able to give much clearer directions as to how it is done. (Some teachers speak of higher or lower breath pressures under certain circumstances but the reader will realize, after reading the foregoing chapters, that such directions are not sufficiently specific.) If a note is too light in quality, the teacher will therefore ask the student to add more chest quality, or thicken the tone, or mix the chest register with the head so as to produce a tone which combines characteristics of both registers.[2] This mixture is attempted over the whole of the range. In trying to obtain these tones, the student may eventually use his breath, vocal cords and resonators correctly, but he will have very little idea of what he is doing and most students do not benefit greatly from this most negative instruction.

[1] Haydn Hemery, *The Physiological Basis of the Art of Singing* (H. K. Lewis & Co. Ltd., London 1939).

[2] It should be understood that the student must be given an idea of the tone he is to conceive but this in itself is not enough. He must also be given the clearest possible instructions on technique if he is to progress satisfactorily.

If a teacher has an instinctive or real understanding of pitch quality and the need for the head tone, the 'mixture' he tries to obtain will be correct for every note and the student *may* eventually be capable of singing an accurate, evenly rising scale. Various procedures are advocated but a common one is to begin by lightening the whole of the voice and gradually increasing the power. Others practice only in the middle of the range and gradually try to extend up and down. Both these procedures can take a very long time and would not be necessary if the principles of voice production were clearly understood and the student shown how to conceive of and attack each note accurately.

On the other hand, if a teacher has no understanding of pitch quality, he may try to 'mix the registers' in such a way as to get the same type of tone throughout the range. This can only be done either by forcing the top or lightening the bottom of the student's range, or both. If this unnatural objective is achieved, it can be very harmful as it is usually necessary to resort to resonance and vocal cord adjustments that will eventually damage the voice in an attempt to keep the quality exactly the same throughout the range.

'Mixed Registration'

One or two writers mean by this term to condemn quite rightly a production which is not in accord with the correct pattern of pitch quality change or with the requirements of the vocal mechanism. Unfortunately, they have chosen a term which is almost identical to the term 'mixing the registers' defined above and used by other teachers in attempts to invoke what they consider to be correct vocal quality. If such teachers have correct pitch quality concepts they may thus achieve a measure of success using a term similar to that used for condemning the production perpetrated by other teachers with incorrect pitch quality concepts but who use the same term as themselves.

'Taking the Chest Register into the Head'

This is a term used when attempts are made to correct faults by 'mixing the registers'. If, in the opinion of the teacher, the higher notes are too light in power and quality, he may try to strengthen them by asking the student to give the higher notes more of the characteristic quality of the lower notes.

The ineffectiveness of the upper notes may have many causes. By the instruction to 'take the chest register into the head', it is virtually impossible to correct all these various faults. A certain amount of extra power may be obtained but the same or other faults will remain.

If the teacher has the wrong conceptions of pitch quality, he may try by this instruction to keep the full, rich quality of the bottom notes throughout the range, with the harmful results described. This term is also used to describe the attempts of an untrained singer if he is singing on the above lines, i.e. a teacher will say that he is taking his chest voice into the head.

In the case of a voice which is forced on the higher notes as the singer attempts to take up the lower pitch quality into the upper pitch quality zone, a teacher with correct pitch quality concepts may say that the lower or chest register has been carried up too far, forcing the upper or head register out of existence or weakening it, and then add that the head register must be brought down to meet the lower register!

'Taking the Head into the Chest'

This term is used when trying to correct the production if it is desired to make the lower notes sound more like the higher notes, i.e. having the added brilliance of the stronger head tone. Here again there are so many technical problems that may be involved and which are not corrected by simply asking the student to 'take the head into the chest', or 'extend the higher register downwards'. Such an instruction may only serve to replace one technical fault by another, e.g. the attempt to mellow the often too open sound of an untrained singer's low notes may be achieved by closing the throat instead of by adjusting the breathing correctly. Again, the instruction to 'take the head into the chest' may simply achieve a lowering of intensity with the same production faults although sounding less unpleasant to the listener on this lower intensity. On the other hand, the singer may use a somewhat more beautiful production as it is easier to sing on a lower intensity, but he will not be using the potential strength of his voice. Much demonstration and trial and error is necessary by this method until the correct tones are produced at the correct intensity, if at all.

If there is disparity between the upper and lower notes, strong lower notes may be weakened so that they 'blend' with the weaker notes of a singer's undeveloped upper range. Thus, instead of developing the higher notes and the overall power of the voice, uniformity of tone is achieved by making a baritone sound like a light baritone, a dramatic soprano like a lyric soprano.

Tenor Quality

In fact, there is no such thing as tenor or baritone quality, only differences in pitch quality and the differences between individual voices which may vary in quality between one tenor and another as much as between a tenor and a baritone. There need be no difference at all in the quality of the same note sung first by a baritone and then by a tenor if their voices happen to be similar in all respects except tessitura. One cannot tell the difference between the top notes of a baritone such as Battistini and the same notes sung by many a tenor. On the other hand, it is quite possible for a very fine and strong tenor voice to sound much richer on a certain note than a light baritone singing exactly the same note.

People who speak of tenor and baritone quality are usually ignorant of the concept of pitch quality and of the methods of developing the full tonal potential of individual voices, due in large part to their having a completely artificial conception of how a baritone and tenor should sound.

It must be remembered that practically the whole of a baritone's tessitura lies in the lower pitch quality zone whilst that of a tenor falls much more in the upper pitch quality zone. The difference in tone quality could be quite considerable between an untrained baritone and tenor, each singing on a rather restricted range. With correct training, there need be little or no difference in quality between two such singers where their respective ranges overlap. Unfortunately, however, the quality differences originally arising from differences in tessitura are usually greatly intensified by teachers who have no understanding of pitch quality. They insist on too high a proportion of lower pitch quality attributes throughout the range of a baritone, irrespective of pitch, while the voice of a tenor is distorted by reducing these to a minimum, particularly on the lower notes, in order to try and keep an unnatural uniformity of tone throughout the range of each singer, objectives which can only be achieved by incorrect use of the vocal mechanism.

Register Weakness

When certain notes in a singer's range are weaker than others, they are described as being weak in that register, e.g. a voice may be described as having a weak upper, lower or middle register, or a teacher may say that he has a weak chest or head register. The weakness in these notes may have nothing whatsoever to do with any actual weakness in the larynx; it may be purely a matter of too little breath flow or incorrect vocal cord setting. However, people who use this term usually believe that there is a weakness in the larynx although they have no knowledge to back up this belief. Of actual muscle weakness of the larynx, they usually know nothing at all. To distinguish actual weakness of the laryngeal muscles from 'register weakness' as described above is most important. Unless the cause of weak tone is diagnosed clearly and accurately, attempts to develop the voice must be correspondingly vague and haphazard. They must also of necessity be over-cautious. Thus, if it is known that weak tone is due to incorrect technique, it is often possible to make marked and rapid improvement to the voice, an improvement which would be impossible if such weakness were incorrectly diagnosed as being due to immaturity of the laryngeal muscles.

LIMITED USEFULNESS OF THE REGISTER THEORY

In conclusion, it should be said that it is sometimes possible for the singer to be helped by a mental concept having no basis in fact. In so far as the above terminology has helped to engender correct concepts of pitch quality, it may have helped to produce certain favourable results. However, this is a very roundabout way of instilling correct pitch quality concepts and it does not answer the problems of voice production in a positive manner. Such instruction is rather like asking a student pastry cook to produce a lighter, fluffier or richer cake without telling him what changes in ingredients, proportions or method are called for.

Too much 'chest tone' in the voice may be due to a vocal cord action out of proportion to the pitch and intensity of the note. Correction, on the other hand, may call for adjustment to other aspects of technique—breath flow, support or resonation—as well as, or instead of, adjustment of vocal cord action. The possible combinations are considerable. To ask the student merely for 'less chest tone' or 'more head tone' in such circumstances, even if supplemented by instruction on breathing, is hopelessly inadequate.

And finally, another difficulty in teaching by such methods is that in reaching out for such vague notions, it is very difficult for the student to hang on to those aspects of his technique that should remain comparatively stable. In attempting to achieve what is being asked of him by such nebulous concepts, he tends to let the resonance setting wander and is less able to concentrate on maintaining his basic support. Small wonder that so many students spend years vainly trying to achieve professional standards. The whole exercise is extremely frustrating both to teacher and pupil and only a specially gifted singer can make progress by such methods. By specially gifted in this context I mean one who is capable of improving his technique in spite of such inadequate methods of instruction, not necessarily more gifted in the final analysis than a singer who, although unable to benefit from such instruction, may when his technique is brought under control as a result of more positive methods, prove to be a more sensitive and expressive singer than the former and in possesssion of a finer vocal instrument.

SECTION FIVE

Development of the Vocal Mechanism

XVI

The Dialectics of Tension and Relaxation in Singing

There has been a great deal of discussion over the years on the necessity for relaxation in singing on the one hand, and tension on the other. Before one can discuss development of the vocal mechanism, therefore, it is necessary to reach an understanding of this question which is one of fundamental importance.

One of the greatest factors in the misunderstanding of this problem is the psychological fear of tension. Tension is not something that is either present or absent and whose existence can only bring tragedy. This fear of tension can only exist where there is ignorance of the correct nature and use of tension. It is right and proper to fear the results of tension wrongly applied, as uncontrolled or misdirected tension can and does cause serious trouble. It can not only result in bad voice production but can ruin a voice completely. But it is wrong to fly from the very mention of the word 'tension', as many singers do, without making any effort to understand it. In essence, this attitude is reminiscent of that of primitive man living in mortal terror of raging floods and the ravages of wild beasts. Civilized man learnt to control the swollen streams for irrigation and energy, and tamed wild animals to help him in his work. We must have a similar, practical approach to tension rather than one of primeval fear of it. We must know how to use both tension and relaxation for our own purposes, in this case the full realization of the beauty, power and interpretative range of a voice.

Many singers spoil their performance by having too much tension on certain muscles. However, this is often due to a lack of tension in other muscles, which makes the use of these unwanted tensions the only means left to the singer to produce anything resembling a singing tone.[1] Take away these tensions without replacing them by others and it is impossible to sing at all. Unfortunately, for reasons enlarged

[1] See pages 163 and 179

upon below, critics of such singers can recognize the presence of badly placed tension but have little or no understanding of the bearing upon faulty production of lack of correctly placed tension.

Teachers who do not study the action of the individual muscles also speak of relaxation and tension in the vaguest terms. The exponents of relaxation are particularly general in their statements and, unfortunately, are in the great majority.

Perhaps those who have contributed most to this state of affairs are some of our greatest singers. An example can be quoted of one of the finest singers of our time who, when asked if he could put into one sentence the most useful advice he could give to the young singer, answered to the effect that the student should not worry about his breathing as this was something that he himself never did. Unfortunately, in giving this advice he forgot that the immature student does not have his years of training and experience, and perhaps not the same natural co-ordination.

This 'do as I do' advice is also used in connection with the question of relaxation. A singer who, after years of training and experience, has acquired such a degree of control over certain muscles that they take up the desired tension without conscious effort on his part, too often concludes that this is how the singer should feel and tries to make his students relax in the same way. If he thinks back at all to his earlier days when he must have used more conscious effort, he illogically assumes that this was wrong and the reason why he did not then sing as well. He does not think for a minute that this effort may have been a necessary stage in his development. He does not realize that this 'do as I do' advice is about as sensible as that of a weight-lifter who tries to help a young man struggling to lift a 200-lb weight with such encouragement as 'Do not try so hard, young man. Look at me, it is quite easy. Be more relaxed.' Obviously, the correct advice would be to lift lighter weights until the muscles have been built up by correct exercises to be capable of lifting the 200 lb. with greater ease. A voice must be developed in the same way. It is true that a great singer can be *more* relaxed. However, this is not because his muscles are more relaxed but because they are stronger and capable of greater tensions with less effort. Every physical training instructor knows that muscles are developed by placing them under certain tensions, but a teacher of the above type would have us believe that the voice is different in some mysterious way and can only be developed by relaxation. They confuse ends with means.

Then we have the teacher who may not sing himself but who can hear the beautiful, relaxed style of a truly great singer with a fully developed voice. He sounds so relaxed, surely he must be relaxed? But this is a very superficial, groundless observation to say the least, and one that is not so easily made in other fields. So does a tightrope artist appear to be relaxed, so does a dancer as he seems to float through the air and move with such grace and effortlessness. Yet we all know that if the dancer were really relaxed he would present a very clumsy and ungainly appearance and if the tightrope walker relaxed, he would soon fall. This appearance of relaxation is only the façade which gives such pleasure to the audience, but behind the delicate façade there are struts and reinforcements without which the whole edifice would collapse. The dancer spends years on strenuous exercises until the appearance of utter relaxation is achieved and the tight-rope walker has tremendous muscular control as well as a fine sense of balance.

Another important factor is that some people have the ability to tense muscles more easily than others, depending on their physical and psychological endowment. Such people are often described as having greater vitality. When the 'vitality' of any person is sapped, either through illness or fatigue, he must use much more conscious effort to perform the same operation that he does automatically when fit and well. In the same way, a person with a less vital personality and physique must put more conscious effort into performing the same operation than someone with greater 'vitality'. Factors similar to those which allow one man to run faster or endure longer, training apart, will enable one person to apply more tension where needed to the muscles used in singing. A vital, dynamic person may well place tension unconsciously on muscles which should be out of action and will need to relax these tensions consciously; but even he rests before a lengthy performance in order to conserve his energy and restore his 'vitality' for the establishment of other necessary tensions. It should now be obvious that unqualified advice to relax from a naturally dynamic teacher could completely ruin the chances of a less dynamic person who, however, with correctly applied tensions, could be equally successful.

What is needed in singing is not a state of relaxation or of tension but a state in which every muscle concerned maintains whatever tension or relaxation is necessary at any moment for the desired tone. To achieve this, the tensions on individual muscles need to be adjusted and controlled, and a primary object of training is the ability to exercise such control with the minimum of effort. The discussion of relaxation or tension is futile and meaningless unless considered in this way, bearing in mind the problems of individual singers. In order to understand the relationship between the various muscular tensions we must first be able to see the voice as a whole. To show the lines along which the problem should be tackled, let us compare the voice with an electrical power system.

First we have the generator capable of producing great quantities of power from a source of energy, for instance, coal or water. Then we have the cables that conduct the power and finally the light globe with a filament that converts the power into light. There are also resistors whose purpose is to block the flow of current where desired. The converter is capable of handling only a certain amount of power, the cables can take no more than a certain maximum of current and the bulb must be in proportion to the size of the filament.

Now let us look at the voice. First we have great reserves of energy which can be controlled and used to place the breathing muscles under certain tensions, thereby acting as a generator which converts the breath into breath pressure. The breath pressure is then converted into sound vibrations by the vocal cords which serve the voice in the same way as the filament serves the electric light globe. Then we have the pharynx and mouth cavity which are like the globe and which must always be in a definite relationship to the vibrations from the vocal cords.

If there is anything wrong either with the generator or the convertor or if there is too much resistance anywhere, the light will flicker or there may be danger of a fuse. In the voice we have no place for resisters. The amount of breath pressure must never be greater than the vocal cords are capable of converting into the type of sound required. If too much or too little pressure is being generated, if the converter—the vocal cords—are too weak, if the pharynx and mouth cavity are incorrectly adjusted or the constrictor muscles are in action, all this will show in the voice.

If all muscles are correctly tensed (or relaxed as the case may be) all channels will be open for the voice to flow through. But if not, they will act as resisters to the voice and, even if sufficient power is being generated, it will be choked off before it reaches the audience. As already explained, if certain muscles are too relaxed, just as much harm can be done as if they or others are too tense. If the muscles for opening the mouth are too relaxed the mouth will close and if the extensor muscles of the pharynx are too relaxed the throat will close.

THE DIALECTICS OF TENSION AND RELAXATION

If the working of the voice is not properly understood, one of two things can happen. Firstly, and by far the worst, the voice will be like a faulty circuit with the tension on the various muscles completely out of line with each other. The breath pressure may be too great for the strength of the vocal cords and incorrectly balanced tensions elsewhere may still further choke off and impair the voice. The result is forced, unpleasant singing, unsteadiness and, if continued, deterioration of vocal quality.

The alternative is a voice in perfect alignment but working at low efficiency. The breath pressure generated will be low, the vocal cords perhaps weak but quite adequate for the intensity used, and other muscles and the pharyngeal adjustment in line with this smaller voice. The tone will be pleasant and there will be no signs of strain but the voice will be comparatively ineffective, like a small globe in a large room. Such voices are not badly produced in the sense of being under strain but they are only giving out a comparatively ineffective glow when their bodies and their vocal apparatus are potentially capable of producing a radiant light.

The teacher must be able to tell at every stage where the weakest part of the voice is and know how to strengthen it. Some muscles must be strengthened by carefully chosen exercises, *but it is not sufficiently understood that other muscles are often strong enough without exercise and only need to be brought into action as required.*

It must also be remembered that it is easier for a student to achieve the desired control when singing on a low intensity, and such a voice may reach a very high degree of refinement, but it will never have the dynamic qualities needed to dominate an audience no matter how long the owner continues to study on these lines. A voice which has been developed to a correct basic intensity is more difficult to control and time is needed for the pupil to achieve sufficient mastery to handle it with the precision and accuracy required for a cultured performance.

A voice of the second category may be more difficult to control in the early stages but the foundation will have been laid so that when the necessary technique is acquired, the final result will be much more rewarding. The first is like a beautifully cut glass imitation while the second, until complete mastery is achieved, is like a rough, unpolished jewel. Voices may differ in size and quality just as there are all kinds of jewels but no one should be content with a mere imitation of his own true voice whether it be comparable to the largest diamond or the smallest semi-precious stone.

XVII

Development of Breath Control

NATURE OF TENSIONS USED IN SINGING

What happens when a muscle tenses? It bunches up and shortens and we often, therefore, use the term 'contract' instead. Such bunching up and shortening can be seen when the biceps are tensed. This contraction or shortening may alter the position and shape of fleshy parts like the tongue and lips, or draw together two or more points to which the muscles are attached (usually bones or cartilages). The efficiency of the movement usually depends on one of these points remaining more or less stationary while the other point of attachment is drawn towards it. Thus an action may be dependent not only upon the main muscle involved, but also on associated 'fixation' muscles which hold steady one point to which the main muscle is attached.

Whenever we make a movement we tense the muscles which make this possible. When we make the reverse movement another group of muscles comes into tension. The muscles responsible for an action and its reversal, e.g. the muscles which move the arm inwards and those which move it outwards—are in antagonism and are known as antagonistic muscles.

A muscle has no power to elongate but may be stretched by forces which move its point of attachment. When one muscle contracts and shortens to perform an action, its antagonist is usually relaxed and made to stretch. If such a muscle is not capable of being stretched sufficiently, it will hamper the efficiency of its antagonist.

It is also possible to perform a movement or hold a position in which both groups of muscles are in action together. When two groups of muscles which function antagonistically come into equalized tension, they are said to be in equilibrium or balanced. For example, one may raise the arm in an easy, relaxed manner or one may stiffen

228

the whole arm before commencing the movement so that both groups are in action throughout the lowering and raising of the arm. In the latter case, while the arm is moving, the raising muscles will be under slightly greater tension than the lowering muscles, or vice versa, but if the arm is held in a mid position with both groups tensed, these antagonistic muscles will be in equilibrium.

In developing the voice, the action of every muscle involved must be thoroughly understood by the teacher so that exercises may be given to enable certain muscles to contract more vigorously while, in other cases, care must be taken to do nothing which will increase the power of a muscle to contract. Rather must they be made more flexible and capable of being stretched more easily. In the first case, the muscle is strengthened so that it is capable of establishing and maintaining greater degrees of tension or contraction. In the second case, the muscle is made supple so that it has greater elasticity and will stretch more easily. The difference can be compared roughly with two pieces of elastic. One is thick and strong and its virtue lies in the fact that it will grip tightly any object which it encircles or hold together in close approximation objects which may be attached to either end. The second piece is much lighter and will not grip tightly, but is more useful in circumstances where greater stretching properties are required.

A person with all muscles very highly developed for strength is not so capable of quick and agile movements, hence the difference in training between a boxer and a weight lifter. In singing, it may be desirable in some cases to increase either the strength or the flexibility of both a muscle and its antagonist. In other cases, one muscle must be strengthened and its antagonist made more flexible. In each case, different exercises must be given. Thus, to establish an open throat, the opening muscles must be strengthened and the antagonistic, closing muscles must be made very flexible. On the other hand, the principal muscles involved in breathing—the diaphragm, intercostal and abdominal muscles—must be kept in a much closer state of equilibrium and each under a high degree of tension.

A muscle which has been made flexible has a much greater range of movement than one which is merely allowed to relax, and offers the least possible resistance to its antagonist. It therefore makes the work of its opposing muscle much easier and more efficient with less effort on the part of the singer. *For this reason, flexibility is all too often confused with relaxation.* However, if the pupil is told to relax before certain muscles are strong enough and others sufficiently

229

supple, it is impossible for him to avoid bringing wrong muscles into tension. Hence his voice is forced in spite of all his efforts to relax. While certain muscles have insufficient strength and others are not sufficiently flexible, the singer must use more energy and more conscious control in bringing the correct muscles into tension and he may appear more tense than he ought. However, as his muscles develop correctly this will disappear.

In practice, the establishment of tensions requires (a) the use of energy (*applied tension*) and (b) a certain potential strength in the muscles concerned (*built-up tension*).

To make this quite clear, let us take the case of a weight lifter. He may be capable of lifting a weight of 200 lb. when exerting himself to the utmost, but if he only wishes to lift 100 lb. he will use less energy and thus *apply* less tension to his muscles. However, if he wishes to lift more than 200 lb. he must perform exercises to increase the strength of his muscles and the amount of built-up tension. When the strength of his muscles has been thus increased, he will not only be able to lift more than 200 lb. but he will also lift the 100 lb. weight with much greater ease and the necessity for less applied tension than previously. The amount of tension previously applied to lift 100 lb. will now enable him to lift a greater weight.

In singing, the amount of applied tension is very much higher than most people realize but, even so, it is strictly limited because after a certain point the application of more tension will bring into action supporting muscles which will interfere with correct production. The introduction of supporting tensions can be easily understood if we visualize a person sitting in a relaxed position and lifting an object from a table. If the object is light, he will lift it with his hand and there will be a minimum of activity in the muscles of his arm; his body will remained 'relaxed'. If, however, he is required to lift a heavier object, he will have to apply more tension to the muscles of the hand and arm and he may find that he is bracing his body in support. If he wishes to lift the heavy object without bringing in these supporting tensions, he has no alternative but to increase the power of the muscles in his hand and arm so that less applied tension is needed.

DEVELOPMENT OF VOCAL POWER

An intelligent understanding of the nature of muscular tensions and of the inter-relation of the various groups of muscles that control the vocal mechanism is essential not only in order to correct faults in the use of the voice but also in order to understand the problems that arise continually during its development. Without such understanding, the voice is more often than not kept on a low intensity and prevented from developing its potential power.

The amount of applied tension required on the different muscles varies according to the intensity, pitch and colour of the note and this must be continued even when the built-up tension is increased if the correct muscular balance for perfect production is to be maintained.

Once the maximum permissible applied tensions have been established, however, all further tension increases must be achieved by increasing the built-up tension—the strength of the muscles. In this way, the *actual* tensions on the muscles concerned are increased without fundamentally disturbing the delicate balance of applied tensions necessary to correct breath-vocal cord relationships and the inhibition of interfering tensions—both essential for the production of the most satisfying tone and for care of the voice. Any temporary disturbance in the ratio of applied tensions as the built-up tension is increased is easily adjusted by the teacher who is aware of the factors involved.

If the muscle tonus is lowered through illness or fatigue, attempts to compensate by increasing the applied tension can only partially succeed for the reason given above, i.e. muscles which are harmful to correct production will come into tension in support.

Similarly, during training, if the built-up tension is not yet sufficient, increased power can be obtained by increasing the applied tension above the normal. Up to a point, this may be helpful to the student in strengthening his muscles and giving him, by the method of exaggeration, an idea of the great amount of applied tension needed and by making him accustomed to using these tensions; but care must be taken not to cause strain. Even so, by this method it takes many, many years to strengthen the muscles sufficiently. *It is far better to increase built-up tension not by singing, but by physical training without the use of the voice.* The amount of built-up tension may thus be increased to a great extent without presenting any problems. It is the amount and, particularly, the distribution of applied tension that must be carefully controlled.

In most cases where development to the voice takes place under present methods, it is indirectly as a result of the student being trained to increase the amount of applied tension whilst singing, a most inefficient method, to say the least.

When the above is understood, it is easy to diagnose two of the main causes of what is commonly known as forced tone. This may be caused, in the first place, by attempts to increase the power of the voice by excessive increase of applied tension rather than by increase of built-up tension and, secondly, to errors in the balance between the various applied tensions even when the general level is approximately correct.

Increases in the power or size of the voice over its whole range as muscles are developed and strengthened must not be confused with a singer's ability to apply tension to his muscles as an effort of the will. The former increases in power, resulting from development of muscles, are referred to as increases in the 'size' of the voice; the term 'intensity' refers to degree of amplitude of vocal cord vibrations as a result of *applied* tensions on the respiratory muscles and this again must not be confused with changes in dynamics as defined on page 151.

ENERGY AND TENSION IN SINGING

We have already discussed the difference between applied tension and built-up tension and, before going any further, it should be remembered that tension is not needed simply to create higher breath pressure. It is also needed to control the expulsion of too much breath and to establish the correct balance between volume of breath and vocal cord tension so that the pressure of breath against the vocal cords is correct for every pitch.

Applied tension is achieved by the use of energy and will-power, while built-up tension can be achieved only by the use of suitable exercises.

Much of the controversy about breathing arises out of the fact that the amount of energy and effort needed by the singer in tensing the necessary muscles *seems* out of all proportion to the intensity of the tone as compared to speech. The explanation is firstly that the breath pressure is not necessarily proportionate to tension—in fact, as we now know, much of the tension used is to *reduce* pressure. Secondly, effort is needed not only to establish tensions but also to maintain them. A simple analogy is the carrying of a weight. In normal, everyday life most of us rarely carry anything heavier than a few pounds. When it is necessary to lift a heavier object, extra energy is summoned and the muscles concerned are put under greater tension. But if the weight has to be carried for any distance, it soon becomes apparent that although the weight remains the same the muscles cannot continue to support it without further increased effort. It may eventually become impossible to continue at all, no matter what effort is exerted.

An untrained singer can usually put his muscles under sufficiently high tension to sing a few bars at a high intensity, but he cannot proceed further unless he exerts himself to a very great extent and, even then, he cannot maintain it for very long. This is partly because his muscles are weak and cannot hold even a moderately high tension for long, and partly because they are not used to holding tension for any length of time. *The singer must not only increase the strength of his muscles but also the time for which they can hold tension.* He must increase his ability to sustain these tensions which is partly mental, as well as his physical strength.

Even when muscles are strong mental effort is still needed to keep them under tension. As the muscles tire there is a desire to relax this effort but the desire must be resisted. If the mental effort is maintained, physical adjustments occur which enable the muscular activity to continue; but if the effort is relaxed, the muscles will also relax. While singing, therefore, a continuous fight must be waged against this desire to relax the muscles whose tension is necessary to correct technique. If the muscles have a high tone, they will achieve higher tensions as a result of the same mental effort but they will tend to tire in exactly the same way. Thus, the same kind of will power is needed by the singer as by the athlete.

However, as the degree of applied tension, although great, is strictly limited as explained previously, the strength of the muscles must be increased. To what degree should this be done?

If one performs certain visible actions like lifting a weight or running at speed, it is easier to conceive of and relate to the action the amount of tension needed. One can see and wonder at the muscles of a weight-lifter but, in singing, there is hardly any movement of the body or any visible manifestation of the tensions used. Good singing should sound effortless so we can obtain little assistance from the sound of the tone as far as this point is concerned.

If the listener finds it difficult to relate the amount of muscular tension needed to the tone being produced, the student is in an even worse position because he cannot hear his own voice from the outside. He cannot hear it as would a listener standing a foot away, much less as it would sound to a listener in the auditorium of a large hall. *He must therefore throw away any preconceived ideas he may have as to the amount of tension needed and be prepared to build up more than he ever imagined necessary.* It is one of the most difficult tasks of the teacher to make the student understand this.

Unfortunately, the tensions cannot be measured easily and herein lies one of the great difficulties in the attempt to demonstrate in a book the need for the use of very great tension. However, this is not an insurmountable difficulty if tackled in a logical manner instead of the more or less dogmatic way in which it is generally treated. First, let us see what the scientist has to say on this point.

Power Sources of Sound

'When the steam engine was first invented it had to replace the horse as a source of power. The pumping of water from the mines was done by pumps worked by horses. Before the mine-owner would introduce the new invention he had to know how many horses it would replace, and so be able to compare fuel costs with fodder costs. The horse-power was originally the rate at which an average horse could do the work over an average working day. It is now fixed in terms of the rate at which a weight can be lifted, and is the power required to lift 550 lb. one foot per second. The watt is approximately 1/746 of a horsepower. The engine in a motor-car is generally rated in horsepower. The large dynamo is rated in kilowatts, the kilowatt being 1,000 watts, or about $1\frac{1}{3}$ horsepower. Very small sources of power are rated in microwatts, the microwatt being one millionth of a watt. Some idea of the magnitudes involved in these units will be possible if we note that 1 watt is the power required to raise a weight of 1 lb. steadily by about $8\frac{1}{2}$ inches per second; that a man doing hard continuous manual labour develops a power of about 100 watts; and that this is in turn the power required to keep alight a 100 watt electric lamp.

'When we come to consider the power of a source of sound, however, we are not thinking of the power required to drive the source and maintain it in vibration, but of the power actually radiated as sound. These two things may be very different. The musical instrument is a "transformer". It is supplied with power by an engine or a performer. Much of this power is used to overcome friction and is wasted in other ways. Only a small proportion is transformed into audible sound. Thus a large organ may require an engine developing 10 kilowatts (10,000 watts) to blow it, yet all that appears as sound may be 12–14 watts. A pianist may use energy at the rate of 200 watts in a very loud passage without more than about 0·4 watt being radiated as sound. The human voice is one of the most efficient transformers, yet of the energy put into the production of a note by a vocalist only about 1 per cent goes to charm the audience and the remaining 99 per cent is, from this point of view, completely lost.'[1]

Next, it is necessary to understand the relationship between the magnitude of physical stimulus and the corresponding sensations produced. Research on this question is summarized in Weber's Law which states that the increase in stimulus necessary to produce a just perceptible increase in sensation is proportional to the original stimulus. A change of about 25 per cent in stimulus is needed to distinguish differences in loudness between two notes. From Weber's Law a useful scale of intensity/loudness relations has been devised based on a ten-fold increase in sound energy as follows:

Increase in loudness

1	2 times	3 times	4 times, etc.

Increase in sound energy (stimulus)

10 times	100 times	1,000 times	10,000 times, etc.
$\times 10^1$	$\times 10^2$	$\times 10^3$	$\times 10^4$

From these figures, some idea can be gained of the proportion of additional tension needed for even a small increase in the size of the voice.

Even when the above facts are known, it is still often difficult for the pupil to realize just how much muscular tension is needed in singing in relation to the actual size of the voice. The following illustration may be helpful to teachers in tackling this problem.

Let us compare learning to sing to climbing a high and difficult mountain which is divided into four camps. The first stage is always comparatively easy. The second stage is usually more difficult, the third requires even greater effort and perseverance, while very few people may reach the summit even though the final distance is no greater than from stage 2 to stage 3; in the last stage, every foot advanced takes a terrific toll of energy. The ratio of energy to distance in fact becomes greater as the higher levels are gained.

Yet if a climber could be taken to stage 3 by aeroplane, he would have no advantage over one who began at the bottom in the conquering of the last stage provided that the latter had had adequate rest before the final assault.

In increasing the size of the voice, we are faced with a similar

[1] Alexander Wood, *The Physics of Music*, p. 33 (Methuen, London 1944, sixth edition 1962).

problem. If we divide this training into four stages, we can appreciate that the last stage in the development of any voice is the most difficult. But, like the climber of the mountain, if a beginner commences his training with strong muscles and a naturally well-developed voice, he will find the last stage of his training no less difficult than a student who commenced with a much weaker voice although, of course, his overall training period will be much shorter.

This same law applies to all physical achievement. A man can make very rapid progress in weight-lifting at the outset but as he goes on it becomes increasingly difficult to add even a few more pounds; similarly for a runner to increase his speed by even a small fraction.

In practice, when a singer understands the working of both groups of muscles connected with breathing, and applies the necessary great increases in energy and tension, provided these tensions are correctly balanced, the result is a great increase of power with no loss of quality and no signs of strain and this the listener cannot fail to hear. Why then is there so little unanimity on this point amongst singing teachers? Surely the answer is now obvious.

First let me repeat that a singer who does not understand his breathing mechanism usually adds tension to both groups of muscles in incorrect proportions. Also these errors in production become increasingly evident as the intensity is increased, particularly if the resonators are also badly adjusted as is usually the case.

Let us first take the case of teachers who do believe in the need for energy and tension. This is rarely based on real understanding but is usually due rather to accident of experience; they may have had close contact with singers with well-produced voices who acknowledged that they used a lot of energy whilst singing. These teachers must then realize the need for energy and effort even though they do not understand why, and fail to get perfect results from their own students. In time, such teachers may obtain good results by trying as best they can to eliminate strain without reducing the level of energy and tension used.

And now, what of the teachers who believe in relaxation and have little use for energy and tension. They may have known or studied only with the type of singer described in Chapter XVI, or with incompetent singers who used tension and energy indiscriminately. Their own teaching experience, because of their limited knowledge and the natural tendencies of uninformed singers, has been that increases of tension produces very bad results. They have no experience of correctly balanced tension and correctly used energy because they do not know the factors essential to their establishment. No wonder, then, that these teachers are against the use of energy and tension when they do not know how to use them without causing strain.

At present, statements on tension and relaxation can be likened to the varying results obtained from an experiment by different scientists each of whom has omitted to take one or more important factors into consideration. Only when all the factors in breathing are known and understood can we expect greater unanimity on this point amongst singing teachers.

Before concluding this section, it must be stressed that when the tension on the breathing muscles is increased, adjustments must be made in other parts of the vocal mechanism to correspond. Failure to do this can result in forced tone, but the cause of this must be correctly diagnosed and not attributed to excess tension on the breathing muscles when the fault lies elsewhere.

Perhaps, however, the main reason for controversy lies in the fact that there is a need for a certain mental relaxation in great singing born of complete confidence in one's technical ability. Until the singer has this technical command and then learns to have complete confidence in the correct functioning of his muscles, he will be unable to relax completely all the muscles which need to be out of action. But this has nothing to do with relaxation of other muscles which need to be under tension, nor with the need for keen mental awareness of artistic problems.

BREATH CAPACITY

In discussing the breath capacity needed by the singer, two factors must be taken into consideration, (*a*) the physiological needs of the body in gas exchange and (*b*) the mechanical requirements of phonation.

BREATH REQUIREMENTS OF ORDINARY SPEECH

In normal quiet breathing an adult takes in a shallow breath approximately 16–18 times per minute. During the use of the voice in speech, this is somewhat reduced. During ordinary speech, in order to complete a long sentence, expiratory reserve volume is used and in order that oxygenization of the blood may be maintained even though the frequency of breathing is reduced, the range of the respiratory movements is automatically increased as a result of chemical stimulation described above, and the succeeding breaths are increased by calling upon the inspiratory reserve volume. There is no need for the speaker to anticipate the need of breath by taking in a deeper inspiration in advance as the mechanical needs of speech are sufficiently met by using the expiratory reserve volume and bodily needs are met by increase of tidal volume as a result of reflex processes.

BREATH REQUIREMENTS DURING SINGING

In singing, the length of phrases necessitates that breaths are taken in less frequently than during speech. In a simple experiment, the words of several songs and arias were spoken at the same rate as required for the song while breath was inspired unconsciously as far as depth was concerned but only at the intervals which would be permissible whilst singing. It was found that people with good chest development or those experienced in the use of the voice, e.g. advanced singers, actors or public speakers, were able to speak the words of most songs without the need consciously to increase the depth of respiration. People without these advantages were often unable to do so.

In certain schools of voice training, the breath capacity is not increased but the singer is enabled to sing longer phrases as a result of being taught to produce his voice in such a way that the amount of breath used for mechanical purposes during singing is less than that used during speech. The singer is taught to hold back the breath by placing tension on the breathing muscles which achieve this purpose. If such procedure resulted in the creation of beautiful and powerful voices, there would be no need to increase breath capacity. However, this is not the case. By this method, a teacher may develop the power of the voice, increase the range, and enable the pupil to sing longer phrases but the quality of the tone suffers, particularly on the lower range where most breath is required; and a correctly produced, sustained pianissimo will be out of the question.

The amount of breath needed by a singer has not been scientifically measured, i.e. it has not been calculated by measuring the diameter of the glottis or the size of the resonators or by any other such means. One can only arrive at an appreciation of the amount of breath needed empirically, by a process of trial and error and analysis of the tones produced. Because the mechanical requirements of singing are so little understood, many prejudices and misconceptions exist which prevent such experiments being carried out correctly. In the following pages an attempt is made to increase understanding of the mechanical factors involved in voice production as far as breath volume is concerned and some of the more common prejudices will also be discussed.

Breath volumes in singing are affected by the following factors:

(a) *Decrease in Breath Volume due to increased amplitude of vocal cord vibrations*

It has been indicated that increase in amplitude of the vocal cord vibrations results in a need for less breath volume. As the amplitude of the vibrations and thus the power of the tone is greater in singing than in speech, it follows that less breath volume is needed because of this factor in singing.

(b) *Increase in Breath Volume due to need for greater depth of vocal cord vibrations*

The depth of vocal cord in vibration during speech is not usually great. In singing, however, it is essential to improve the quality of the voice and a greater mass (depth) of vocal cord in vibration provides such a distribution of energy among the various partials of the note as will produce a richer quality. For this factor, more breath volume is needed in singing than in speech.

Thus, while the increase in amplitude of the vibrations reduces the amount of breath required, the need to vibrate a sufficient depth of vocal cord may increase it. To what extent one cancels out the other can only be discovered as yet by practical experience in the studio. Many teachers are aware that the power of the voice can be increased without increasing the breath expenditure, and this is so, but they may not realize that any deficiency in tone quality may be due to insufficient breath. However, unless the co-ordination between breath flow and all the mental and physical controls over the vocal mechanism are thoroughly understood, attempts to improve the tone by increasing breath capacity and breath flow may not produce desirable results. Ignorance of these factors has even led many teachers to conclude quite erroneously that it is undesirable to increase breath capacity.

EFFECT OF ELASTIC RECOIL ON BREATH EXPENDITURE

Another factor to be considered is that of elastic recoil. As explained above, the greater the volume of breath, the greater the force of elastic recoil. The greater the volume of breath in the lungs (either through increased chest measurements or by consciously increasing the extent of the inspiratory movement, or both) the more quickly will the breath flow out during expiration and the greater must be the muscular forces in opposition to this recoil if breath flow is to be checked.

The muscular forces required to increase the power of the tone, as explained above, are fixation of the ribs and tension on the abdominal muscles. These forces oppose the elastic recoil of the lungs and thorax so that as these muscles are strengthened there is a tendency to use less and less breath. *This is quite necessary up to a point, but there comes a time during the singer's development when the amount of breath used in relation to the power of the voice is not adequate for providing the best tone quality.* The more the muscles are strengthened, the greater this tendency becomes. If the singer has sufficient breath available for the purpose of phrasing, he could theoretically provide more breath by exercising conscious independent control over the diaphragm so that more breath is used in relation to the same abdominal tension. In practice, however, there is a limit to the extent to which this independent control can produce the required amount of breath and, after a certain point, it can only be produced by increasing the breath intake and consequently the force of elastic recoil.

More than enough breath should be available by elastic recoil, and the singer can then reduce the flow by muscular action if necessary, and must learn to do so. If, however, there is insufficient breath, as is more likely to occur at the end of a phrase, there is little or nothing the singer can do. If breath capacity is sufficient, it is easier to set up habits of proper breath control and when these habits are sufficiently subconscious, then singing becomes what one may call 'natural' over the whole range of the voice. The pre-requisite to this 'natural' state is strong muscles and sufficient breath capacity. *To attempt to sing naturally, as advocated by many teachers, before these physical requirements are met, is out of the question.*

Phrasing

Understanding of breath requirements and elastic recoil is of considerable help in phrasing. It is obvious that if a phrase requires a lot of breath, it will be advisable to take in a larger quantity at the commencement of the phrase. However, what is not so obvious is that the amount of breath required does not depend solely on the length of the phrase. Breath requirements must be calculated according to the following factors:

(a) *Length of phrase.*

(b) *Pitch of the notes.* The higher the pitch the less breath is needed; the lower the pitch, the more breath. The amount of breath intake will also be influenced by the distribution of these notes, i.e. whether the high notes lie at the beginning or end of the phrase.

(c) *Dynamics.* The varying amounts of breath required for pianissimo, fortissimo, and normal voice are indicated in Fig. 50.

(d) *Colour.*

Of course, this calculation is not required for every phrase of a song. The singer will do this automatically to a great extent when his basic technique is correct, but the above rules are of considerable assistance during training and when special difficulties arise.

Need for Parallel Development of Breath Capacity and Muscular Strength

If increased chest capacity and inspiratory effort increases the force of elastic recoil without corresponding increase in the strength of the opposing muscular forces, the singer finds himself with a large volume of breath which he is unable to control. Thus, for a beginner or for a singer with weak inspiratory muscles, a large breath capacity is an embarrassment rather than an advantage. The greater the chest capacity, the greater must be the strength of the muscles which oppose the elastic recoil, and the greater must be the skill of the singer in controlling these forces. In fact, the advantages of taking in more breath cannot be fully appreciated until the muscles are strengthened. *Development of the muscles must go hand in hand with development of chest capacity for best results.* Only in this way can the power of the tone be increased simultaneously with greatest enhancement of tone quality.

When this dual development is not understood, it is easy to understand how prejudices arise against the intake of a great deal of breath. For example, a teacher who is opposed to the use of muscular tension will find that increase of breath intake produces numerous difficulties for his students. They are unable to produce a flowing line, and their tone may sound breathy and weak. The only way in which such a teacher can avoid these difficulties is to limit the amount of breath intake. In this way, a student may learn to sing with a beautiful musical line, but with thin tone, and he will never develop the full potentiality of his voice. The difficulties and errors which are attributed to the intake of too much breath are in reality, due to weak muscles and consequent inability to control that breath correctly.

If a singer's abdominal muscles are developed and he understands and has command over all the factors in control, I have found that it is always beneficial to increase his breath capacity as much as possible. Such an advanced singer need never fear that he has too much breath. He should be afraid only of having too little. If he has taken in more breath volume than is needed in production, this can be controlled, and can only be beneficial. If he has too little breath he can never produce the tone which should be rightfully his; he must either resort to straining or remain content with inferior tone on all or part of his range.

It is only the inexperienced singer with a less developed technique who may sometimes find it a disadvantage rather than a help to take in a complete, full breath. In this case, careful calculation of breath intake may help him over difficulties in the rendition of a song but such limitation of intake must be recognized as an interim measure and not as a fundamental part of his technique. For example, if the first notes of a long phrase require little breath, the singer may find that the large breath intake required to complete the phrase will tend to increase the rate of air flow beyond that required for the first notes. Very careful calculation of breath intake will make such a phrase easier to sing correctly. With further development, the singer will be able to control a large amount of breath even in such difficult circumstances and will find the increased intake beneficial.

Normally, a person having a large chest capacity will also have strong abdominal muscles. Occasionally, by nature or by unbalanced development, one finds a singer with a large breath capacity but weak breathing muscles. This is more often encountered in the training of the female voice. In this case, because of the weak abdominal muscles, the amplitude of the vocal cord vibrations is smaller and the opening of the glottis greater; the rate of breath flow is higher as the weak inspiratory muscles are unable to oppose the elastic recoil. Such a singer will benefit from exercises which increase the tension simultaneously on both sets of muscles so that breath expulsion is checked at the same time as the amplitude of the vibrations increases through increased abdominal tension. *The voice may undergo great development by this means before the singer has to learn to use muscles independently in order to flow sufficient breath.* The old exercise of singing before a lighted candle without causing it to flicker is useful for this type of student because it will help to tighten both the diaphragm and abdominal muscles. However, there comes a time when this exercise no longer serves a useful purpose. In fact, if continued beyond a certain stage, it will prevent the student from using sufficient breath for the production of good tone in much if not all of his range. Unfortunately, this exercise and others of a similar nature are too often used without real understanding in circumstances where they are far from being beneficial.

Invariably those who advise against the intake of large quantities of breath also show lack of understanding of control factors. E. T. Evetts and R. A. Worthington[1] state that mezza-voce in simple music in an easy compass can be produced as in speaking with no consciously increased breath intake and that sufficient breath is not unconsciously provided only when singing the long sustained passages of more sophisticated music using the voice to its full power. First of all, it is not clear what these writers mean by 'full power'. Do they mean fortissimo singing or simply the normal singing intensity of a voice whose overall size has been fully developed? Secondly, when reading such a statement, the reader must ask himself what the writer means by mezza-voce. I have heard many students whose 'mezza-voce' was no more than singing the words to tune and in a higher pitch than used for speech, but at little more than speaking intensity and with no great beauty of tone. *In fact, on numerous occasions I have listened to actors who had undergone a period of singing tuition, only to find that their speaking voices were decidedly more powerful than their singing voices.*

These writers make the common error of assuming what superficially appears to be obvious and relating breath needs proportionately to the power of the tone. They do not distinguish clearly between increased amplitude of vocal cord movements and differences in loudness due to resonatory factors. They imply that less breath is needed for pianissimo whereas it is in pianissimo that any insufficiency of breath capacity is most seriously felt unless the singer is to remain content with the anaemic pianissimo so often heard today.

To reinforce arguments against increasing the breath intake, certain singers are often cited because of the inability of an observer a few yards away to see when a breath is taken. However, here again, the argmnent is incomplete. As explained above, when the breath is inspired correctly large quantities can be taken in with very little

[1] *The Mechanics of Singing* (Dent, London 1928).

noticeable movement. Further, many singers are fortunate enough to be endowed with such efficient resonators that they can produce a tone of considerable size and quality even with little breath. One cannot, however, assume that because such a singer uses less breath his voice would not be even better if he took in more. But while incomplete breathing may not prevent him from being successful, it could prevent a less fortunate singer, who might otherwise have a very worthy voice, from reaching a sufficiently high standard to succeed in a singing career. Individual requirements vary and this must be taken into account.

Another widespread fallacy is that operatic singing, because of the powerful tones required, necessitates the use of more breath and therefore a larger chest capacity than other types of singing, lieder for example. In fact, the breath requirements for opera and lieder are fairly similar, but for different reasons. The size of the tones conceived in opera calls for a larger amount of breath, but this is somewhat compensated for by the fact that the higher tessitura and the higher average intensity of opera calls for less. In leider, on the other hand, breath requirements for the size of the tones conceived are less unless much pianissimo is used, but breath requirements for the lower tessitura and lower average intensity are somewhat greater.

A brief outline of a singer's development will summarize the foregoing and help to give the reader a clearer understanding of the factors involved in breath control and development. Most beginners have small breath capacity and weak breathing muscles. Their voices are limited both in range and dynamics. Because of weakness of the inspiratory muscles, these pupils use a great deal of breath which results in an inability to sing long phrases and the need to replenish their breath supply frequently. If attempts are made to increase the power of such voices without increasing the breath capacity, what happens? The breathing muscles are strengthened, greater abdominal tension results in closer approximation of the vocal cords as the amplitude of their vibration increases, and greater tension on the inspiratory muscles results in the flow of less breath. The voices become more powerful, the range is higher and the singers are enabled to sing longer phrases without taking in additional breath. But here development must stop. *Without further increases of breath capacity, longer phrasing can only be obtained by sacrificing tone quality, particularly on the lower range, and correctly produced, sustained pianissimo will be unattainable.*

DEVELOPMENT OF BREATH CONTROL

EXERCISES FOR DEVELOPMENT

The development of the breathing is not a simple process of steady improvement. Like all physical and mental development, there are periods of growth, sometimes quite rapid growth, alternating with periods of consolidation. These periods of consolidation require psychological and physical adjustments on the part of the student which must be thoroughly understood by the teacher.[1]

On the *physical* side, the developmental problems are purely ones of muscle training and increase of chest capacity similar to those encountered by any physical culturist. It is a matter of suitable exercises, time and patience to build up the muscle tonus so that the muscles will hold the necessary tensions without too much effort on the part of the student.

The muscles which are usually the weakest, particularly in the case of female students, are the abdominal muscles. These must be strengthened by suitable exercises such as the following.

1. The pupil should sit on a chair with his feet under a divan or other heavy object. He should then lean over backwards, with hands on head, until his head touches the floor, then return to the sitting position.

2. The pupil should lie on the floor, feet together and toes pointed out. He should then raise his feet slowly together to the vertical position, and lower them slowly without letting them touch the floor. Raise feet again and repeat. The effectiveness of this exercise is considerably enhanced if weights are attached to the feet.

The number of times these exercises should be repeated depends solely upon the fitness of the student. He should not be allowed to go beyond his capabilities in an attempt to obtain quicker results as there is a limit to the speed at which muscles can be developed. To exceed this is most foolish. At the same time, to err in the opposite direction and take these exercises too easily will unnecessarily delay the student's progress. Exactly the same principles of muscular development that apply in weight-lifting should be applied when developing those muscles which must be strengthened for singing. The same applies to exercises for chest development.

[1] See pages 186–7.

DEVELOPMENT OF BREATH CONTROL

FROM PHYSICAL TO MENTAL CONTROL

No matter what method of breathing is advocated, there are two opposed schools of thought on the matter of control. One claims that the control of the breath can and should be effected mentally; the other school insists that a purely mental control is impossible. The unfortunate thing about this controversy is that both are right, but each only half right. Here is another example of the failure to appreciate the different requirements of the beginner and the advanced singer. The facts are that at the commencement of training, physical control is essential; mental control can be exercised only by the more experienced singer. Yet, one or other type of control is usually recommended exclusively by its advocates to all pupils whether inexperienced or advanced.

Physical control implies that the singer is conscious of his breathing muscles and controls them directly by thinking of their action in relation to every note. He thinks of the pitch, intensity, and the resonance adjustment needed to produce the desired quality, and *calculates* the tension on the breathing muscles almost simultaneously before attacking each note.

In the beginning of a singer's training, a direct physical control over the breathing muscles is the only possible control. It is the only one he is capable of using and the only one that will enable him to progress satisfactorily to a stage when this control is no longer necessary. Even this control is impossible until a certain muscular strength has been built up by appropriate exercises. Yet many teachers expect to achieve results by mental control when the student's breathing muscles are so weak that even conscious, willed effort cannot create the necessary tensions. This muscular strength must be built up and physical control firmly established before the student can make further progress.

However, physical control is at best only a crude, clumsy method of controlling the breath. By this method, it is quite impossible to supply the exact quantities of breath to the vocal cords. It gives only approximate quantities which are quite inadequate for the delicate handling of the breath essential in singing. A finer control is needed. Physical control should only last until a high degree of command has been established over the breathing muscles and the student has an appreciation of the degree of tension necessary for any intensity and quality on every pitch. Once this has been established, a change over to indirect or mental control should be made.

Mental control implies that the singer no longer thinks directly of his breathing muscles. He thinks only of the quality he wants, the pitch and the intensity. If the first stage of the training has been accomplished satisfactorily, his breathing muscles will respond to his mental concepts of tone with a high degree of accuracy.

The next step is to achieve *absolute* accuracy. In the middle and lower parts of the singer's range this is comparatively easy, but on the top it is more difficult. The gaining of complete command is a matter of practice and experience. By the time a student is ready to attempt mental control, he should have been taught to know the correct tone qualities as they sound to him throughout his range. He should also be able to recognize the tone quality produced by having too little breath and that produced by having too much. He now conceives of the quality and intensity he wants before attacking each note. He no longer thinks of his breathing muscles but as he sings, he listens most carefully to the tone he is producing. If his judgement has been accurate, the tone quality he hears will be correct. If not, he must adjust accordingly. And, of course, the teacher must be present to confirm or correct the student's conceptions. The more experienced the latter becomes, the more accurate will be his judgement.

The difference between these two controls is perhaps made clearer in the following illustration. We are so familiar with the physical properties of the everyday objects surrounding us that we handle them accurately without thought, but if we are presented with articles made from unfamiliar materials we are more careful. It will take a certain amount of experience before we can handle them with accuracy. For example, if we over-estimate the weight of an object and the energy needed to lift it, we will raise it with a sudden, jerky movement. If we underestimate, we will fail to lift it all and have to try again. If we found ourselves completely surrounded with un-familiar objects, we would make endless mistakes if we tried to handle them all without thinking. *To a student, every note is unfamiliar and remains so for a long time as their properties are continually changing as his vocal mechanism develops.* If he tried to sing without conscious calculation of the effort required, he would make endless mistakes and would gain little from his experience. Only when he is much more advanced can he 'reach out' for every note without thought of the muscular action involved.

For a student of singing, therefore, understanding of the breathing rules is as important as knowledge of technique to the pianist. They are an essential foundation to his training even though he never consciously thinks of them once mental control has been firmly established, as an experienced pianist no longer thinks of his fingering. Yet no one would deny the necessity for it in early training.

If the changeover is made according to the foregoing procedure, the singer will judge the tensions accurately and the breathing muscles will be his willing and accurate servant instead of a clumsy and inefficient one. Until then, the breathing muscles, instead of being his servant, will be his master and prevent his control of the breath being beautiful, even and accurate. It is easy to understand the error made by so many singers who become teachers. They assume that as they never worry about their breathing muscles, they can tell the student to do likewise, not realizing the suppleness, strength and automatic judgement they have built up over the years.

It is the responsibility of the teacher to decide when the student is ready for this next step in the control of his voice. If the student attempts mental control before he has sufficient command of his breathing muscles, and before they are sufficiently supple and strong, he will fail to obtain results.

The reluctance to accept mental control lies in the fact that it is not clearly enough understood and never clearly described. Teachers who realize the inadequacy of a purely physical control and who themselves use mental control fail to analyse correctly the process by which a student can also gain this control. Some of these teachers, in trying to improve on a purely physical control of the breathing, advocate what they call 'laryngeal control', but as they do not explain very clearly how to control the laryngeal mechanism, the term is not very helpful. The student is not thereby assisted, in the first stage, to establish the correct tensions on the breathing muscles, and in the second stage to sing the notes and listen to the sound produced so that he can analyse the tone quality and make the necessary adjustments in his technique, in the same way as a violinist plays, listens to the tone, and adjusts his technique if necessary until it is so well established that constant analysis is no longer necessary.

All that has been said about mental control of the breathing applies equally, of course, to control of the laryngeal mechanism and the co-ordination between all aspects of technique. The singer has in his singing palette a wide range of tone colours which he has learnt to produce and remember by the above physical means and he should think directly of these tones in the final stages of his training. If he needs correction or if a new conception of tone is required for a new work in his repertoire, this can be given him by return to the physical methods described, but his final aim must be to cast off these physical aids and simply sing with all the colours at his command. In this way, he is thinking in terms, not of sensations or of areas of his facial anatomy which can give him only a very limited scope for variation, but is working directly in terms of tone concepts which can be varied to an enormous extent.

When physical control is discarded, the achievement of indirect control leaves the mind free to concentrate fully on interpretation. In fact, in the final stage, the singer should not even think of quality or intensity as such. He thinks only of the words and music and the feeling behind them, and his tone colours and dynamics arise naturally out of his interpretation and feeling. Achievement of mental control is the last step before attainment of the state of mental relaxation mentioned on page 237—the passivity of great singing where such physical command is attained that the singer is completely unaware of the physical processes that complement his interpretative ability.

XVIII

Practice

The question of practice is one of great importance. How much should a singer practise and of what value is practice in the development of a voice? In the old days, and even today, the study of singing entailed long hours of scales and exercises for many, many years. Is this necessary? Or can it, in fact, be harmful?

To answer these questions we must understand the twofold purpose of exercises. There is first of all a physical need to strengthen muscles and develop their flexibility; secondly, there is the need to develop the singer's skill and mastery in the use of his voice.

Certain muscular development must be given primary importance because until muscles are developed, the singer's scope is very limited. In early methods of training muscular development was accomplished by singing exercises but this was a very, very slow process. Today, with the increased knowledge at our command, most muscles can be developed by specially devised physical exercises without using the voice at all. It is a much quicker method and there is the added advantage that the voice remains fresh. The respiratory muscles and the chest are developed with body-building techniques; while the mouth, lips and tongue, whose flexibility is required for resonance control, are also developed by non-vocal methods. The only part of the vocal equipment that requires singing exercises in order to increase strength and flexibility is the laryngeal mechanism, and the exercises must be carefully chosen so that the right ones are given for the desired result. Too often, exercises are given to students with no understanding of their real value and purpose.

In practically every case, however, the weakest point in a singer's equipment is not the larynx, which is usually capable of working under far greater power than is imagined. It is the state of the respiratory muscles and the muscles of resonance that is usually responsible for holding back the singer's progress and which must be tackled

250

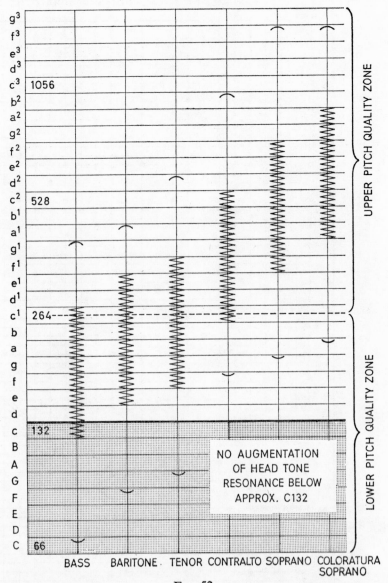

FIG. 52

Brackets indicate the approximate potential range of a fully developed voice in each category. Shaded areas represent the tessitura or lie of the voice—the area within which the singer's best tone is achieved and where the greater part of his singing lies.

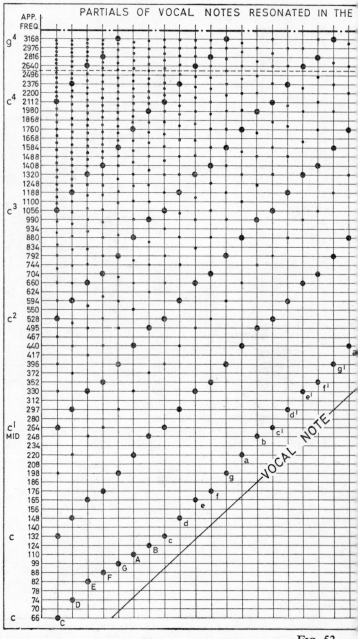

FIG. 53

252

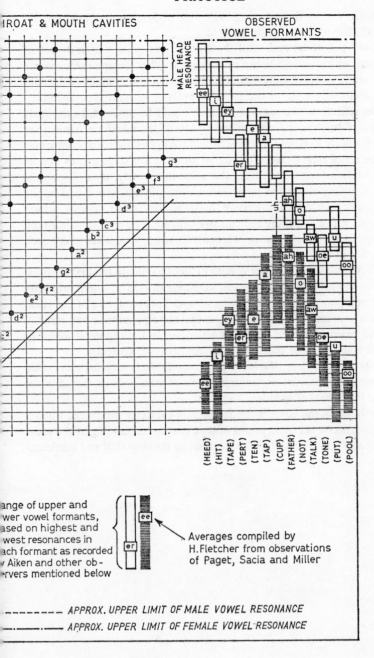

THROAT & MOUTH CAVITIES

OBSERVED VOWEL FORMANTS

MALE HEAD RESONANCE

(HEED) (HIT) (TAPE) (PERT) (TEN) (TAP) (CUP) (FATHER) (NOT) (TALK) (TONE) (PUT) (POOL)

Range of upper and lower vowel formants, based on highest and lowest resonances in each formant as recorded by Aiken and other observers mentioned below

Averages compiled by H. Fletcher from observations of Paget, Sacia and Miller

_ _ _ _ _ _ _ APPROX. UPPER LIMIT OF MALE VOWEL RESONANCE

_ _ . _ _ . _ _ APPROX. UPPER LIMIT OF FEMALE VOWEL RESONANCE

253

first. Only when these are in a high state of development are exercises for the larynx essential or desirable.

Until this time, and until the student has quite a high degree of control of his voice, the use of scales and other singing exercises can be harmful. In fact, only when the production is very much under control is it really wise for the singer to practise without supervision.

On reflection, the reasons for this should be obvious. In the early stages of his training, the different parts of the vocal mechanism are not properly balanced in strength and a singer's ability to control his voice is not established. To practise alone at this stage means that he is spending long hours using the voice incorrectly. By doing so, he can not only strain the vocal mechanism physically but bad habits of tone and control become fixed in his mind, habits which become more and more difficult to eradicate. The enthusiastic young singer cannot therefore be warned too strongly against over-much practice at this stage.

Very little vocal practice should in fact be done in the first months. These first months of the student's training should be aimed primarily at developing the muscles, giving him an understanding of the vocal mechanism and instilling correct mental concepts of tone and control. Vocal practice is then increased according to the degree of development and ability of the student to use his voice correctly.

It is much better in singing to practise a lot less and think more. One constructive thought, one concept thoroughly understood, can do more good than hours of practice.

Only when the voice is fundamentally correctly produced, when a singer has correct conceptions of tone and understanding of the vocal controls should he undertake exercises to develop skill and musicianship.

APPENDIX I

Air Pressure

The earth exerts a gravitational force on all objects whether they are allowed to fall or left to lie on a surface, e.g. a table or floor. The force of an object against such a surface is called a pressure and is the weight of the object. The conventional manner of stating the weight of an object is to give the complete weight of the whole object, whether this be expressed in pounds and ounces or in kilograms and grams.

On the other hand, the conventional manner of expressing pressure is not to give it as the total pressure of the complete object but as the weight or force exerted by each given section of the object. This is known as the force per unit area and is usually given either in lb. per square inch or in grams per square centimetre.

The earth also exerts a gravitational pull on the atmosphere so that air has weight and exerts a pressure which cannot obviously be measured on scales but in the following manner. A glass tube about a yard long, closed at one end, is filled with mercury and stopped up. The tube is inverted and lowered into a bowl of mercury. The stopper of the tube, now underneath the surface of the mercury in the bowl, is then removed. It is found that the mercury does not all drop from the tube into the bowl but remains in the tube to a height of about 29·9 inches (or 76 cm.). This is because the downward pressure of air on the surface of the mercury in the bowl presses the mercury against the opening of the tube so that it offers a resistance to the downward gravitational force of the mercury contained in the tube. If the pressure of the air was less, the pressure exerted on the mercury in the bowl and thus against the opening of the tube would be less, the downward gravitational force of the mercury in the tube would meet with less resistance and would fall to a lower level. If the air pressure is increased, the greater downward pressure on the mercury in the bowl would force the mercury higher up the tube. Thus, the weight or pressure of air per square centimetre supports and is equivalent to the weight of a column of mercury 76 cm. high and 1 sq. cm. cross-sectional area. In English units this is approximately 14½ lb. per square inch. However, in most diagrams, air pressure is expressed in terms of the height of mercury remaining in a tube as a result of such pressure. The same experiment can be carried out using water instead of mercury in which case the water rises 33 feet as it is much lighter than mercury.

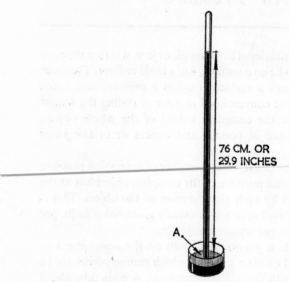

76 CM. OR
29.9 INCHES

A.

FIG. 54

To understand air pressure, it is also necessary to know *firstly*, that whereas solids only exert a downward pressure, gases transmit pressure equally in all directions. This can be easily observed in a balloon, in a gas where the molecules are much more separated than in a solid verted, the hand holding the covering card can be removed and the pressure of air will keep it in position and support the water. *Secondly*, the pressure exerted by a gas such as air is due not so much to the actual weight of the molecules in the gas but rather to the movement of the molecules of which the gas is composed. The molecules of a material are considered to be in a state of motion which is very rapid in a gas, where the molecules are much more separated than in a solid or liquid and have greater freedom of movement. Thus the molecules are constantly colliding with each other and with the surfaces with which the gas is in contact, giving the effect of a continuous push or pressure, which we call the pressure of the gas. If the volume of the gas is compressed, the molecules become more crowded so that collisions are more frequent and the pressure on the walls of the containing vessel or other surface is greater.

To measure the pressure of a gas or to measure air pressure other than that of the atmosphere, a device known as a manometer is used. One of the simplest forms of manometer is a U-shaped tube into which is poured a quantity of mercury (or some other similar liquid). If both ends are left open to the air, the level in each limb is the same, as each limb is exposed to the same pressure. For the experiment, one end is left open to the air and the other connected to the gas container. The limb open to the air is being subjected to atmospheric pressure. If the pressure of the gas to be measured is greater than that of the atmosphere, it will force the mercury out towards the opening, as in Fig. 55. The excess pressure over atmospheric pressure is equal to AB cm. of mercury and the pressure of the gas is thus equal to atmospheric pressure (76 cm. Hg.) plus AB cm. of mercury.

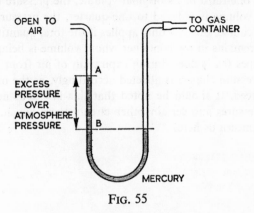

FIG. 55

If the pressure of the gas to be measured is less than atmospheric, the greater pressure of the air will force the mercury towards the gas container and can be calculated in a similar manner by deducting from atmospheric pressure the difference in the levels of the two limbs.

A manometer of this type, built on a stand and fitted with a gauge, is very useful equipment for a singer. (A convenient size for the bore of the tube is about 2 mm.) If he blows into one end, using a piece of rubber tubing, the manometer will indicate the air pressure in the lungs. The pressures obtained in this way are not the same quantitatively as would apply during phonation using the same muscular tensions, because the changing state of the open glottis during singing is not taken into account. However, it does show that pressure is increased when the tension is increased on the diaphragm and abdominal muscles, and dissipated when the tension on these muscles is reduced. It also shows that the greater the air intake, the higher the pressure that can be obtained. Its main usefulness to the singer is in giving him an indication of the strength of his muscles. The stronger his muscles become, the higher the reading he can obtain.

Boyle's Law. If any gas is compressed into a smaller space—in other words, if the volume of the gas is reduced—then the pressure rises. The ratio of pressure increase to volume change follows a law, known as Boyle's Law, which applies to all gases or mixtures of gases. The law states that *at a constant temperature the volume of a fixed mass of gas is inversely proportional to the pressure.* Thus, if the volume is halved, the pressure is doubled; if the volume of the gas is reduced to one-third of its original volume, the pressure is trebled; and if the volume is reduced to one-quarter, the pressure is quadrupled. Of course, this law only applies if the total quantity or mass of the gas remains in the container whose volume is being reduced. If gas escapes (as it does during expiration of air from the lungs) then the pressure change is affected accordingly, as the mass of the gas is reduced. It should be noted that this law does not hold at extreme pressures and certain other circumstnces which, however, need not concern us here.

APPENDIX II

Breath Flow and Tone Quality

Measurements of intra-thoracic pressure and breath flow during singing were carried out at Edinburgh University by M. H. Draper, Ph.D., M.B., B.S., using a technique similar to that used in the studies described on page 93. The subject was standing in a steel tank incorporating a yoke of sponge rubber in the lid as a neck seal. Changes in the volume of air in the tank, indicating volume changes in the chest, were recorded on a spirometer. This method of measuring the volume changes left the mouth entirely free so that the singing could be quite uninhibited.

The pressure of the air in the trachea immediately below the vocal cords was calculated from measurements of oesophageal pressure, recorded from a small latex balloon which was passed through the nose until it lay in the oesophagus at about the level of the bifurcation of the trachea.

The most important fact to emerge from the experiments was that the effect of changing the quality concept is to alter the air flow. A mouth dominant resonance setting (open quality) has a low air flow and this is consistent with visual observation of the vocal cords which were seen to be set much closer together when an open tone was sung.

A throat and head resonance setting has a greater air flow at the same intensity and the vocal cords are set wider apart.

In the experiments, best quality was always associated with the highest air flow. Thus, two notes sung at 10 cm. water with a breath flow of 96 mls./sec. were of bad quality (too open), while two notes of the same pitch sung at about the same pressure but with a flow of 180 mls./sec. were of excellent quality.

When changing the vocal cord setting from pianissimo to fortissimo, consistent good quality, i.e. neither too open nor too closed, is achieved by altering both pressure and flow. A good-quality fortissimo note had a flow of about 100 mls./sec. and a pressure of 7 cm. water, while a pianissimo note of too open quality had the same breath flow and a pressure of only 4·4 cm. water, the relative intensities of the two notes being 9 to 6·5 on a tape intensity meter. A higher flow of breath on the pianissimo note would have given improved quality and made it more closed and mellow. The reason why the same flow resulted in a difference in pressure on each note was due to a difference in vocal cord setting. To improve the quality on the pianissimo note, it would be necessary to alter the tension on the breathing muscles so as to flow more breath while keeping the same concept of the size of the tone.

All attempts to sing loudly with insufficient breath resulted in too open tones if the air flow was not increased accordingly. The breath control theory, viz. if you can only reduce air flow, you must then produce good-quality singing, was seen to be incorrect. The loudness which can be attained by introducing mouth resonance and low air flow is dissonant and not acceptable. Rather one has to learn to achieve increased intensity by other means and this demands greater control over breath flow and pressure levels by the singer.

Good quality was found to be the result of the various quality concepts of tone being co-ordinated with appropriate breathing patterns. Thus, the interesting situation arose that when the singer was instructed to restrict the air flow but keep the quality good, he could not do this. The following experiments were particularly instructive. The singer was instructed to sing g^1 396 with a large breath intake but a restricted flow, and no instruction about quality. This resulted in a good-quality note—flow 162 mls./sec., pressure 16 cm. water: the subject did not succeed in obeying the instruction to restrict air flow. The experiment was repeated and the flow dropped too low in relation to the slight lowering of intensity— flow 104 mls./sec., pressure 14 cm. water, and the quality of the note was quite different, i.e. too open.

On another occasion the singer was instructed to produce a note of good quality. The resulting note was, in fact, of poor quality and reference to the spirometer reading confirmed that the singer had omitted to take in sufficient breath and the flow was much lower than normal for a good-quality note. In other words, the mental concept of a good-quality note was not sufficient to produce the tone conceived. Correct breath flow through control of inspiration and expiration was also a necessary factor.

Similar experiments, repeated after an interval of six months with another subject, confirmed the above.

NOTE. When these experiments were made, prior to publication of the first edition, the role of the resonators and of the laryngeal mechanism in determining vocal quality was not as clearly understood, hence the descriptions of tone quality in terms of resonance which are no longer used, i.e. mouth and throat resonated tones.

Bibliography

AIKIN, W. A., *The Voice, an Introduction to Practical Phonology* (Longmans, Green, 1932).

BARTHOLOMEW, W. T. O., 'Definition of Good Voice Quality in Male Voices', *Journal of the Acoustical Society of America*, vol. 6, 1934.

CAMPBELL, E. J. MORAN *The Respiratory Muscles and the Mechanics of Breathing* (Lloyd-Luke Ltd., London, 1958).

COMROE, FORSTER, DUBOIS, BRISCOE, CARLSEN, *The Lung, Clinical Physiology and Pulmonary Function Tests* (The Year Book Publishers Inc., Chicago, 1955).

CUNNINGHAM, D. J., *Textbook of Anatomy* (Oxford University Press, 1951).

DRAPER, M. H., LADEFOGED, P., and WHITTERIDGE, D., 'Expiratory Pressures and Air Flow during Speech', *British Medical Journal*, 18 June 1960, vol. i, pp. 1837–43.

DUEY, P. A., *Bel Canto in Its Golden Age* (King's Crown Press, Columbia University, New York, 1951).

HELMHOLTZ, H., *On the Sensations of Tone*, translated from the German by Alexander J. Ellis (Dover Publications, Inc., New York, 1954).

HOLLINGSHEAD, W. H., *Anatomy for Surgeons*, vol. 1 (Cassell, 1954).

JONES, DANIEL, *The Pronunciation of English* (Cambridge University Press, 1950).

KEITH, SIR ARTHUR, 'The Mechanism of Respiration in Man', in *Further Advances in Physiology*, edited by Leonard Hill (Edward Arnold, 1909).

NEGUS, V. E., *The Comparative Anatomy and Physiology of the Larynx* (Heinemann, 1949).

PAGET, SIR RICHARD, *Human Speech* (Kegan Paul, 1930).

PRESSMAN, J. J., 'Physiology of the vocal cords in phonation and respiration', *Arch. Otolaryng.* 35:355, 1942.

BIBLIOGRAPHY

Pressman, J. J., 'Sphincter Action of the Larynx', *Arch. Otolaryng.* 33:351, 1941.

Russell, G. Oscar, *Speech and Voice* (Macmillan, New York, 1931).

Seashore, C., *Psychology of Music* (McGraw Hill, 1938).

Wood, Alexander, *The Physics of Music* (Methuen, 1944), sixth edition 1962.

Index

Amplitude, of sound waves, 63
  of vocal cord vibrations, 135–43,
    150
Articulation
  of consonants, 193–9
  of vowels, 180–5, 199–200

Bartholomew, W. T., 169–70, 189
Battistini, 218
Beethoven, 203
Behnke, Kate Emil, 210
Bel canto, 203
Breath, capacity, 212, 237–44
  pressure (see Pressure)
  ventilation, 82–8
  volumes, 81–2, 89, 91–2
Breathing Mechanism
  control of, 94–103
  description of, 69–81
  exercises, 245
  mechanics of, 88–93
  physiology of, 81–8
Breath control in singing, 133–44
  rules of, 139–41

Campbell, E. J. M., 75, 77, 79, 80,
  91–2, 94, 100, 135
Caruso, 30–1, 155, 209
Chest tone, 160, 174, 189, 207,
  214–19
Colour, 145, 164–7, 172–5, 201–5
Consonants, 193–9
Constriction, 121, 161–4, 178
Covered tone, 155, 188–9

Damping, 34, 49, 55–8, 63, 121,
  171–3, 175, 201–5

del Monaco, Mario, 32
De Reszke, 30
Development, 223–49
Draper, Ladefoged, Whitteridge,
  93, 100
Draper, W. H., 259
Duomarco, Rimini and Recarte,
  94, 99, 100
Dynamics, 63, 150–61, 201–5

Edge, 152–67, 192, 207
Elastic Recoil, 79–80, 88–93, 101,
  103, 133
Energy, 232–7
Evenly rising scale, 51, 146–9
Evetts and Worthington, 243
Expiration, control of, 100–3
Exercises, larynx, 156
  abdominal muscles, 245

Falsetto, 211, 213–15
Fischer-Dieskau, Dietrich, 154
Fletcher, H., 65
Fortissimo, 152 (see Dynamics)
Forward Production, 174–5, 192
Frequency, 45

Gallicurci, 32
Garcia, 31
Gigli, 37
Green and Howell, 77
Golden age, 30–40
Gounod, 204

Harmonics (see Partials)
Head tone, 160, 169–71, 174,
  187–91, 207, 214–19

INDEX

Helmholtz, H., 35
Hemery, Haydn, 215
Horne, Marilyn, 192
Hum, 170–1, 191

Inspiration, control of, 95–100
Intensity, 45, 50–1, 149–51, 201–5
  (see Dynamics)

Jones, Daniel, 155

Keith, Sir Arthur, 72

Lamperti, 22, 31
Laryngeal Mechanism
  action of, 109–13
  control of, 145–67
  description of, 104–9
  indirect control of, 109, 162–4,
    178
  in relation to breathing, 133–44
  position of, 109, 178, 162–4
  rules of control, 146–9, 157, 159
  weakness of, 109, 212–14, 218–19
Legato, 156
Lieder, 154, 201–5
Lip position, 127, 173, 184–5

Melba, 30
Mental control, 246–9
Mezzo forte, 152 (see Dynamics)

Nasal resonance, 191
Negus, V. E., 134–6, 138
Nodules, 109, 163, 178–9 (see Vocal
  cords, health of)

Operatic technique, 201–5
Operatic tone, 20, 34–7
Oxygen debt, 87–8

Paget, Sir Richard, 171, 176, 191
Partials, 34–6, 45–9, 252–3
  resonance of, 53–63
Patti, 32
Phrasing, 240–1
Pianissimo, 143, 150, 152, 157–9,
  175, 238 (see Dynamics)

Pitch quality, 47–50, 158–60, 201–4,
  208–10
Practice, 250–4
Pressman, J. J., 109, 111, 135–6,
  145, 150, 163, 207
Pressure, air, 255–8
  intra-abdominal, 79–80, 94, 99–
    100, 135
  intra-thoracic, 80, 91–3, 133–44
Psychology, 151, 154–5, 157, 210–
  211, 225, 245

Quality, 34–8, 45, 47–50, 61–3 (see
  Pitch quality, Partials, Edge,
  Head tone, Chest tone)
  in relation to breathing and vocal
    cord vibrations, 138–9, 141–2,
    149–50
  instrumental, 64, 172–3
  tenor, 218
  vowel, 64–5, 172–3

Range, 159, 170, 213–14, 251
Registers, 207–20
Resonance, 49, 52–65
  vocal, 168–77
Resonators, control of, 178–92
  description of, 114–29
  size of, 63–4
Rules of Voice Production, 139–41,
  146–9, 157, 159
Russell, Dr. Oscar, 27–8, 120, 128,
  171, 181, 208

Scale, evenly rising, 51, 146–9
Schubert, 154, 203–4
Seashore, C., 59
Selectivity, 56–8, 171–3
Sound, amplitude of, 63
  analysis of, 33–8, 43–65
  attributes of, 45
  energy, 43, 48–9, 55–7, 59–63
  power sources of, 234–7
Staccato, 156
Stanley, Douglas, 158, 162, 179
Strauss, Richard, 20, 204
Support, 81, 103, 144, 150–1,
  156–60, 165–7
Sutherland, Joan, 192

INDEX

Tenor quality, 218
Tension, dialectics of, 223–7
　　nature of, 228–37
Tessitura, 212, 251
Tetrazzini, 30, 32, 209
Throat, closed, 125–6, 128–9, 164,
　　178–83 (see Constriction)
　　open, 125–7, 164, 178–86
　　openings, 186–7
Timbre, 45, 62

Upper partials (see Partials)

Verdi, 204
Vibration, forced, 54–5
　　free, 52–3

of springs, 45–51
　　stationary, 53
Vocal cords, health of, 109, 178–9,
　　141–3, 163, 170
Vocal cord vibrations (see Laryn-
　　geal Mechanism)
　　amplitude of, 135–43, 150
Vowels, articulation of, 180–5,
　　199–200
　　formants, 65, 175–7, 253
　　quality, 64–5, 172–3, 176
　　resonance of, 171–3, 175–7

Wagner, 20
Whisper, 135–7, 151–2, 175–6
Wood, Alexander, 62, 235